TO KILL A DEMOCRACY

TO KILL A DEMOCRACY

INDIA'S PASSAGE TO DESPOTISM

DEBASISH ROY CHOWDHURY
AND
JOHN KEANE

OXFORD
UNIVERSITY PRESS

OXFORD
UNIVERSITY PRESS

Great Clarendon Street, Oxford, OX2 6DP,
United Kingdom

Oxford University Press is a department of the University of Oxford.
It furthers the University's objective of excellence in research, scholarship,
and education by publishing worldwide. Oxford is a registered trade mark of
Oxford University Press in the UK and in certain other countries

Published in the United States of America by Oxford University Press
198 Madison Avenue, New York, NY 10016, United States of America

British Library Cataloguing in Publication Data
Data available

Library of Congress Control Number: 2021938150

ISBN 978–0–19–884860–8

Printed and bound by
CPI Group (UK) Ltd, Croydon, CR0 4YY

Contents

Tryst With Democracy

A Distant Rainbow

There's an old proverb that tells how all nations are slaves to imaginings about their origins, blind pride in their finest hours, pure joy in those moments when it's said extraordinary things were achieved that others thought beyond reach. India is no exception to this time-tested truism. The story runs like this: back in the mid-twentieth century, against formidable odds, the people and leaders of India courageously mobilized to snap the chains of imperial domination and set out on the rough road to democracy. They built a democracy that's today not only the planet's biggest, but a democracy that breathed fresh life into its ideals and boosted India's global reputation as a country that survived a murderous Partition, defeated an empire and blessed the fortunes of self-government by its people, and for its people, in radiant style.

Like other national stories, India's rests on a belief in a beginning that ranks as the beginning of beginnings: that magical moment of birth of Indian democracy, just before sunset on the 14 August 1947, when the Indian tricolour was raised over the old imperial Parliament, to flutter in the late-monsoon Delhi sky, blessed by a distant rainbow. Later that evening, just before midnight, runs the founding story, Jawaharlal Nehru, boyishly slim, dressed in a white achkan with a red rose in his lapel, stood before the Constituent Assembly to declare that the half-century struggle for full independence from British rule was finally over. The four-and-a-half minute speech by Nehru is said to be among the most compelling made by any modern world leader.

Nehru's words combined humility with ambition and the yearning, expressed in formal English spoken with an upper-class accent, to start something new in a world broken and battered by war, cruelty, and domination. 'It is fitting', he said forcefully, into the All India Radio microphone, 'that at this solemn moment we take the pledge of dedication to the service of India and her people and to the still larger cause of humanity.' The world was now One World, he continued. Peace and freedom had become indivisible. Local disasters now produced global effects. Beginning with India, democracy thus had to be brought to the world, so that power and freedom were exercised responsibly. 'Long years ago', he said, 'we made a tryst with destiny, and now the time comes when we shall redeem our pledge, not wholly or in full measure, but very substantially.' He added: 'This is no time for ill-will or blaming others. We have to build the noble mansion of free India where all her children may dwell.'

The allegory of India's tryst with democracy notes the formidable obstacles confronting its transition from a trampled British colony to a proud power-sharing democracy. Nehru and his Congress party envisaged an Asian democracy that wasn't simply a replica of the West. It had to solve two problems at once. The new democracy had to snap the chains imposed from the outside by its colonial masters; and unpick the threads of colonial domination at home by creating a new nation of equally dignified citizens of diverse backgrounds. Democracy was neither a gift of the Western world nor uniquely suited to Indian conditions. India was in fact a laboratory featuring a first-ever experiment in creating national unity, economic growth, religious toleration, and social equality out of a vast and polychromatic reality, a social order whose inherited power relations, rooted in the hereditary Hindu caste status, language hierarchies, and accumulated wealth, were to be transformed by the constitutionally guaranteed counter-power of public debate, multiparty competition, and periodic elections (Figure 1).

Efforts to build an Indian democracy are said to have done more than transform the lives of its people. India fundamentally altered the

Figure 1. A polling station in Delhi, 1952, during the first general election

nature of representative democracy itself. During the first several decades after independence, a new 'post-Westminster' type of democracy resulted, in the process slaughtering quite a few goats of prejudice. None of the standard political science postulates about the prerequisites of democracy survived. They had spoken of economic growth as its fundamental precondition, so that free and fair elections could be practicable only when sufficient numbers of people owned or enjoyed such commodities as automobiles, refrigerators, and wirelesses. Weighed down by destitution of heart-breaking proportions, the country managed to laugh in the face of academic insistence that there was a causal—perhaps even mathematical—link between economic development and political democracy. Millions of poor and illiterate people rejected the imperial and pseudo-scientific prejudice that a country must first be deemed materially fit for democracy. Struggling against poverty, they decided instead that they must become materially fit *through* democracy.

This was a change of epochal significance, say those who tell the India Story, as it's been called.[1] In contrast to post-1949 China and many postcolonial countries, India's transition to democracy did not just show that Mugabe- and Stroessner-style dictatorship and military rule were unnecessary in the so-named Third World. Indian democrats proved that political unity within a highly diverse country could be built by respecting its social differences. They showed, despite everything, that the hand of democracy could come to include potentially billions of people defined by a huge variety of histories and customs that had one thing in common: they were people who were not Europeans, and did not want to be ruled by them. In this way, the region defied the common-sense rule of the white sahibs of Britannia that democracy takes root only where there's a demos bound together by a common culture. Churchill had said so repeatedly. In contrast, say, to the colonies of Australia or Canada, India was the white man's burden, he insisted, a muddled place that was immune to purposeful change in the Western way, which meant that the British were condemned to play the role of custodians of a pagan wilderness in need of law and order. 'The rescue of India from ages of barbarism, tyranny, and intestine war, and its slow but ceaseless forward march to civilisation constitute . . . the finest achievement of our history', he crowed. Then he grumped. 'India is an abstraction', he said, 'a geographical term. It is no more a united nation than the Equator.' This fact posed a special difficulty.

> There are scores of nations and races in India and hundreds of religions and sects. Out of the three hundred and fifty millions of Indians only a very few millions can read or write, and of these only a fraction are interested in politics and Western ideas. The rest are primitive people absorbed in the hard struggle for life.

Hence India had no democratic future. It was preposterous to suppose that 'the almost innumerable peoples of India would be likely to live in peace, happiness and decency under the same polity and the same form of Government as the British, Canadian or Australian democracies.'[2]

Indian democrats rejected such poppycock. They instead thought of India as a society brimming with different hopes and expectations about who Indians were and what their government should do for them. They bearded the woolly predictions of experts who said that French-style secularism, the compulsory retreat of religious myths into the private sphere, was necessary before hard-nosed democracy could take hold of the world. The Indian polity was home to hundreds of languages. It contained every major faith known to humanity. Social complexity on this scale led Indian democrats to a brand-new practical justification of democracy. Democracy—say champions of the India Story—was no longer regarded as a means of protecting a homogeneous society of equals. It came to be seen as the fairest way of enabling people of different backgrounds and divergent identities to live together as equals, without civil war.[3]

The Greatest Show on Earth

The India Story has had a great run. Despite many disquieting twists and turns in the country's nearly three-quarters of a century as an independent republic, the broad story has mostly endured. The world sees India as a democracy and the majority of Indians say they're attached to 'democracy' (63 per cent) and satisfied with its achievements (55 per cent).[4] There are at least three overlapping explanations for the long life of the India Story.

The first reason is the usual focus on India's achievements in the field of government since independence—the performance of its state institutions, political reforms, and elections. The new republic of India is seen to have managed to resolve its boundary challenges and to establish itself as a sovereign territorial state with an impressive written constitution. The Indian state crafted a durable peace with its humbled British masters by choosing to remain within the British Commonwealth. The French and Portuguese enclaves on Indian soil were annexed. The new Indian republic survived the turmoil and hell of the Partition of 1947, when perhaps as many as 16 million people were forced to cross borders and a million or more suffered

murderous pogroms. A new written constitution was adopted (on
26 November 1949). Its principal hand was the political leader of
the lowly 'untouchable' caste and law minister, B.R. Ambedkar. 'We,
The People of India', began a document soon to be renowned for its
length and sweeping breadth, and for its redefinition of democracy to
include the rule of law as a weapon to be used against abuses of power
in the hallowed name of 'the people'. Its soberly written preamble
described India as a 'sovereign democratic republic'. It stood for social,
economic, and political justice for all its citizens; liberty of thought,
expression, belief, faith, and worship; equality of status and of opportunity; and fraternity that would assure the dignity of 'the individual
and the unity and integrity of the Nation'.

It was within this visionary constitutional framework that the new
republic hosted its first parliamentary general election, which began
in October 1951 and took six months to conduct. It was the grandest
show the world had ever seen. The aim: to create a countrywide electoral system that extended a fair vote for 4,500 seats to 176 million
Indians aged 21 or over, 85 per cent of whom couldn't read or write.
The methods: in quick time, 224,000 polling booths were built;
2 million steel ballot boxes were manufactured and delivered to site;
16,500 clerks were hired on six-month contracts to type and collate
the electoral rolls; 56,000 presiding officers and 280,000 support staff
supervised the voting; and 224,000 police officers were assigned to
polling stations. At each polling station, to assist voters who were
mainly illiterate, multiple ballot boxes were installed, each one with a
separate political party symbol: an elephant for one party, an earthen
lamp for another, a pair of bullocks for the Congress party. Helped by
Indian scientists, the newly established Election Commission actioned
plans for preventing fraudulent voting by finger printing each voter;
the indelible ink, of which nearly 400,000 phials were used, lasted at
least a week. Voter turnout was 60 per cent. It was an election in
which 75 political parties wooed the votes of 176 million adult women
and men. A total of 489 seats in the federal Parliament and 3,375 seats
in the state Assemblies were filled. Nehru's Congress party claimed

victory in eighteen of the twenty-five states and won an outright majority of seats (364 of the 489) in the directly elected lower house called the Lok Sabha, or the House of the People (the upper house, called the Rajya Sabha, or Council of States, comprises members elected by state legislatures and a few nominated by the president). The socialists were routed. The communists claimed second place, which was an impressive result for a newborn democracy that probably included more hardcore believers in Stalin than the Soviet Union. In the interests of a fair and equal franchise, there were even efforts by the Election Commission to dismantle patriarchal barriers to women's participation in the election. The diffidence of many women to allow their names to be entered on the electoral register—preferring instead to be X's wife or Y's mother—was publicly criticized and officials were instructed to record the actual name of such women voters. They sometimes refused. An estimated 2.8 million female voters were turned away, yet the public uproar that followed was the beginning of an unfinished democratic revolution against male prejudice.

The political institution-building that took place after independence was substantial, but the chroniclers of the India Story go further, by emphasizing how, during later decades, India's gravity-defying adventure with democratic politics was strengthened by institutional repairs and experiments with new governing procedures. They give the example of the Parliament's breathtaking decision (in 1993) to extend democracy 'downwards' and 'sideways' by extending local self-government (*panchayat*) to all of India's 600,000 villages (Figure 2). The three-tiered reform created some 227,000 'village councils' at the base; 5,900 higher-level or 'block councils' comprising representatives drawn from the village councils; and standing above these over 470 'district councils'. Similar structures (municipal corporations and councils) were erected in the cities, so that overall, the ranks of the country's elected representatives—some 500 members of Parliament (MPs) and 5,000 state representatives—were swelled by another 3 million newly elected local representatives. There were design flaws, and this momentous move towards greater democratization was not welcomed by all.

Figure 2. A village council meeting in Gadchiroli, Maharashtra

States unevenly implemented the new structures, and fiscal decentralization failed to keep pace with political decentralization. Local
governments were unable to legislate or take either the states or the
central government to court over jurisdictional disputes. Dirty tricks
were played on the weak by the strong. Village assemblies often didn't
take place, or they were inquorate, or their records were falsified by
village oligarchs. Women candidates and voters suffered harassment.
Elected local government leaders (called *sarpanches*) from the lower
castes were physically prevented from assuming office. Even though
there was talk of excluding political parties from this new domain
of self-government, foul party-political games were played. And,
when all else failed, the dominant castes used violence to have their
way. And yet, in the India Story, despite all this, the *panchayat* reforms
produced benefits. Not only was *panchayat* voter turnout generally
higher (on average 60 per cent) than for state and national elections. The local government reforms helped democratize Indian

democracy. New political spaces were created for the downtrodden, especially women (one-third of seats was set aside for them). Groups such as *Dalits* (the lowest in the Hindu caste structure, officially classified as Scheduled Castes, or SCs) and tribal people known as *Adivasis* (literally, 'original inhabitants', officially classified as Scheduled Tribes, or STs) were also guaranteed seats in proportion to their actual numbers.

Equally gravity-defying was the creation of a new model of secularism—not the secularism of the French or American constitutions, but in effect a new vision of guaranteeing the political equality of all Indian religions, which implied the need for government policies to fight religious fanaticism and to correct the imbalances of power within and among different religions. India's secular democracy, say its defenders, came to resemble a modern palimpsest bearing traces of many ancient faiths and ways of life, a legally protected canvas of many different colours, not a patchwork quilt of loosely connected or cantankerous faiths kept from each other's throats ultimately by the gun barrels of the state.

The India Story tells how the legal requirement to reserve spaces in the national and state legislatures, and in public sector employment and educational institutions, first for SCs and STs and then for the middle castes, clumped together as 'Other Backward Castes' (or, OBCs), had democratizing consequences, especially in the field of elections. The reforms stimulated a new kind of democratic class struggle driven by lower-caste assertion of regional caste-based political parties headed by iridescent leaders. Among them was Mayawati, the first woman to become chief minister of the most populous state of Uttar Pradesh, a leader who delivered thumping speeches about the importance of creating an 'egalitarian society' freed from discrimination based on caste or creed; and the former chief minister and political boss of Bihar, Lalu Prasad Yadav, who portrayed himself as the 'messiah' of the backward castes, Muslims and Dalits. Bearing names like the RJD (Rashtriya Janata Dal), the SP (Samajwadi Party), and the largest Dalit-based party, the BSP (Bahujan Samaj Party), these parties intensified political competition, both in the states and at the federal level in Delhi. A record thirty-one different parties, many of them defending a one-point programme and most of them elected from the regions, filled the Parliament following the 1996 general elections. Despite repeated splits, these splinter parties pushed the young Asian democracy to the point where, from the mid-1990s, no government in Delhi was formed without their help.

The India Story stresses that the political empowerment of the powerless was perhaps Indian democracy's greatest achievement. Unlike any other democracy on the face of our planet, the Indian poor—despite multiple obstacles and in the absence of compulsory voting—turn out at election time in proportionately greater numbers than the affluent middle and upper classes.[5] In the United States, the motivation to vote is lowest among the poorest (in the 2008 elections, when overall voter turnout was 57.1 per cent, it was 41.3 per cent; among the wealthiest it was 78.1 per cent). In India, the pattern is just the opposite. In the first two general elections in India, overall voter turnout was under 50 per cent. In the 1977 elections, the figure reached around 60 per cent, where it has consistently remained, the increase due largely to the growing political involvement of the poor, women, and young people. In the 2019 national election that returned Narendra Modi to power with a thumping majority, the turnout reached a record 67 per cent. The trend, says the India Story, is living proof that a big majority of India's citizens have grown convinced that the ballot box is a means of earthly redemption—that elections are uniquely democratic moments when citizens display their dignity as equals and express their differences as members of particular communities.

The India Story undoubtedly captures the important ways in which the country has experimented with democratic self-government. The long and interesting list of achievements doesn't just include a robust written constitution, a three-tier system of government driven by stronger local self-government and a quasi-federal division of powers between states and central government, and the introduction of compulsory quotas for marginalized groups. Fiercely fought student elections, popular protests, and creative instruments such as public interest litigation that enable public-spirited individuals or courts to take up the cause of victims of arbitrary power, have also provided traction to the India Story. According to one Indian political scientist, 'the new political community of democracy is being forged and in the process there is a democracy of communities emerging.' Describing India as a democracy engaged in the process of democratizing itself, the interpretation quietly supposes that history is on its side, and that Indian democracy, for the sake of overcoming imperfections, now needs further reforms.

> After seven decades the Indian democratic system has, by and large, acquired...the legitimacy that it requires for its smooth and proper functioning...Because it has done so, and stabilised, we have the luxury to analytically move to the next historical stage of intellectual inquiry of identifying its blemishes and expressing our discontent with its limitations.[6]

Along similarly sanguine lines, another leading Indian scholar notes that democracy is 'a raw, exciting, necessary and in the end ultimately disappointing form of politics.' It 'encourages people . . . to refuse to be ruled by those who deny them recognition'. He goes on to observe that while in India 'the idea of democracy has released prodigious energies of creation and destruction', its promise is widely believed and now serves as a material force shaping the lives of many millions of citizens. 'Democracy . . . has irreversibly entered the Indian political imagination', he concludes. 'A return to the old order of castes, or of rule by empire, is inconceivable: the principle of authority in society has been transformed.'[7]

Darling of the West

Apart from gradual democratization and a robust history of elections and institutional innovation, there's a second and rather unexpected reason for the credibility of the India Story, to do with outside

reinforcement. It may sound odd to put things this way, but in a curious twist of fate, an upside-down species of Orientalist prejudice has
nourished the India Story. In recent decades, especially among
American speechwriters and politicians and their political allies, outsiders have come to speak effusively of India as an important global
partner whose commitment to commonly shared values such as 'liberal democracy' augur well for a close relationship in matters of trade
and technology, diplomacy, and military strategy.

The diplomatic love affair of Western powers with democratic
India is comparatively recent. Things weren't always so rosy, especially
during the early decades after Indian independence, when Nehru
personally dominated the making and unmaking of Indian foreign
policy. Democracy stopped at India's borders; Nehru's foreign policies
were India's. The results were distinctive. Whole continents (Africa
and Latin America) and policy areas like trade and commerce were
virtually ignored. Nehru had little affection for the time-tested rule
that democracies always fare better when they band together, under a
tent of multilateral, publicly accountable, cross-border institutions. His
suspicion that the United States was plotting to become the region's
next imperial power, combined with his general disdain for global Big
Power Politics, led him to forge an alliance with Tito's neo-Stalinist
Yugoslavia, and did so in the name of the doctrine for which he
achieved global fame: 'non-alignment'. Nehru liked to defend it by
referring to the Five Principles (*Panch Sheel*) of world order, which
included non-aggression; peaceful coexistence; respect for the
principle of the sovereignty of states; non-interference in their
domestic affairs; and equality among the world's states and peoples.
The mix contained incompatibles; and democratic virtues like
respect for equal civil and political freedoms inside states went
missing, which helped Nehru turn a blind eye to the violation of
the same principles, for instance in his long-standing support for
the Soviet Union and its imperialist, anti-democratic command
over the 'captive nations' of central-eastern Europe. After the
death of Stalin in 1953, relations grew especially warm with the

Soviet Union, which provided capital and technical assistance for India's state-led industrialization.

The blinkered foreign policy produced mixed results. Indian energy was put into cultivating relations with the totalitarian People's Republic of China (though the disastrous 1962 war with China and the failure to resolve bellicose tensions over the Tibet border dogged Nehru until his death in office). Nationalist statesmen like Gamal Abdel Nasser praised Nehru as the voice of human conscience. Yet there were smouldering tensions with the United States, captured by the perhaps apocryphal but telling anecdote that has Secretary of State John Foster Dulles demanding to know whether India was for or against the United States, to which Nehru replied: 'Yes.'

The anti-American tone set by Nehru's foreign policy hardened in post-Nehru India. When in the early 1970s Pakistan was plunged into civil war and a war with India that ended with the creation of Bangladesh, the United States sided with Pakistan, its partner in the rapprochement with China. In that same period, India scrapped its non-alignment policy by signing a twenty-year Treaty of Friendship and Cooperation with the Soviet Union. 'By 1971', Henry Kissinger later wrote, 'our relations with India had achieved a state of exasperatedly strained cordiality, like a couple that can neither separate nor get along.'[8] Tensions with the United States festered after India exploded its first nuclear device (in May 1974), in an operation code-named Smiling Buddha. It was not only the first country to do so outside the United Nations Security Council. India also blocked calls by the United States to allow outside inspection of its nuclear facilities.

The turning point in India's relation to the West, and to the United States in particular, came after the collapse of the Soviet Empire in 1989–91. India was plunged into confusion about how the country might behave in a unipolar world dominated by the United States. Further disagreement between the two states about nuclear weapons erupted; a period of stand-off followed the 1998 nuclear test by India and the decision of the Clinton administration (in May 1998) to recall its ambassador and impose economic sanctions on India. Yet despite this friction, the United States, looking for allies against China, began to regard India as a geopolitical prize. Rich in resources, blessed with a giant domestic market, strategically well positioned, prone to antagonism with China, and blessed with the title of the world's largest democracy, India came to be regarded as a potential major partner in consolidating US power in the region and beyond as part of a coalition to contain the next rising global power, China. According to this geopolitical reasoning, the goal of American foreign policy was to consolidate a partnership between two polities that would in the end come to resemble each other, and to see eye to eye on most major foreign policy matters.

And so, an American charm offensive was launched. It began with President Clinton's visit to India (March 2000). It yielded a jointly signed vision statement that set out a charter for future political engagement between the two countries, backed by an agreed programme of 'institutional dialogue' about bilateral deals. Despite anti-imperialist rumblings at home about dealing with the Americans, India's diplomats negotiated a full lifting of sanctions. US Secretary of State Condoleezza Rice and her officials presented to Indian Prime Minister Manmohan Singh (March 2005) an outline of a 'decisively broader strategic relationship' laced with talk of helping India 'become a major world power in the 21st century'. Agreements covering cooperation in maritime security, humanitarian assistance, disaster relief, and counterterrorism, the lifting of a three-decade moratorium on nuclear trade with India and naval exercises prepared the way for a visit (March 2006) by President George W. Bush. 'I'm honoured to bring the good wishes and the respect of the world's oldest democracy to the world's largest democracy', he said, to warm applause. 'The partnership between the United States and India has deep and sturdy roots in the values we share. In both our countries, democracy is more than a form of government, it is the central promise of our national character.'

During the next two decades, American leaders repeated the melody. The serenading of India as a democratic partner hit a new high as the Obama administration announced a 'pivot' to Asia. 'India and the United States are not just natural partners. I believe America can be India's best partner', said President Obama during his second visit to India (2015), drawing applause from his invited Delhi audience. 'The world will be a safer and a more just place when our two democracies— the world's largest democracy and the world's oldest democracy— stand together.' Spiced rhetoric of this kind flavoured the 'Namaste Trump' mass rally in February 2020, in the world's largest cricket stadium (since renamed Narendra Modi Stadium) in Ahmedabad. 'America loves India. America respects India', said the American president. 'And America will always be faithful and loyal friends to the Indian people.' Never mind that more than one-third of the estimated 125,000 people who had turned out to see him left before the end of his nearly thirty-minute speech, or that another third had turned their backs by the time Mr Modi spoke after the American president. The important thing was that in Ahmedabad and several cities, giant billboards trumpeted the old trope of the 'world's oldest democracy' meeting the 'world's largest democracy' (Figure 3). Modi's efforts to

Figure 3. The world's 'oldest democracy' and 'largest democracy'

use his stadium hosting of Trump to turn geopolitics into a heavily advertised spectator sport broke with his predecessors' careful attempts to strike a balance between the United States and China. Under Modi, India has hedged against neighbouring China by openly courting the distant US. India has signed a joint strategic vision statement for the Asia–Pacific and the Indian Ocean region, a Defence Framework Agreement, and a landmark defence logistics pact with the United States, giving each side access to the other's military facilities. Together with Japan, the United States and Australia, India is party to the Quadrilateral Security Dialogue, the 'Quad' initiative designed to promote multilateral dialogue and an 'Asian arc of democracy'. Defence, intelligence, and trade ties with the United States have reached new highs in recent years. There's also been much eulogizing by Modi about the need for India, the 'world's largest democracy', to 'overcome the hesitations of history' by forging tighter links with its 'liberal democratic' American partner.

Emergency Rule

Apart from the Western validation of Indian democracy and India's own institutional evolution, there's a third—less obvious—reason why the India Story has enjoyed a long life. It is, ironically, an egregious attempt to destroy India's democracy that reinforced faith in its democracy. This happened under the watch of Indira Gandhi, during a stormy period now known as the Emergency.

The tempest was unleashed by the lacklustre showing of Mrs Gandhi's Congress party in the 1967 general elections, which it managed to win, but with a reduced majority and loss of control over eight state legislatures. Indira Gandhi responded by resorting to the old populist tactic of appealing over the heads of her party apparatus, directly to voters, especially to its millions of poor. The aim was to strengthen her hand and build a new-style Congress government by disrupting the so-called 'vote banks' system, through which local party barons (known as the Syndicate) organized whole groups of voters through patronage networks, in return for which they received perks and privileges from the central Congress leadership. Through posters, loudhailers, and television and radio sets, the slogan 'Abolish Poverty' (*Garibi Hatao*) was plastered everywhere. Constitutional protection for the privileges of the regional royalties was abolished; banks were nationalized; and Prime Minister Gandhi surprised millions by calling a general election one year early.

In that general election (1971), Mrs Gandhi's move to nationalize Indian politics by distracting attention from regional and local concerns was richly rewarded—with a handsome landslide victory. Then military conflict with Pakistan erupted. Mrs Gandhi's swift, iron-fisted approach resulted in both victory and the secession of Bangladesh and (in the 1972 regional elections) another round of political success. The way was now open to shrink democracy into elections and rebuild Congress into an election-winning machine that resembled a large, lumbering elephant with Mrs Gandhi in the saddle, garlanded with flowers, under a parasol, looking down imperially on intrigued and admiring crowds (Figure 4).

Figure 4. Indira Gandhi addressing a public rally in Maharashtra (1972)

Many citizens and representatives grew worried that Indian parliamentary democracy was about to be strangled by a dictatorship. Street protests erupted. Political writers like Rajni Kothari—among the earliest researchers of the Indian scene—pondered the nature of democracy for the first time since independence.[9] Local communities mobilized. Millions began to feel that parliamentary democracy was becoming an empty shell—and that the rods of iron-fisted rule had to be cut. Mrs Gandhi's demagogy backfired. In the name of democracy, she and her cronies were blamed personally for all that was perceived to be wrong with India.

Her response was dictatorial. Convicted in the Allahabad High Court of electoral malpractice, disqualified from Parliament, and debarred from holding office for six years, Mrs Gandhi moved swiftly. Summoning powers that the Constitution (Articles 352–60) had cunningly borrowed from the British Empire, Mrs Gandhi manoeuvred the president into declaring a state of Emergency, in June 1975. It lasted for twenty-one months. It was not exactly martial law. The army didn't take sides. Soldiers never strutted city streets, weapons cocked, but democratic rights were suspended. Opposition leaders found themselves behind bars. Newspapers were censored, hundreds of journalists arrested, and foreign correspondents were forced to leave. There was spreading talk of the Constitution as a millstone around the necks of those who wanted to improve the lot of Indians.

This wasn't the first time that state power was used so ruthlessly. Non-Congress governments in the states were routinely sacked by the Congress-ruled centre, as in Kerala, where a democratically elected communist state government was toppled.[10] But the ferocity of this nationwide crackdown and the suspension of fundamental rights proved shocking. Its intensity and toughness served as a reminder that the constitution makers had designed a state to deliver more than the red roses of democracy. They blessed the Indian state with extraordinary law and order powers to deal with what B.R. Ambedkar had called the 'grammar of anarchy' and 'the bloody methods of revolution'. In June 1975, their prayers were posthumously answered.

Parliament and cabinet were bypassed. Sidestepped as well were the old structures and party faithful of Congress. Mrs Gandhi cultivated a brand new power base: the so-called Youth Congress run by her trusted younger son, Sanjay, himself surrounded by young men of dubious backgrounds, dressed in kurta pyjamas, the midnight's children of Nehru's India, all keen to hallucinate on whiffs of political power. Governmental power, meanwhile, moved rapidly towards the centre of the centre—to the Prime Minister's Office in Delhi, a city that in turn Mrs Gandhi decided to adorn. Like the British before her, 'Madam' moved to make her own mark on the capital by commissioning the Lieutenant Governor of Delhi to 'Make Delhi Beautiful'. Her picture was posted everywhere. Slums were bulldozed. Trees were planted. The Emergency was to endure—and to be remembered.

Remembered it was, but not in the way that the Leader's advisers and flatterers had expected. Such was their arrogance that in 1977 they managed to convince Mrs Gandhi to go to the polls. The Leader was misled. Dressed in fine hubris, she came to the election table, only to be forced to eat humble pie. The election aroused tremendous passions. It emboldened groups—farmers, the poorer castes, untouchables—whose voices previously hadn't counted for much. They rounded especially on the hubris of government and its policies, symbolized by the abusive vasectomy programmes championed by her son, Sanjay. Votes piled up against the Leader, to the point, for the first time in the history of Indian democracy, where Congress lost control of the central government. The motley alliance known as the Janata Party swept the polls, winning a majority of parliamentary seats. Morarji Desai became the first non-Congress Prime Minister of India. Many Congress party loyalists deserted 'Madam', who lost her own parliamentary seat.

How Democracies Die

The political defeat of the Emergency gave credibility to the India Story. More than a few observers reassuringly noted how Indian

citizens had set a global example: they had demonstrated that demagogy could be defeated using democratic means, and that the arrogant
could be humbled, taught that they couldn't make a table eat grass.
The saga convinced many observers, both inside and outside the
country, that India was a consolidated democracy, and that it was a
polity blessed with political resilience, and with great powers of
renewal. India's reputation as the world's largest and most successful
new democracy was strengthened.

The spirited defeat of the Emergency told by the India Story reinforced the belief that India was a robust and resilient democracy
because it had defied the standard textbook treatments of how living
democracies miss their step, stumble, and collapse to the ground. The
most common understanding of how democracies meet their end—
let's call it the sudden death view—supposes that democracies normally die in a puff of smoke, in a hail of gunfire, or (as in ancient
democracies) with the rumble of chariots and the cut and thrust of
spears and swords. More than a few ancient assembly democracies
were certainly destroyed in this way, by sudden military invasion
backed by conspiracies of the rich, or by single-minded tyrants. This
was the fate of Athens, the region's most powerful assembly democracy, which despite the spirited resistance of its citizens suffered military defeats and eventually succumbed to an invasion by the
well-armed kingdom of Macedon.[11] Proponents of this catastrophist
way of thinking note that twentieth-century representative democracies similarly suffered a quick death at the hands of military force. The
armed annexation of the Sudetenland and (in March 1939) full military occupation of Czechoslovakia by the Nazi Wehrmacht, and the
follow-up Nazi invasions of Luxembourg, Belgium, and the
Netherlands, are cases in point. Parliamentary democracy was killed in
a trice by aerial bombardment, tanks, and invading troops. Sudden
death was later the fate of Chile's Salvador Allende. In a grave moment
of high political drama, the president of a democratically elected socialist
government bid farewell to his country in a live radio broadcast, then

took his own life as armed troops, helicopter gunships, and air force jets bombarded the presidential palace.

Observers fond of the sudden-death view point out that during the past generation, especially during the Cold War, military *coups d'état* were the chief cause of the death of democracy. The data appears to be on their side.[12] It shows that during that period, around three-quarters of power-sharing democracies met their end in this way. More recent examples of quick-death casualties include the forceful Israeli crushing of the electoral victory of Hamas in the Palestinian legislative elections (2006) and the military *coups d'état* against the governments of President Mohamed Morsi in Egypt (2013) and Yingluck Shinawatra in Thailand (2014).

All the evidence seems to confirm the sudden-death account of how democracies are killed off. And yet it doesn't, at least according to a second way of thinking about how democracies come to an end. Champions of this alternative view say that the death of democracy requires that we pay close attention to the power struggles that unfold, often quite slowly, within the institutions of government. This slow-motion politics explanation emphasizes that democratic breakdowns are always the result of strings of overlapping political developments. The explanation shifts attention from the high drama moments towards the complex background dynamics that produce breakdowns of democratic government. Not catastrophic events, but drawn-out and deep-seated political processes are the ultimate cause of the break-down of democracy, it says. Those who think this way agree that democracy is best defined narrowly, as popular self-government based on the periodic election of representatives. They agree as well that the causes of the demise and downfall of democracy in this sense are traceable to breakdowns of consensus within the high-level institutions of government. But in their autopsies, this second approach wants to emphasize that the collapse and expiry of democracy is normally a protracted process principally driven by political factors, such as the short-sightedness and miscalculations of political leaders, bitterly disputed election results, the dysfunctions and failures of government institutions, and the manoeuvrings of the armed forces.

The slow-motion politics explanation emphasizes the cunning and creativity of political actors and the indeterminacy of the political dynamics in which things can go in more than one direction. The death of democracy is never a foregone conclusion. Democide happens because it is chosen by political actors in political circumstances not of their choosing. Critically important, runs the argument, are the bitter contests between political forces favouring the maintenance and/or reform of a democratic political system and those who don't care about its fate, or who actively want its overthrow. The explanation notes that in any given crisis of democracy—late 1920s Weimar Germany, Bolivia in late 2019—the political dynamics are normally stormy, sometimes terrifying, and always radically confusing. There are nevertheless identifiable patterns. Usually, a democratically elected government loses its grip because the formidable problems and challenges it faces begin to seem insoluble. There are loud cries for the removal of the government. In the shadows, anti-government forces hatch plans to give it the boot. Disloyal opposition flourishes. There are wild rumours, talk of conspiracies, street protests, and outbreaks of uncontrolled violence. Fears of civil unrest spread. The armed forces grow agitated. The elected government responds by bolstering its executive powers, for instance by granting itself emergency powers, proroguing the legislature, reshuffling the military high command, and imposing media blackouts. Things eventually come to the boil. The moment of denouement arrives, often in the shape of a constitutional putsch: court challenges and legal defeats of the government by forces paying homage to the Constitution yet in reality bent on dissolving not only the government but constitutional democracy itself. The government can also be infiltrated by the enemies of democracy. Or it can face fierce opposition in the streets by forces of disorder pressing for a political transition. Whatever the micro-dynamics, the drawn-out drama reaches its climax. The government collapses. The army moves from its barracks onto the streets to quell unrest and

to occupy key government and media institutions. Democracy is buried in the grave it has dug for itself.

Champions of the slow-motion politics explanation point out that
the same outcome can happen when a democratically elected government sets out purposefully to wreck democracy. The mortal
wounding of democratic government from the top happens in slow
motion, but what makes it difficult to spot is the way the degraders of
democracy dismantle governing arrangements, including free and fair
elections, in the name of democracy. The 'mafia state' account of
Orbán's Hungary is an example of this kind of interpretation.[13] It
explains how multiparty, power-sharing democracy, in the name of
'the people', slowly but surely, can be destroyed from within by a
dominant power group cleverly manipulating the mechanisms of free
and fair periodic elections. This explanation, a variant of the slow-
motion politics approach, sees mafia politics as the democratic enemy
of democracy. In contrast to the traditional understanding of mafia as
underground wealth and power networks whose octopoid tentacles
are wrapped around the throat of the state, mafia politics builds a
mafia state. It sucks life from power-sharing democracy committed to
the principle of equality. Mafia governments led by big-mouthed
demagogues do everything they can to concentrate political power in
their own hands. They publicly attack journalists and independent
media, public service bureaucracies, independent judiciaries, and
other power-monitoring institutions. They are gripped by an inner
urge to destroy checks, balances, and mechanisms for publicly scrutinizing and restraining power. Mafia politics has no taste or time for
institutional give-and-take politics. Hence, mafia governments, acting
in the name of 'the people', use media to hit hard against their targeted 'enemies'. They spread uncivil language, pick political fights
with their opponents, and tighten border controls against 'foreigners'
and 'foreign' influences. Their eyes are constantly on the next election.
With luck and good timing, and helped along by degraded and neutered political institutions, mafia governments go on to win subsequent
elections. There are more celebrations in the streets. For millions,

victory in the name of 'the People' is sweet. The Godfather demagogue is delighted. There is talk of more political triumphs to come. But, mortally wounded, the core governing institutions of democracy suffer a slow and painful death.

'Bread, Fish, Wastrels and Frauds'

At first glance, these two sets of explanations of how and why democracy withers and dies seem very different. But they aren't. Worth noting is their shared concern with what transpires within the meeting rooms and hallways of government: their common preoccupation with political struggles and dramas that unfold within high-level governing institutions, including on the battlefield of elections, which are thought of as the quintessence of democracy. More important to note is the way these explanations of the death of democracy have long served to fortify the India Story, whose disciples have regularly pointed out that in all the years since independence the country only once experienced an organized and declared political challenge to its governing arrangements. The difficulty is that the story is now challenged by a recent development: mounting fears, even among opposition political parties, that Indian democracy is threatened by what is being called an 'undeclared' political emergency. Indian public intellectuals are also sounding the alarm. The historian Ramachandra Guha, who once described India as a '50-50 democracy', has downgraded it to '30-70'. Political thinker Pratap Bhanu Mehta warns that Modi's Bharatiya Janata Party (BJP) is spreading the cult of 'propaganda' and 'Our Leader', and normalizing the dangerous 'use of state power to suffocate the opposition'. Psephologist and political activist Yogendra Yadav similarly reports that 'there has never been a simultaneous assault on the three D's of the Indian Republic—democracy, diversity and development.'[14]

Global democracy reports and rankings have begun to reflect these concerns. A 2019 report by the Economist Intelligence Unit classified

India as a 'flawed democracy'; the country fell ten places to 51st position out of 167 states and territories, its lowest ever ranking. The
Freedom in the World 2020 report by Washington-based Freedom House
ranked India among the 'least free' democracies. It pushed India down
to the 83rd position, along with Timor-Leste and Senegal, in a list of
195 countries and territories. The following year, it downgraded India
from 'free' to 'partly free'. The sharpest decline in India's democratic
credentials was registered by the *Democracy Report 2020* compiled by
Sweden's V-DEM Institute. 'India has continued on the path of steep
decline', it noted, 'to the extent that it has almost lost its status as a
democracy.' Ranking the country below Sierra Leone, Guatemala,
and Hungary, the V-Dem report revealed that the quantitative markers of democracy in India began to slide around 2000, but that the
decline became particularly steep since the 2014 election of the Modi
government. In its 2021 report, V-DEM declared India had turned
into an 'electoral autocracy'.

These quantitative surveys do offer helpful snapshots of the degradation of political life, for instance mounting physical attacks on
minorities, government clampdowns on academic freedom, intimidation of journalists and Internet blackouts (highest in the world).
There are rising concerns about the recent cult of a supreme leader
who enjoys an iron grip over his party and government and rock-solid
numbers in the Parliament. Worries are surfacing about the declining
independence of governing institutions. Overnight, the Modi government pulled from circulation high-denomination banknotes—
86 per cent of the cash in circulation—and crashed the economy,
without so much as a murmur of protest from the Reserve Bank of
India. Inconvenient data that might show the government in a bad
light is routinely suppressed. The much-vaunted civil service is suffering a partisan makeover. The military is happy to be used as a political
tool, in ruling party advertisements after clandestine cross-border
attacks. The higher judiciary has become increasingly compliant, and
mainstream media resembles a government echo chamber. The steep
decline of the country's democracy ratings is strongly linked to the

information blockade and mass arrest of local leaders in the erstwhile state of Jammu and Kashmir; a citizenship registration exercise in the north-eastern state of Assam that disenfranchised nearly 2 million people; and the ruthless crackdown on peaceful protests against a special citizenship law that the country's Muslims fear will be used against them.

All these political developments help explain the serious damage that's being done to the India Story, but the surveys don't capture the most concerning trend: the slow-motion crumbling of the social foundations of Indian democracy. India is confronted not only by an undeclared political emergency. For many decades, the country has been suffering an undeclared social emergency. Understanding its dynamics, and its political consequences, requires that we move beyond the narrow confines of previous state- and election-centred explanations of how democracies die. These state-centred explanations fail not only to register the familiar point that right from the outset India's democratic adventure was frustrated by 'some of the vilest forms of social distinctions known'.[15] In the pages to come, we go further by explaining why India is today a prime example of a democracy menaced by its failure to protect and nurture its social underpinnings. Ambedkar feared that Indian democracy would be plagued by gaps between the struggle for good government founded on one-person-one-vote political equality and a social base stricken by huge 'graded' inequalities ruinous of 'unity and solidarity'. His fears were long ago vindicated. Under Modi, the decomposition of social life continues, but we emphasize in this book that the whole trend has been decades in the making and that responsibility for failures in such social policy areas as health and education are also traceable to the inaction and incompetence of successive political parties and governments in Delhi and the states. The drivers are many, but the net result is that social decline is ruining the spirit and substance of democratic politics. Slowly but surely, Indian democracy is experiencing social death. The India Story has lost its credibility. India is not the world's largest democracy. India is the world's largest case of endangered democracy.

There's a bigger point here, one that's relevant for the study of democracy, its flourishing and demise, and its possible mutation into a strange new kind of government we call despotism. The key point is that when assessments of democracy and how they are killed concentrate exclusively on governmental dynamics and political games of thrones, they are simply unable to grasp the fundamental significance of the social substructures of any given democracy. Yes, paying attention to high-level political dramas and dysfunctions is important, for these can and do have ruinous and reshaping effects on elections, political parties, legislatures, executive leadership, courts, and the army. But the great weakness of the sudden-death and slow-motion politics explanations is their neglect of the social foundations on which any given democracy rests. Democracy is much more than high-level dynamics centred on political parties, elections, legislatures, governments, prime ministers and presidents, civil service bureaucracies, the police, and the armed forces. These institutions of government always rest upon, and draw their strength from, interactions among millions of people living their daily lives in a variety of mediated social settings that stretch from family households, personal friendships, and local communities through to distant workplaces, sporting and leisure venues, and places of worship. Seen in this way, democracy at the 'upper levels' of government can function and be durable only if citizens 'down below' in everyday life live to the full its norms of equality, freedom, solidarity, and respect for social differences. Democracy is much more than monitory democracy—periodic elections plus a plethora of watchdog bodies that publicly scrutinize, check, and restrain those who exercise power. Democracy is a whole way of life in which people from different walks of social life see eye to eye, rub shoulders, cooperate and compromise, and generally think of themselves as the equals of one another. To speak metaphorically, democracy is a form of social life and self-realization that feeds upon what Hindus call *ātman*, a shared sense that every living person is bound to others in breath and body, mind and soul, by the innermost essence of equality.

Said differently: democracy understood as the self-government of people through their chosen representatives can happen only when citizens live together non-violently in various social associations and communities and treat each other as equals worthy of respect and dignity. Democracy is more than pressing a button or marking a box on a ballot paper. It goes beyond the mathematical certitude of election results and majority rule. It isn't the same as attending local public meetings or watching breaking news stories scrawled across a screen. Periyar E.V. Ramasamy, the celebrated Tamil founder of the Self-Respect movement, saw this. Several decades before and after independence, Periyar warned repeatedly that democracy could degenerate into the 'political gambling' of elections. In the hands of elected politicians, it might deteriorate into squabbles over 'bread and fish' among 'wastrels and frauds'. And if that happened, as he expected it would, the rituals and rivalries of elected government would sap the spirit and substance of a democracy committed to the social equality and freedom of its members.[16]

Periyar correctly spotted that a well-functioning democracy requires a special kind of social life. Democracy is freedom from hunger, humiliation, and violence. It's public disgust for callous employers who maltreat workers paid a pittance for scraping shit from latrines and unblocking stinking sewers. Democracy is saying no to brazen arrogance. It's the rejection of caste and religious bigotry and every other form of human and non-human indignity. Democracy is not being forced to travel in overcrowded buses and trains like livestock. Democracy is not having to wade through dirty water from overrunning sewers, or breathing poisonous air. Democracy is respect for women, tenderness with children, jobs that bring satisfaction and sufficient reward to live comfortably. Democracy is hygienic living conditions, and answering nature's calls in safety and privacy. It's public and private respect for different ways of living. Democracy is humility. It is the willingness to admit that impermanence renders all life vulnerable, that in the end nobody is invincible, and that ordinary lives are never ordinary. Democracy is sharing and caring for others. It's freedom from fear and the right not to be killed. It's equal access to decent medical care and sympathy for those who have fallen behind. Democracy is a learned sense of worldly wonder. It's the everyday ability to handle unexpected situations wisely. It's the rejection of the dogma that things can't be changed because they're 'naturally' fixed in stone. Democracy is thus insubordination: the refusal to put up with everyday forms of snobbery and toad-eating, idolatry and lying, bullshit and bullying. Democracy is the defence of the social footings that put springs in the steps of people freed from the curse of indignity.

Indian scholars have analysed these sentiments with great finesse and eloquence. Amartya Sen pioneered a 'capabilities approach' that makes the case for maximizing people's freedoms to achieve well-being.[17] Democracy is 'an insurrectionary faith open to the weakest of mortals', writes a young thinker convinced of the need to take stock of Indian democracy in fresh ways, with a raw intensity, by challenging prejudices about the necessity and normalcy of social inequality. 'What Indian democracy needs', says another thinker, 'is a new sense of the relationship between public and private: recognizing that there are some things states are particularly bad at, but also recognizing that we will be impoverished unless all enjoy the minimum bases for social self-respect and acknowledge each other through projects we hold in common.'[18] Intellectuals outside India agree. Democracy is 'a kind of society', a whole way of life committed to the principle that people considered as equals can 'make the best of themselves', said a distinguished twentieth-century scholar of democracy. It is 'not merely a mechanism of choosing and authorizing governments'. The 'egalitarian principle inherent in democracy' requires that in their everyday lives, including the jobs they hold, people develop and fully enjoy their personal and collective capacities. The cultivation of social relations is 'a necessary condition of the development of individual capacities'. The 'maximization of democracy' requires that citizens enjoy the 'absence of impediments' and an 'adequate means of life' and 'protection against invasion by others'.[19]

Fine principles, excellent words, but what happens to a democracy when governments and citizens allow its social footings to be damaged, or destroyed? The coming pages dwell on this fundamental question, but consider briefly just a few initial indicators. India today is the fifth largest economy and among the most socially unequal countries in the world. Article 39C of the Indian Constitution requires the state to 'direct its policy towards securing that the operation of the economic system does not result in the concentration of wealth and means of production to the common detriment'. Reality is more brutal. India's richest 1 per cent own more than four times the total wealth held by 953 million people who make up the bottom 70 per cent of the population. The wealth of these billionaires increased by almost ten times during the past decade, and their total wealth is now larger than India's annual state budget. Nearly three-quarters of the new wealth generated yearly goes to this richest 1 per cent, while the wealth of the poorest 50 per cent of the population rises by just 1 per cent. Muslims and the scheduled castes and tribes are among the biggest losers. According to a 2018 Oxfam India report, a minimum wage worker in rural India would need to work for 941 years to earn as much as the yearly salary of a top executive at a leading Indian garment company. The disparities are compounded by discrepancies among Indian states, which are at various stages of development. The numbers are stark. In 1960, the three wealthiest states were 1.7 times richer than the poorest three. By 2014, this gap had almost doubled, with the three wealthiest states three times richer than the poorest three. Over 50 per cent of the population in Bihar and over 40 per cent in Madhya Pradesh and Uttar Pradesh are 'multidimensionally poor', while in Kerala it is just 1 per cent of the population and between 4 and 7 per cent in Punjab, Goa, Sikkim, and Tamil Nadu.

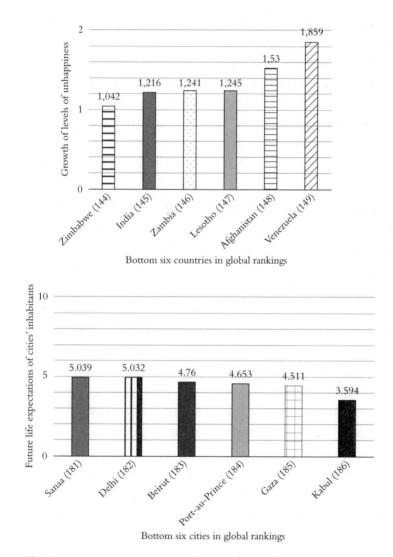

Figure 5. Declining national happiness and city dwellers' future life expectations rankings

These everyday disparities find expression in surveys that go beyond conventional indices such as GDP, wealth distribution, and income levels. Take social happiness levels (Figure 5). When happiness measures include such factors as access to food and housing, locally available healthcare facilities, personal safety, and the freedom to make daily choices, then according to the 2020 UN World Happiness Report, India ranks a lowly 144 (out of 153 countries and regions), just ahead of Malawi (145) and war-ravaged Yemen (146). It stands among the six countries where unhappiness has risen the most in the past decade, along with Zimbabwe, Zambia, Lesotho, Afghanistan, and Venezuela. A higher percentage of people in Gaza are more upbeat about their future than the citizens of Delhi, where everyday feelings of personal safety run low. Delhi is among the bottom six cities, out of 186, where future life expectations are the lowest, right behind Sanaa (Yemen) and just ahead of Beirut. A majority (51 per cent) of its residents feel that neighbourhood crime is a serious problem. Most households (95 per cent) are worried about the safety of their unaccompanied men if they haven't returned home by 11 p.m. Things are worse for women. In Delhi, 87 per cent of people start worrying by 9 p.m. if a female household member is out alone. Only 1 per cent say they aren't worried when a female member of the household is out at any time of the day. The same studies show that virtually all Delhi women are forced to act as if everyday social life is hostile terrain. They typically avoid walking alone, or in unfamiliar places. They know there are definite no-go areas. They're forced to dress modestly, conceal their personal belongings, and travel only on crowded trains and buses or, if they can afford the fare, in licensed taxis.

Social indicators such as these tell us a great deal about the roots of the deep disorders now facing Indian democracy—much more, say, than statistics on voter turnout or surveys of citizens' shifting party preferences. *To Kill A Democracy* pays attention to the circular relationships and destructive feedback loops that connect the dilapidation of social life with the killing of democratic politics and governing institutions. It does so for reasons that are typically ignored by the prevailing understandings of how democracies meet their end.

Most obvious is the fact that the decaying social substructures of Indian democracy openly contradict and degrade the high-minded *legal ideals* of the Indian Constitution, the preamble of which solemnly promised justice, liberty, equality, and dignified solidarity to all its citizens. The splintering and shattering of social life induces a sense of legal powerlessness among citizens and breeds cynicism towards the judiciary. It becomes vulnerable to political meddling and state capture. Massive imbalances of wealth, widespread violence, famine, and unevenly distributed life chances also make a mockery of the *ethical principle* that in a democracy people can live as citizen partners of equal social worth. If democracy is the self-government of social equals who freely choose their representatives, then large-scale social suffering renders the democratic principle utterly utopian, or turns it into a grotesque farce. Inadequate diet, poisonous air, and contaminated water *maim and kill citizens*. Fear of violence, rotten healthcare, widespread feelings of social unhappiness, and daily shortages of food and housing *destroy people's dignity*. Indignity is a form of generalized social violence. The vast majority of the society, including well-educated people with good jobs and assets, do not escape its clutches. Everybody suffers, rich and poor alike. Indignity spares nobody. It kills the spirit and substance of democracy. When famished children cry themselves to sleep at night, when millions of women feel unsafe and multitudes of migrant workers living on slave wages are forced to flee for their lives in a medical emergency, the victims are unlikely to believe themselves worthy of rights, or capable as citizens of fighting for their own entitlements, or for the rights of others. Ground down by social indignity, the powerless are robbed of self-esteem. No doubt, their ability to strike back, to deliver millions of mutinies against the rich and powerful, is in principle never to be underestimated. But the brute fact is that social indignity generally undermines citizens' capacity to take an active interest in public affairs, and to check and humble and wallop the powerful. Citizens are turned into subjects who are forced to accept the normality of bossing and bullying. They put up with state and corporate restrictions on basic public freedoms. They must get used to big money, surveillance, baton charges, preventive detentions, police killings, and soldiers on the streets.

But the scandal doesn't end there. For when millions of subjects are daily victimized by social indignities, when in other words there is a swelling of the ranks of subjects who feel 'disesteemed' (James Baldwin), the powerful are granted a licence to *rule arbitrarily*. Millions of humiliated people become sitting targets. Some of the downtrodden and many in the middle and upper classes turn their backs on public affairs. They bellyache in unison against politicians and politics. But the disaffected do nothing. They wallow in the mud of resignation. Complacency wins. Cynical indifference breeds voluntary servitude. Or the disgruntled begin to yearn for political redeemers and steel-fisted government. The powerless and the privileged join hands to wish for a messiah who promises to defend the poor, protect the rich, drive out the demons of corruption and disorder, and purify the soul of 'the people'. This has several observable effects. *Demagoguery* comes into season. The disempowerment of citizens encourages boasting and bluster among powerful leaders who stop caring about the niceties of public integrity and power sharing. They grow convinced they can turn lead into gold. But their hubris has costs. When democratically elected governments cease to be held accountable by a society weakened by poor health, low morale, and joblessness, rulers are prone to blindness and ineptitude. They make careless, foolish, and incompetent decisions that reinforce social inequities. The elected rulers encourage big market and government players—poligarchs we call them—to decide things. Those who exercise power in government ministries, corporations, and public/private projects aren't subject to democratic rules of public accountability. Like weeds in an untended garden, corruption therefore flourishes. Almost everybody has to pay bribes to access basic public services. The powerful enjoy unbridled power. *Institutional democracy failure* happens. Finally, in the absence of redistributive public welfare policies that guarantee sufficient food, shelter, security, education, and healthcare to the downtrodden, democracy morphs into a mere facade. Elections are regularly held and there's abundant talk of 'the people'. But democracy begins to resemble a fancy mask worn by wealthy political predators. Self-government is killed. Strong-armed rule by rich and powerful poligarchs in the name of 'the people' follows. Cheer-led by lapdog media, *phantom democracy* becomes a reality. Society is subordinated to the state. People are expected to behave as loyal subjects, or else suffer the consequences. A thoroughly twenty-first-century type of top-down rule we call despotism is born.

Social Emergencies

Health of a Democracy

Universal Suffering

A hospital bed wasn't given to Amarpreet Kaur's father until the very end.

On the morning of 4 June, as Delhi prepared to wind down the 2020 Covid lockdown, the young HR executive and her family reached the capital's LNJP Hospital. Her 68-year-old father had high fever, was having trouble breathing, and had tested corona-positive several days earlier. He desperately needed to be admitted to a hospital, yet no hospital in Delhi would touch him. The one that had done the test had stopped taking calls from the family. Calls to all other hospitals, public and private, had proven futile. All of them said they had no spare beds. Finally, one government helpline suggested they take him to LNJP, which supposedly had sufficient beds. But when they took him there, the hospital staff said they couldn't admit him. The family spent hours pleading with them, but they refused to yield. Kaur's father, sitting in a car outside the hospital's emergency block, was visibly sinking. A desperate Kaur sent out an SOS tweet appealing to the Delhi government for help. 'He won't survive without help. Pls help', she begged.

By now her father had fainted, and the family decided to take matters into their own hands. They seized an empty gurney and wheeled him into the emergency room. Still, nobody was willing to attend to him. 'We ran to the first doctor we found and fell at his feet. With folded hands, we begged him to take a look at our patient', wrote Kaur's husband Mandeep Singh later, in a first-person media account.[1] It was already too late. Around noon, Kaur tweeted: 'He is no more. The govt failed us.'

India's chronic failure to provide decent public healthcare had claimed one more victim. The pestilence had broken the back of a crumbling and unequal health system. As Covid cases surged, hospitals found themselves severely lacking in test kits. Doctors didn't have sufficient personal protective equipment (PPE), often making do with raincoats and motorbike helmets to protect themselves. Thousands of health workers had tested positive for the coronavirus, including LNJP's medical director. When PPE was supplied, doctors and nurses complained they were substandard. Doctors at two Delhi hospitals also went on strike as they hadn't been paid for months. Nationwide, 600,000 of the country's one million community health workers known as ASHA (Accredited Social Health Activists) struck work in demand of better and timely wages and elementary safety equipment such as sanitizers and gloves. Just weeks earlier, Modi ordered a grand flypast by the air force to shower flower petals on hospitals as a mark of appreciation for health workers. On the ground, they had been all but abandoned.

Except for pockets of public healthcare excellence, such as Kerala, it was more or less the same story across the country. Frontline healthcare workers were overworked and underequipped, Covid tests were hard to get, hospital beds even harder. Even treatment for non-Covid patients had become next to impossible. Hospitals had mostly suspended procedures such as chemotherapy and dialysis, even for terminally ill patients. On the rare occasion they were still available, private healthcare facilities were charging exorbitant rates for procedures and medicines. In Noida, a city adjoining Delhi, an eight-month-pregnant woman died in an ambulance in the course of a frantic, thirteen-hour search for a hospital bed. She was refused admission by eight hospitals. For any medical intervention, hospitals demanded Covid test results. But Covid tests were difficult to obtain. Government

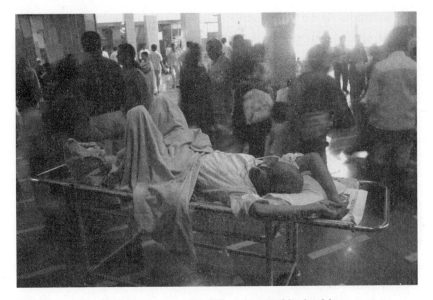

Figure 6. The pestilence exposed India's rotting public healthcare system

policy was to restrict tests to a bare minimum, in what one High Court described as an attempt to 'artificially control the data'.[2] The fewer the tests, the fewer the cases, and the greater the appearance of order even as the situation reeled out of control. A Delhi grandee of the Congress party took to Twitter after his family's harrowing ordeal trying to get his wife tested in the national capital: 'Despite growing up on a hospital campus & knowing every medical professional of consequence, I had to move heaven and earth just to get her tested. Delhi's health systems are broken.' For lesser beings in lesser cities, it was infinitely more hellish (Figure 6).

Despite being among the countries conducting the least number of tests, India nevertheless raced to the top of the Covid charts. A hastily announced lockdown had badly damaged the economy, devoured livelihoods overnight, pushed people into hunger, and triggered an unprecedented exodus of migrant workers from the metros back to their communities in the hinterland. The government now seemed to be in an equally mad rush to lift the lockdown and salvage whatever was left of the economy. The steady stream of reverse migration turned into a torrent. As the floodgates opened, a city disease brought by rich people in aeroplanes from faraway lands was spreading out into the villages, where 70 per cent of Indians live. The risks multiplied as the public healthcare system is even more diseased in rural India, and the people even less resourced to buy private cure.

When India announced the world's most stringent lockdown towards the end of March 2020, it was thought the drastic move would help slow the spread of the coronavirus, and give the federal and state governments sufficient time to shore up the public healthcare infrastructure. There was much to be done. According to government data collected a week before the lockdown, there was just one isolation bed for every 84,000 Indians, one quarantine bed per 36,000, one doctor per 11,600, and one hospital bed per 1,826 people. Nearly 20 per cent of India's 739 districts didn't have a single bed with intensive care facilities. With the government spending on healthcare having historically been around 1 per cent of GDP, the health infrastructure was simply too broken. The plan to buy time to fix it with a lockdown had failed. Seven decades of negligence of citizens' health would not be reversed with two months of patchwork. The pestilence hadn't gutted India's health system, it merely showed it up for what it was. A supposed democracy had for nearly a quarter of a century subjected its people to murderous inequity by not provisioning for basic universal healthcare. It had celebrated the equality of its people and their votes, even while treating their bodies as unequal. Now the show was over. It was payback time.

The Great Leveller

The Indian Constitution upholds the right of its citizens to enjoy human dignity. The country's Supreme Court has ruled that this means the right to health is integral to the right to life, and the government has a constitutional obligation to provide health facilities. But healthcare is not a fundamental right in India. There is no universal healthcare system. Instead, it has a three-tiered health system, in which the poorest go to the notionally free and suitably ramshackle public hospitals; the rich and upper middle classes access super-speciality private hospitals with hotel-like lobbies and airconditioned suites, respectful doctors, and state-of the-art equipment; and the rest take refuge in low-to-middle-end private nursing homes that are a scaled-down version of the five-star corporate hospitals.

The Covid-19 outbreak laid bare the denial of decent healthcare to the poor by this long-tolerated caste system of healthcare. Media buzzed with reports and outrage on the meltdown of the health infrastructure. Editorial writers urged the need to go back to the basics to guarantee a dignified life for all. That state-run public hospitals were mostly hellholes suddenly seemed to matter more than before, even to people who had never needed to visit public hospitals because they could buy private care. It was more evident every passing day that, like all pestilences, this one was an equal opportunity killer. Too bad that a democracy that is animated by issues such as a uniform civil code for all religions had never invested any political energy in uniform health-care. For, the pestilence didn't discriminate between classes or religions or castes. It was the public hospitals that were leading the fightback while private health institutions lay low—refusing patients, curtailing even standard services, and raising insurmountable paywalls with predatory prices. Private hospitals account for two-thirds of hospital beds in India and 80 per cent of available ventilators, but were handling less than 10 per cent of the critical load.[3] The infernal public hospitals, run by an uncaring state fit only for the helpless poor, were suddenly the only option for even upper-class corporate executives like Kaur who wouldn't ordinarily bother with them. The pestilence was a great leveller.

In Mumbai, the country's richest city, people were dying waiting for hospital beds and even when, on the off-chance, they did find a hospital open to taking in a Covid patient, there was no ambulance to be found. There were few government ambulances, and private ambulances—unaffordable for most—were hard to find. In Bangalore,

India's Silicon Valley, a hospital bus driver who tested positive walked four kilometres to the chief minister's home with his family after failing to find an ambulance to take him to the hospital, then stood there shouting for help. The state's health minister declared that 'only God can save us.'

As the Covid crisis deepened, it was evident that the almighty was all that Indians could count on. In hospitals across India's financial capital, coronavirus patients were sharing beds or lying on floors and in corridors waiting for beds to clear up. Sometimes patients were even sharing wards with unclaimed corpses. State and city governments across the country had been making grand announcements of shoring up the capacity of government hospitals. They forced private hospitals to reserve beds for coronavirus patients and converted large venues such as planetariums and stadiums into quarantine centres. There was sufficient capacity to tackle the crisis, they assured their people repeatedly, but the situation on the ground told a very different story. In the rich, western state of Gujarat, which has just 0.33 hospital beds per 1,000 people, the state High Court described the Civil Hospital in capital Ahmedabad 'as good as a dungeon, may be even worse'.[4]

If India's richest cities and states so withered in the onslaught of the pestilence, the situation in its poorer hinterland was predictably more alarming. Less than a week before Kaur's father breathed his last in Delhi, a searing video of wailing Covid patients in neighbouring Uttar Pradesh, one of the poorest states, went viral on social media. In the video, the patients were seen protesting against the horrendous facilities at the government hospital where they were admitted. 'You have turned us into animals. Are we animals? Don't we need water?' a patient in the video shouted, as others stepped out of their wards and joined in. They complained the toilets were unusable and the food inedible, and urged the authorities to take money from the patients if the government was short of cash, but at least treat them as humans. There were so many videos like these on social media, filmed by Covid patients recording the alarming state of hospitals in Uttar

Pradesh, that the authorities banned patients from taking their mobile phones into isolation wards.

Chronic Disease

The apocalyptic scenes of reverse migration, the panic over food within just days of the lockdown, the failure to arrange for suitable transport to systematically transfer migrant workers to their places of origin in order to minimize contagion risks, and the calamity confronting Indian hospitals from the earliest days of the pestilence: all of this pointed to a deeper social malaise caused by government inaction, mismanagement, and dereliction of duty. Indian state structures are not just ineffective, or proof of what has been called a 'flailing state'.[5] Their incompetence and lack of public accountability show that democracy failure—government bumbling, data fudging, ineptitude, and offloaded responsibility—play an important role in the social emergencies afflicting India. Economists have long warned that unregulated markets fail and, as a result, produce great misery among their victims. Democracies fail too, when elected governments are unchecked by watchdog mechanisms of democratic scrutiny and restraint. When democracy is in short supply, social policy failures multiply. The equation is almost mathematical: without effective democratic accountability, state institutions typically do nothing or they make neglectful or foolish or outright reckless decisions that wound the lives of their citizens. As in some other democracies, most strikingly in the United States, decades of inadequate and uneven state provisioning of basic social services have spawned a deeply unequal society, skewed further since the early 1990s by a lopsided market liberalization that has allowed the state to turn its back on its most fundamental responsibilities by privatizing public goods and resources. Consequently, historical inequities are reproduced and disparities deepened. Daily indignities and the unjust denial of the most basic rights become commonplace. So does the coarsening of politics.

Uttar Pradesh, India's most politically important state with a population the size of Brazil's, typifies the connections between weakened social foundations and rough politics. Ruled by Yogi Adityanath, a Hindu hardliner who rode to infamy and power with his rioting private army, rabid rabble-rousing, and unabashed Muslim-baiting, Uttar Pradesh was identified by the federal government as the state least prepared for Covid-19. Each of its seventy-five districts on average is home to about 2.7 million people, but nearly half of the districts didn't have a single bed with intensive care facilities. Seventy per cent of the districts had fewer than 100 isolation beds before the lockdown.

Not that Uttar Pradesh needed a pestilence to expose the mouldering innards of what passes for a public healthcare system. The state is building the world's biggest statue—a 725-foot bronze installation of the Hindu god Ram, costing $420 million, overtaking Gujarat's 600-foot jumbo of one of India's founding leaders and first deputy prime minister Vallabhbhai Patel—but struggles to pay for basic healthcare. In August 2017, sixty-three children died in five days at government-run Baba Raghav Das Medical College and Hospital (commonly known as BRD) in the state's Gorakhpur city, Adityanath's hometown and power base. The hospital's liquid oxygen supplier refused to refill the stocks after its repeated pleas for dues went unheard. 'We want to inform you that the gas plant has only 2 or 3 days of stock available ... We don't take any responsibility for this', the company wrote in one of its last letters to officials in a desperate attempt to wangle the 6.3 million rupee dues accumulated over ten months. The government didn't move a finger. Then the day arrived when the oxygen ran out, and the children admitted at BRD began to gasp for air, and die untimely deaths.

A national outcry followed what Nobel Peace Laureate Kailash Satyarthi called a 'massacre'. In an anguished tweet, he asked, 'Is this what 70 years of freedom means for our children?' and pleaded with the Uttar Pradesh government to fix 'decades of [a] corrupt medical system'. But the government chose instead to fix the bad press. The new chief minister, Adityanath, couldn't afford to be seen failing in his own city. So his government flatly denied that the disruption in oxygen supply had anything to do with the deaths; shifted the blame to four doctors, including BRD administrators, and a few other hospital employees; and promptly dispatched them to prison. The most prominent scapegoat was Dr Kafeel Khan, a young paediatrician who had become a media darling for his efforts to procure oxygen cylinders the night liquid oxygen ran out and panic spread. He paid for his initiative—and for being a Muslim guardian of compassion, in sharp contrast with Hindu far-right icon Adityanath's indifference—by spending the next eight months in a dank prison cell with 150 other inmates (Figure 7).

The Gorakhpur oxygen story eventually petered out as the media glare moved elsewhere, chasing breaking news. All blame was laid at the door of the arrested hospital administrators and encephalitis, a

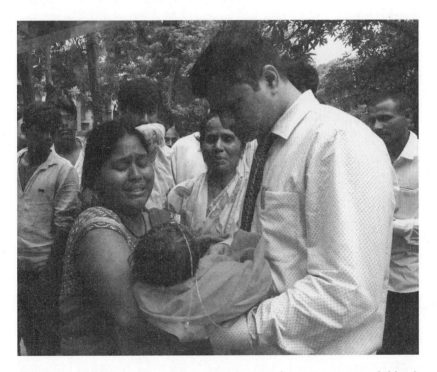

Figure 7. Dr Kafeel Khan (right), sent to prison for trying to save children's lives when oxygen ran out at BRD Medical College Hospital, Gorakhpur, Uttar Pradesh, 2017

catch-all term for a host of ailments. Encephalitis lends death a ring of inevitability and absolves the authorities, even though many of the factors that cause the deaths attributed to this mosquito-borne disease are avoidable and have less to do with the disease itself than with the low quality of general administration and mismanagement of sanitation, elementary healthcare, and roads and transport.

Along with poor sanitation, local-level primary health centres are inadequately staffed and equipped, preventing them from diagnosing and treating encephalitis patients in time. Patients are thus brought from hundreds of kilometres away to government hospitals such as BRD. Underfunded and understaffed as they are, these hospitals easily break under the mounting load. These wider afflictions apply to Gorakhpur as much as they do to India's public healthcare system in most parts of the country, yet are only episodically mentioned in political or media conversations, and go unaddressed. Two years after the BRD deaths, the federal government told the Parliament that Uttar Pradesh's 3,500-odd primary health centres still only had a third of the required doctors, and about a thousand of these centres—supposedly the backbone of the healthcare infrastructure—were working without electricity, regular water supply, or all-weather approachable roads. It was much the same story in states such as Chhattisgarh, Odisha, Karnataka, and Bihar.

Media depictions of crises typically reduce them to adversarial frames (in this case, between political parties, between Adityanath and his 'enemies') that require less cognitive energy to be grasped and make them more exciting and easier to consume. Complex information about deep-seated structural problems devoid of personalized dramas of confrontation are ratings-killers. Thus, the Gorakhpur story, which was one of a social crisis, was dumbed down into a political battle. It was about dead children and a broken healthcare system with a long legacy, but turned into a battle for survival for its new chief minister, then only five months into the job. Its resolution was suitably political, too. The 'guilty' were found, heads rolled, scores were settled, turfs protected, the people pacified, and the opposition silenced.

In effect, nothing was fixed. Like in much of India, the underlying factors ailing the healthcare system were left to fester. People moved on. Life went on. Till a killer pestilence arrived, and there was nowhere to hide.

Damn Lies

As part of the political response to the oxygen deaths, the Uttar Pradesh chief minister decided he needed a grand showing to undo the damage. Adityanath promised a programme to eradicate acute encephalitis syndrome (AES) altogether. Within two years, he was trumpeting its success, claiming a case reduction of 65 per cent. More patchwork. What really happened was that hospitals such as BRD were told to refuse encephalitis cases from other states, and doctors were pressured not to register encephalitis as the cause of death. Such under-reporting is common in India; an easy-fix means by which elected executives suppress disease numbers. Aided by institutional malleability and corruption, the skulduggery goes unabated. In West Bengal, Mamata Banerjee, a firebrand leader of the ruling regional party, the Trinamool Congress, has put the squeeze on dengue. Dengue deaths are often registered as 'viral fever' or 'mystery fever' or 'fever with thrombocytopenia' or some such. India under-reports dengue by a factor of 282 times, compared to other countries that under-report ten to thirty times.[6] Andhra Pradesh and Orissa similarly manipulate malaria figures.

Data-fudging as problem-solving is standard operating procedure for India's governments, which often fear public exposure of a problem more than the problem itself. Throughout the coronavirus crisis, except for a handful of states and cities that have diligently released data, governments at various levels have played loose and fast with numbers, starting with the restriction of tests to laughably low levels so that fewer cases were reported. Even these low numbers weren't spared. When West Bengal was found to be under-reporting corona

deaths, it said many of the victims died of 'co-morbidity'. The Tamil
Nadu government was found to be reporting only half of the deaths
in the capital Chennai. Uttar Pradesh was releasing patchy data. At the
federal level, the entire administration was geared to bear out the
Modi government's narrative that the curve was being flattened, even
as it kept rising every day to new highs. Officials continued to deny
community transmission even though the locked-down country had
been cut off from the rest of the world for months. Johns Hopkins
economist Steve Hanke placed India among the eight 'that either do
not report Covid data or are reporting highly suspicious data'. Apart
from India, the 'rotten apples' of coronavirus data, as he called them,
included Vietnam, Venezuela, Egypt, Syria, Yemen, Turkey, and China.
Not exactly the company one would expect of a country once seen
as the great democratic hope of the East, as scripted in the 'India
Story'.

State policy that indulges denial is easier than rooting out the
pathogens of death. The result has been a mounting pile of corpses in
an unending spiral of state-driven mass deaths of its most vulnerable
people. BRD's sixty-three victims were among the 802,000 infants
who died in 2017, mostly from lack of access to water, sanitation,
proper nutrition, and basic health services, according to a UN report.
That makes India the country with the highest number of infant
deaths, followed by Nigeria at 466,000, Pakistan at 330,000, and the
Democratic Republic of Congo at 233,000. Some 605,000 of these
were neonatal deaths that were preventable or treatable, such as com-
plications during birth, pneumonia, diarrhoea, sepsis, and malaria.
Based on data from the Global Burden of Disease report of 2016,
another study ranked India 145 out of 195 countries in terms of
healthcare access and quality—behind war-torn Yemen (140), Sudan
(136), and North Korea (120), despite a far higher per capita income
than these countries.[7] China, with a population similar to India's but
with a much higher per capita income, ranked far ahead at 48. But as
the disease data show, even back in 1995, when China's per capita
income was half of India's 2015 per capita income, China was doing

far better on all major health indicators than what India achieved twenty years later in 2015, with twice the per capita income.[8]

Health and Democracy

The superior performance of one-party China on the health front throws up interesting questions about the relationship between public health and democracy. Among recent analyses of democracy, too little research and writing has been done on the subject of bodily wellness. The principle that in a democracy each citizen is entitled to enjoy and make full use of bodily health is not given sufficient emphasis. Feminists, disability activists, and public champions of good health and well-being have reacted against this neglect. They remind us that rationalist definitions of democracy as public deliberation and agreement among 'informed' and 'reasonable' citizens are much too abstract because they downgrade or simply ignore outright the fact of bodies. They insist that the integrity or violation of the bodies of citizens should be integral to the way we think about democratic politics. Bodies are political matters. When bodily sickness or maltreatment blight the lives of citizens, or when their bodily integrity is harmed or destroyed by violence, the spirit and substance of any given democracy are threatened. Emotional and physical pain, mental anxiety, and untreated illness disable democracies. The principle that democratic self-government requires that free and equal citizens, enabled by their governments, are entitled to equal respect of their bodily capacities and differences is violated. Democracy suffers a slow-motion death, one sickness or death at a time. This is why properly functioning democracies are expected, for instance, to pay special attention to increasing life expectancy, to honour and support the disabled, and, generally, to improve the bodily health of their citizens through universal provision of high-quality healthcare. As a result, democracies are *supposed to* perform better in terms of health indicators than non-democratic regimes.

Exceptions like China aside, most studies of the links between democracy and health outcomes do find a positive correlation. The general argument is that representative democracy forces competition for popular support that in turn makes contenders for power more responsive to citizens' healthcare needs. One study, examining the links between political freedom and health expenditures, specifically in Eastern Mediterranean countries, concluded that an increase in the freedom of the press and democracy raises public and private health spending and reduces out-of-pocket health expenditures.[9] Panel data from 170 countries over forty-six years between 1970 and 2016 found HIV-free life expectancy at age 15 improved faster in countries after they transitioned to democracy. It also concluded that free and fair elections lead to increases in government health spending and declines in cardiovascular disease mortality and road deaths. So-called autocracies, it concluded, might have less incentive to finance disease prevention and treatment than democracies.[10] A separate study of similar data from the 1960s to the 2000s showed health policy interventions were superior in democracies.[11] It posited a robust correlation between democracy and life expectancy at birth, vaccination, sanitation facilities, and improved water sources. Democratic governments, it estimated, spent around $160 (in purchasing power parity terms) per capita more on health than permanent autocracies.

The case of India spells trouble for these statistical conclusions that democracy is the nurse of good health. India simply doesn't measure up to the democratic standards of bodily well-being. Even a cursory glance at major health indicators bears this out (Figure 8). Some 2.4 million people die of treatable conditions every year in India. Of these, twice as many people (1.6 million) die of poor-quality healthcare rather than lack of access to it (838,000) because India's death rate from poor care is the worst among a list of 136 nations.[12] Some 122 Indians die per 100,000 because of poor-quality care each year, far more than in peer countries and neighbours such as Brazil (74), China (46), Nepal (93), Bangladesh (57), and Sri Lanka (51). India's average life expectancy has increased by ten years in three decades to 70.8,

Healthcare Access and Quality Index
(Based on death rates from 32 causes of death that can be prevented
by timely and effective medical care, also known as 'amenable mortality')

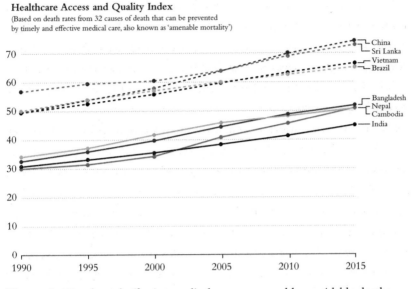

Figure 8. Timely and effective medical care, measured by avoidable deaths

according to a *Lancet* study released in October 2020, but Indians are living more years with illness and disability. India's healthy life expectancy (HALE) is 60.5, similar to Ethiopia (60.1) and Rwanda (59.8), but lags behind Nepal (61.5), Iraq (63.3), Bangladesh (64.4), Palestine (64.4), Brazil (65), Vietnam (65.7), Sri Lanka (66.8), and China (68.4).[13] India reduced its infant mortality rate by over 40 per cent in a decade from 57 per 1,000 live births in 2006 to 32 in 2017, but still trails Cambodia (25), Vietnam (17), Brazil (13), and Sri Lanka (8).[14] Since 2016, even that modest success has faltered; the mortality rate has started increasing in several states.[15] If vaccination rates are likely to be greater in democracies, as comparative studies report, there couldn't be a greater anomaly than India. With the exception of tuberculosis, India's immunization rates are lower than the poorest regions in the world, such as parts of sub-Saharan Africa. The country's share of global measles mortality, which claims 100,000 lives every year, in fact increased from 16 per cent of the global total in 2000 to 47 per cent in 2010.[16] With more than half a million pneumonia deaths every year, India accounts for a fifth of the global total. India leads the five countries with the largest numbers of child pneumonia deaths, followed by Nigeria, Pakistan, the Democratic Republic of Congo, and Ethiopia.[17] India similarly leads in tuberculosis deaths, bearing a third of the global TB mortality, with 421,000 deaths every year.[18]

The figures shouldn't be surprising, as the Indian state's spending of around 1 per cent of the GDP on health compares poorly with 2.9 per cent in China, 4 per cent in Latin America, 2.1 per cent in South East Asia, and 4.9 per cent in Europe. Annual public per capita expenditure on health works out to just 1,500 rupees, or $20.[19] This, along with the limited reach of health insurance, means the average Indian has to pay much of the health expenses out of her own pocket, a whopping 67 per cent, a cost which isn't borne by the state or an insurer and paid at the point of service by the consumer. An estimated 39 million Indians fell into poverty yearly as a result of medical expenses, according to a 2011 study in *The Lancet*. By 2017, the figure had jumped to 55 million every year.[20] Most Indians thus end up not opting for any medical care at all. Among the richest 5 per cent of the population, 98 per cent of people receive some medical care before death. But among the poorest 25 per cent, nearly 40 per cent die without any medical care.[21] A move towards government-funded insurance systems at federal and state levels has had limited and varying success. Modi's government has launched an ambitious insurance programme, popularized as 'Modicare', with a potential reach of half a billion people, to help cover the healthcare expenses of the poorest, but the whole scheme is handicapped by low budgetary allocations and the reliance on profit-seeking private care. As a result, India fares poorly in *The Lancet*'s 'universal health coverage (UHC) effective coverage index'. While India scores 47 on this index, barely beating Timor Leste (46) and is at the same level as Ethiopia, Myanmar, and Nepal, it lags behind Mongolia (48), Ghana and Yemen (49), Bangladesh (54), Iraq (58), Rwanda (59), Brazil (65), North Korea (53), Cambodia (57), and China (70).[22] All-India scores captured by global indices like these in fact do not even reflect the true extent of the crisis in less developed states. In Tamil Nadu, for example, at least 64 per cent of the people are covered by a health scheme or insurance, while it is just 6 per cent in Uttar Pradesh.[23]

All in all, India's health report raises serious questions about the bodily health of its citizens and the democratic responsiveness and quality of its governing institutions—even before the mayhem of the pestilence. Analysing epidemics data from 1960 to 2019—pre-Covid-19, that is—*The Economist* concluded that democracies handle epidemics most effectively.[24] The performance of robust democracies such as South Korea and Uruguay during the 2020 pestilence would seem to validate the point. Their accountability mechanisms and state-provided healthcare, uncompromised by the global rush to blind pro-market reforms, stood them in good stead vis-à-vis democracies that have run down their public healthcare systems and shifted health risks and debts onto individuals and households. The disastrous handling of the Covid-19 emergency by India, along with Brazil, the US, the UK, Mexico, and South Africa, on the other hand, necessitates a crucial qualification of that correlation between democracy and the handling of epidemics.[25]

Private Greed

In India's case, the collapse of the public healthcare system during the pestilence was exacerbated by a mercenary private healthcare sector that turned the crisis into an opportunity. Reports abounded of nursing homes and corporate hospitals charging extortionate amounts for tests and treatment, even concocting false test reports to entrap patients. Media images captured an 80-year-old man in the state of Madhya Pradesh tied to a hospital bed during a dispute over fees for his treatment. His family said the hospital arbitrarily doubled the fees and refused to let him go when he tried to leave.

The horror stories of fleecing were of a piece with an exploitative private health business that has burgeoned as a result of the failure of the Indian state to provide even half-decent healthcare for all its citizens. The failure to regulate and make accountable the private sector is a clear instance of democracy failure. Many private hospitals are known to set revenue targets for doctors and force them to order avoidable tests, medicines, or procedures. The first question a doctor at a private hospital in India is likely to ask a patient is not about their ailment, but whether or not they are insured. The procedures to be advised thereon hinge on the answer, not on the required treatment. A law to rein in private healthcare operators, the Clinical Establishments Act, has remained largely ineffectual. Doctors and private health establishments complained its provisions were unrealistically rigid, and states were reluctant to enforce it, fearing a backlash from the medical profession. As in other public goods vacated for private capital, from education to water, politicians behaving as poligarchs are among the biggest players in the medical business as well. They help private businesses fatten up their bottom line with tax breaks, cheap government land, and other preferential policies while ensuring that public hospitals remain incapacitated. On paper, a commitment of quota of treatment for the poor is extracted in return for such favours, but is badly implemented. Sick politicians themselves seldom go to public hospitals. Many are flown abroad on taxpayers' money for medical care befitting their lifelong services to the people.

Malpractices at private medical set-ups, such as arbitrary and exorbitant billing, poor services, and lack of transparency in diagnosis, are systematically overlooked. The Medical Council of India, which was supposed to set the standards for and monitor the medical profession before it was replaced by a new body in 2020, was largely ineffectual in its sixty-three years of existence. In one of Indian democracy's many failures caused by the malfunctioning or breakdown of its regulatory mechanisms, all that this body effectively did was to register doctors on the medical register of India. Its local chapters were merely elected bodies of professionals, and like all elected bodies, had to be mindful of their members' interests, rather than aggravate them. Proving medical negligence or malpractice has been next to impossible. State medical councils would not act against their own club members; consumer courts lack specialized medical knowledge and are generally dysfunctional; and civil and criminal cases against doctors require testimonies of other doctors, giving doctors a clear advantage in such lawsuits.

Doctors are in any case a rare commodity in India that no government would want to cross. The World Health Organization (WHO) recommends one government doctor for every 1,000 people. India has one for every 11,000. There's a shortage of 600,000 doctors and 2 million nurses, by some estimates.[26] In some states like Uttar Pradesh and Bihar, the numbers are more dire. Bihar has one government doctor per 28,000 people, Uttar Pradesh has one for every 18,000. These figures, again, may not fully capture the doctor shortage problem. The doctor/patient ratio improves if we factor in non-government doctors, but these doctors tend to cluster in urban centres, where greater population density offers better income prospects. The countryside is correspondingly underserved.

Government studies find 700 million Indians have no access to specialist care and 80 per cent of specialists work in urban areas. The result is a profusion of underqualified or poorly trained quack doctors—1 million of them, reckons the Indian Medical Association. In Delhi alone, there are an estimated 50,000. An estimated 57 per cent of those practising allopathic medicine in India are quacks, mostly concentrated in rural areas. So central is quackery to India's health infrastructure that the government has begun issuing licences to allow quacks to practise medicine, and call them a respectable 'Community Health Provider'. These 'CHPs', along with ASHA workers, are key to the Modi government's goal of achieving universal health coverage. As are 'AYUSH doctors', who are basically practitioners of indigenous alternative medicine (AYUSH is abbreviation for Ayurveda, Yoga, Naturopathy, Unani, Siddha, and Homeopathy). They are now being allowed to prescribe modern medicines and even conduct general surgical procedures to meet the critical shortage of doctors. Experiments with allowing licensed quacks to handle elementary healthcare and increase medical access may show promise, but the institutionalization of sub-par medical care for the poor who cannot afford conventional medical care is also proof of a democracy-defying hierarchy of human life in India. The hierarchy violates the principle of equal suffrage and social equality. The prioritizing of urban lives over rural, and the rich over the poor, that is implicit in India's health policy is just ugly social Darwinism.

The reason why India suffers a shortage of doctors is the failure of successive governments to prioritize public health, set up adequate numbers of medical colleges, and train doctors at subsidized rates. Instead, the task of creating medical professionals is increasingly handed over to private businesses, which charge astronomical amounts for the coveted degree. The graduating doctors from these private establishments, seeking to recoup their sunk costs, are naturally more inclined to conform to the usurious practices of corporate healthcare. Not only is demand for health services structurally filtered through money, so is its supply. Caught between an unregulated private health business and the mostly broken public sector, the average Indian citizen is faced by a Hobson's choice of cheap massacres and expensive slaughter. In a country where the top 10 per cent of the population holds 77 per cent of the total national wealth, most don't in any case get to make that choice simply because their daily lives are plagued by other deprivations. Such as food.

A Million Famines

Wails for Rice

There was a time in the not-so-distant past when hunger was considered the product of the laws of nature, or the curse and deathly gift of spirits and deities. In their name, the hell suffered by the hungry was feared, decoded, and accepted. According to this ancient way of thinking, relief from the aching emptiness of hunger was either impossible or obtained only as a gift of the divine. As Mahatma Gandhi observed, people gripped by hunger encounter God only through the taste of bread.

Hunger was universally feared, but its curse was accepted as the lot of life. There were even vigorous defences of this prejudice. Think of the moralizing parson and scholar Thomas Malthus (1766–1834), who drew the conclusion that all famines, extreme scarcities of food, are the God-given laws of the human condition. The poor, lacking 'moral restraint', breed to excess, but as population increases geometrically and food supply rises only arithmetically, the poor, he said, soon find themselves pushed into the unforgiving arms of hunger and famine. Their fate cannot be ameliorated: any relief given to the hungry triggers an increase of their sexual desire and their numbers, a decrease of the food available for the entire body of the poor, and thus a return to the natural condition of famine.[1]

Enter democracy. For its defenders, democracy is an ethic, and a whole way of life, that can't tolerate hunger and famine. In ethical terms, democracy stands for the dignity of people who consider each other as equals. Hunger eats the hungry. It is not a problem; it is an obscenity. Hunger means indignity. It tramples underfoot people suffering hurt. The ethics of democracy are thus the sworn enemy of hunger, as described by writers such as Bhabani Bhattacharya, the Indian novelist of the calamitous consequences of hunger and famine. For him, hunger is democracy's opposite. It brings moral degradation. It breeds desperation and the predation of hoarders and profiteers. Hunger is fishermen's boats chopped up for firewood to sell, child prostitution, illicit trafficking, people too weak to walk, untreated disease, forced emigration from ancestral homes. It is bickering, anger, broken hearts. Hunger is children crying themselves to death, roadside corpses, in uncountable numbers.[2]

When it comes to actual practice, democracy is said to be a potent guardian against the evils of hunger. The mechanisms of democracy guarantee that hunger is no longer treated as the work of fate, or the angry gods, or the harsh laws of political economy. Hunger and famine are instead seen to be the product of human action, or human inaction. As posited by Amartya Sen, they aren't caused by shortages of food but are a product of the scarcity of democracy. In this formulation, while unexpected events such as drought and creeping desertification trigger food crises, famine in the sense of acute hunger can't occur without human complicity, of the kind that brought terrible suffering and death by starvation during the Bengal famine in 1943, when 3 million people are estimated to have starved to death under British occupation. Many of Sen's generation are still haunted by the wails for rice on the streets of the then Calcutta (now Kolkata) from that time.

According to Sen, human complicity with hunger was evident in the death of perhaps 30 million people during Mao Zedong's ill-named Great Leap Forward (1958–62) and the Ukraine famine of the early 1930s, which couldn't have happened under democratic conditions.[3] Hence his remarkable conclusion: 'No famine has ever taken place in the history of the world in a functioning democracy.'[4] In India, a famine on the scale suffered by the Chinese people during the Great Leap Forward 'would have immediately caused a storm in the newspapers and a turmoil in the Indian parliament, and the ruling government would almost certainly have had to resign'.[5]

Independent and democratic India has actually suffered extreme hunger on the scale of famine. Hunger swept through Bihar (1966–67), where reportedly some 13.4 million people found themselves trapped in destitution, thousands of citizens starved to death, with many eyewitness accounts of people eating wild leaves and roots, picking pieces of grain from the dust around railway sidings, and undergoing appalling skeletonization. Famine later descended on Maharashtra (1973), with an estimated 130,000 deaths and, during the 1990s, hunger plagued the people of the Kalahandi and Naupada districts in Orissa. Each of these instances did receive extensive media coverage and triggered protests and political backlash, forcing the government to act. While millions were employed for relief works to tackle the drought in Maharashtra, the crisis in Bihar added to the urgency of finding an alternative agricultural policy to ensure food security, leading to the 'green revolution', or the shift to industrial agriculture by employing modern farming techniques.

Slow Death

The days of catastrophic famine described by Bhattacharya and others now seem to be over. The wailing for rice is a fading memory of an earlier generation. It seems that India is proof positive of the thesis that democracies cannot tolerate famine. But the Indian democracy faces a new challenge: hunger that kills its citizens quietly, in silence.

Consider Mahuadanr. During a visit to this remote village in the eastern state of Jharkhand, it was late afternoon and Sanchi Devi still hadn't had anything to eat all day. There was nothing at home, so in all likelihood it was going to be one of those days when she would just have to make do with salt tea. The problem, she explained, was she had guests. A distant relative was visiting with family, and it would be nice to offer them something. By something, she meant rice. Rice and the wild greens and leaves she manages to find in the nearby fields are all she gets to eat on most days. Asked when was the last time she had *daal*, a common source of protein for Indians, she tried hard to recall but drew a blank. Meat, eggs, or milk, naturally, are out of the question. It would be odd even to ask.

Days like these have taken a visible toll, ageing her far beyond her years, which, she guessed, would be around 50. She lived with her son, his wife, and child in a thatched mud home where the town ends, adjacent to the paddy fields that stretch towards the distant hills. In sowing season, she is hired to work in those fields for about a month, making 100 rupees (just over $1) a day. Sometimes Sanchi does odd jobs for the retired teacher on whose land her mud hut stands. That yields an odd bowlful of rice now and then. It's a bonus, because her family, landless, pays no rent: the work is the rent. For a few months a year, the whole family would go and work in a brick kiln nearby. Her son and daughter-in-law made bricks while Sanchi looked after the 2-year-old granddaughter. The monsoon had just hit these parts. That meant there was no work at the kiln for now. Summer is the season for brick-making. Sowing season for the next crop was still a few months away, so there was no work in the fields either. And hence, no food.

Poor families are entitled to 35 kg of highly subsidized grain through the public distribution system. For some reason, Sanchi had been getting just 10 kg for some time, she said. Shared between the four family members, 10 kg runs out by the middle of the month. It had been a couple of days since the rice ran out when her distant relatives decided to call in. In times like these, when the ration ran out, her son tried finding work as a porter in the town market. She was hoping he would manage to bring home some rice. It would be nice to offer the guests something, she repeated.

Starvation

On New Year's Eve in 2018, Budhni Brijiyan, Sanchi's mother-in-law, died after four days without food. Sanchi had run out of rice and neighbours weren't able to come to the rescue with offers of extra rice. Budhni caught a cold, and her broken body couldn't fight back.

The human body, when blessed with regular nutrition, can normally withstand a month or so of food deprivation. But chronic hunger hollows out the bodies of its victims over their shortened lifetime, to the point when just a few days without food can turn fatal. Conventional famines, triggered by shock events like crop failure, are typically months-long periods of absolute food deprivation for a large mass of people. Low-level famine is a lifelong affliction. It kills slowly and a smaller number of people at a given time and place. That makes it un-newsworthy and almost invisible. As Sen has observed, slow starvations get less media attention than famines. Their slowness, and spatial and temporal dispersion are what distinguish today's starvation deaths from Indian famines of yore. Thanks to the public distribution system, when it is applied properly, there's some food some of the time these days. Then there's work, however infrequent and badly paid, which provides for some more. But for particularly vulnerable groups, such as tribes whose livelihoods have historically been tied to the forests that are increasingly being appropriated for mines and factories, and who now have to depend on uncertain menial work, it may still not be enough. Neighbours' munificence is one way of bridging these critical gaps, but not an adequate, sustainable solution.

Months before her mother-in-law's death, Sanchi's husband died. He came back from work on the fields one day with a foot injury. The family didn't have enough money to arrange an ambulance—*the* ambulance, actually, as there's just one run by a non-profit organization that serves the 100,000 people living in the 106 villages in the area—to take him to the nearest health clinic. He lay at home untreated for a few days, then died. His sister died in a few days as well, of indeterminate illness. His brother had died earlier. Of tuberculosis, they said. There can often be immediate medical triggers such as stomach disorder or malaria for many deaths among the poor, but in whatever form they come, hunger lies at their core. These deaths are conveniently attributed to diseases to avoid media attention and political scandal. But the chronically hungry don't die of pneumonia or tuberculosis. They die because their feeble bodies can't fend off disease anymore. India recorded seventy-nine starvation deaths across eight states in the four years to June 2019. This number was based solely on media reports. Food activists believe it is a fraction of the real figure, which is hard to calculate because of the protracted nature of starvation deaths, their invisibility, and the complex interface of hunger and disease that makes it harder to pin a death specifically on starvation. Government reluctance to acknowledge the deaths for what they are also contributes to obscuring the true extent of the problem. Death by starvation isn't a good look for a political system that calls itself a democracy. It risks accusations of hypocrisy, the fertile soil in which public antipathy towards governments and democratic institutions and their thwarted promises takes root.[6]

Embarrassingly for the Jharkhand government, Budhni wouldn't go quietly. Sanchi and the rest of the family held on to her body for two days because they didn't have the money for the last rites, propelling their plight to the headlines. Finally, the local administration offered the family 2,000 rupees to complete the last rites, and stem the bad press. But the region was by then in the limelight. More reports of hunger deaths emerged, many of them caused by poor implementation and little accountability of the public distribution system. Another democracy failure. A new drive to go digital compounded the problem, as many of the recipients of subsidized food under the old public distribution system fell off the list in the transition to a nationwide biometric identification system. Boondocks like Mahuadanr also lack a steady electricity supply or Internet connection, both key to the digitized food distribution model India is trying to adopt. Many desperately needy households across India have found

Figure 9. Government-provided midday school meals are necessary sustenance for the poorest Indians

themselves excluded as a result. In past years, millions of ration cards have been struck off (some 300,000 in tiny Jharkhand alone). The government says they were found to be 'fake' when biometrically verified, a claim contested by independent studies.[7] The 30 million people thus deprived of rations nationwide add up to about 108 million people—8 per cent of the population—who are already excluded from the public distribution system which is based on the outdated census of 2011 (as calculated by economists Jean Drèze, Reetika Khera, and Meghana Mungikar).

Hungry Nation

The scale of dispersed and slow-motion famine that afflicts Indian democracy should be an ethical and political scandal, but it's hardly ever an election issue. In the world's fifth largest economy, starvation deaths sometimes do cause brief media outrage when they occur, such as the ones in Jharkhand, or when two children died in 2019 in the southern state of Andhra Pradesh after eating mud to quell hunger, or when three sisters died after going hungry for days in the capital Delhi the year before. But a conspiracy of silence by incompetent officials, ephemeral media attention, and the indifference and complacency of well-fed citizens, helps to temper outrage. Avoiding words like starvation—using malnutrition instead—and hiding hunger under the garb of other diseases allow India's million famines to go untreated, debilitating the social foundations of its democracy.

In 2013, the Parliament enacted the National Food Security Act in response to a civil society movement for universal access to food. It made the right to food a fundamental right by guaranteeing subsidized food grains to about three-quarters of the population. The country still scored a poor 94 (out of 107 nations) in the 2020 Global Hunger Index. This index, based on the extent of undernourishment, underweight children, child stunting, and child mortality, classifies India's level of hunger as 'serious'. India shares the rank with Sudan; narrowly beats North Korea (96); fares worse than Congo (91), Nepal (73), Iraq (65), and Sri Lanka (64); and is miles behind China and Brazil (both among the seventeen countries in this index that have low levels of hunger and hence go unranked). The Food and Agriculture Organization of the United Nations estimates that 190 million Indians—nearly three times the population of France—are undernourished (Figure 9).

The extent of hunger is doubly scandalous in a country that produces far more than the 225 million tonnes of food it needs to feed its population a year, yet wastes 40 per cent of it. India, in fact, annually wastes as much food as the UK consumes and which would be enough to feed the 100 million people of its poorest state, Bihar, all year. Some 21 million tonnes of wheat are estimated to rot in India every year, equivalent to Australia's total annual production. Crops are left to rot in the sun without storage or transportation, or eaten by insects and rats in poorly maintained warehouses. State and central governments, irrespective of who's in power, for as long as can be remembered, announce elaborate plans of building infrastructure for storage and transportation so that food isn't wasted. Yet hunger continues to kill with impunity and food wasted with abandon.

In 2018, according to UNICEF, India reported 880,000 child deaths under the age of 5. Since no popularly elected government wants to admit starvation deaths, the cause of children's death is passed off as diseases such as encephalitis or diarrhoea, even though it is mostly hidden starvation—nearly 70 per cent[8]—that robs children of the strength to fight diseases. At least one in two children suffers from deficiency of essential nutrients because of hidden hunger. About 90 per cent of children under the age of 2 don't get what UNICEF considers a minimum acceptable diet.[9] As a result, a third of the country's children, 46.6 million, are stunted. Even though stunting has been declining in past decades, that still makes India the country with the highest number of stunted children. It accounts for more than a third of the global total, with the incidence of stunting higher in the poorer northern and eastern states and among lower castes.[10] A new government survey now finds that stunting has been on the rise again since 2015, reversing earlier progress. The country also has 20 million 'wasted' children (who have low weight for height as a result of muscle wasting from hunger), half of the world's total. More than a fifth of its children are wasted, the highest rate for any country. According to the Hunger Index, the prevalence of wasting has also increased since 2015. Nearly 60 per cent of India's children are anaemic.[11] So are 53 per cent of women of reproductive age, with much greater percentages for Dalit and tribal women.[12] That sets in motion a cycle of death, impairment, and poor life chances for millions of Indians even before they are born. A third of children under 5 are malnourished. Those who survive early low-intensity starvation face a lifetime of deprivation as chronic hunger adversely affects learning, employability, and earnings. Two-thirds of India's working population were stunted as children.[13]

Despite the damage done to social life, hunger finds little mention in the country's political discourse. Election campaigns are not fought over hunger, nor do governments fall for failing to break its deathly grip. Gujarat, one of the richest states, had more than 380,000 malnourished children as of February 2020, according to the state government. The number had actually jumped 140,000 in six months.[14] Gujarat tops the list of Indian states in terms of child wasting. More than 20 per cent of its children show low birth weight, 40 per cent are stunted, 33.5 per cent underweight, and 62 per cent anaemic.[15] But Gujarat also has had the same party in power since 2001. Hungry children are never a political problem. Far from it. So successful is the supposed 'Gujarat model' of economic growth and development that Modi, who ruled the state for a dozen years, was rewarded with national power for his sterling show in the state. That's how invisible hunger is.

India shows how modern so-called democracies fitted out with supposedly free elections and notionally free media can be surprisingly tolerant of hunger in less visible, more geographically dispersed and slow-motion forms. Of late, hunger has reappeared in comparatively rich democracies such as the United Kingdom and the United States as well. Doctors are warning that in the United Kingdom, nearly one in five children under 15 now live in a home where parents cannot afford to put food on the table. In the United States, over 12 million children live in food-insecure homes, and 22 million children rely on free or subsidized lunch at school. Millions of children are left underfed when schools are closed in summer, as the summer meal programme run by the federal government reaches just 4 million pupils.

In India, the highly subsidized prices of food grains sold through the public distribution system nominally targets the poor but creates a dual-price system that gives corrupt intermediaries, such as fair price shop owners and government officials, a strong incentive to divert grains to the open market. As a result, India records a leakage of more than 40 per cent in its public distribution system.[16] The scope for profiteering creates powerful networks comprising state and non-state poligarchs at local levels with a convergent stake to profit from hunger, and hiding it. They are heavily responsible for the damage done to the social footings of Indian democracy. Local administrations never admit starvation deaths. On the rare occasion that such information leaks out, the usual media circus and political blame games follow, devoid of context. All this helps dramatize events but doesn't lead to any awareness of the structural defects underlying crucial public issues, or a public conversation about their mitigation. The drama is heightened by the adversarial media frames of political battles. The opposition demands the government's head. The story gains traction. More people pay attention to the event and debate it, but the talking point isn't hunger, it's the performance of the government, specifically the chief minister. The government swiftly moves to manage the headlines. It denies and disproves the role of hunger in the reported deaths. The office-hungry opposition is thwarted. A ratings-starved media moves on to the next big story. Hunger is forgotten till the next hunger death surfaces. In a perverse way, the political stigma attached to starvation deaths allows its perpetuation. The very mechanisms of democracy that are supposed to guard against mass hunger, namely free media and competitive multiparty politics, become complicit in its reproduction. Low-intensity chronic hunger continues, out of sight. Until, that is, a pestilence and widespread joblessness come calling, and it becomes difficult to be kept hidden anymore.

No Escape

Two months into the Covid lockdown, when many of India's well-hidden secrets tumbled onto its highways, so did its scandalous dalliance with disguised famine. A haunting video of a starving man eating a road-killed dog on the Delhi–Jaipur highway hit the headlines. As millions of jobless migrant workers fled back to their villages, it was a disturbing sight even by the standards of what Indians had come to expect to see on their highways. The lines at soup kitchens grew interminably longer (Figure 10). One survey found that 30 per cent of the workers had no food intermittently for one to two days, while about 10 per cent were out of food for more than seven days, 'facing an

Figure 10. Queues at soup kitchens grew longer as millions lost jobs overnight in the 2020 Covid lockdown

extreme hunger situation'.[17] With their breadwinners rendered jobless and returning home, rural families were plunged into desperate poverty. Many families (35 per cent) were going without food for whole days or skipping meals (38 per cent).[18] The government, belatedly, sanctioned extra food for 800 million people, covered under the country's National Food Security Act, but it failed to deliver rations to millions of households (144 million people in one month) even as it sat on 77 million tonnes of food stock.[19]

There was, however, enough food stock to last two years. So much that plans were afoot to convert the extra rice stock into ethanol for making alcohol-based hand sanitizer. More than 1,550 tonnes of grains rotted in government warehouses in two months of lockdown, even as three-quarters of poor households without ration cards—and now without a source of income—received no rations.[20] In Jharkhand, women raided food trucks on the highways looking for food for their hungry children. The closure of schools in the lockdown aggravated the crisis as free midday meals provided at state schools sustain more than 120 million children, many of them from India's poorest households. In backward regions such as Palghar, barely 100 km from the financial capital Mumbai, where more than 1,100 children died of hunger between 2016 and 2018, the number of those officially categorized as suffering 'moderate acute malnutrition' (MAM) jumped.[21] The pestilence lay bare not just the extent of precarity in India but also the chronic democracy failure in the so-called food distribution system.

India has about 365 million people officially classified as poor, living under the international poverty line of $1.90 a day. Hundreds of millions of others flit between the amorphous classifications of 'poor', 'nearly poor', and 'middle class', sometimes rising above the line, sometimes pushed back into poverty by factors such as medical emergencies and erratic earnings typical of distressed informal labour. As the economy came to a standstill and the pall of hunger spread, senior government ministers continued to make loud proclamations that India had ensured that 'not a single person' had starved. The three top government committees responsible specifically for tackling hunger and required to meet every quarter, didn't even meet once in 2020.[22] This was despite reports of hunger deaths and despair trickling in from different parts of the country. Nearly 100 people died on the special trains that the government itself had arranged, after two months of lockdown, to take migrant workers home. Many were already critically food-deprived by the time they boarded the trains, their hunger made fatal by long journeys that took them back to the same countryside that they had once left to escape hunger.

Ground Realities

The Sack of Singrauli

Two monstrous boiler towers can be seen rising out of nowhere by the unlit highway when crossing the state border from Uttar Pradesh's Sonbhadra to enter Madhya Pradesh's Singrauli district. Like a pair of hungry giants, the iridescent, hydra-headed power plant glares menacingly through the dark, lying in wait, silently spewing its venom.

The thermal power plant is among the ten that make the 1,800 square km Singrauli-Sonbhadra industrial region straddling two states—commonly referred to as Singrauli—the country's energy capital. It supplies about 15 per cent of India's coal-based electricity. The region has several coal mines that together produce 100 million tonnes of coal a year and feed the power stations, which in turn feed a host of other factories, from aluminium to chemicals. All this industrial activity has heavily taxed the environment.

The area is marked by government officials as 'critically polluted'. On an average summer day, Singrauli looks like a town caught in a dust storm. In the areas near the mines and the highways, where trucks plying coal make the air thick with black dust, it's particularly bad. Where it's not coal, it's fly ash from burnt coal of the power plants. Or it's the loose dust that flies off the mountains of dug-up mine top-soils—the filth that layers Singrauli's crops and water bodies and is breathed in by local residents. Visibility, even in the middle of a perfectly sunny day, is low in many parts of Singrauli. And that's just the pollution you can see. Singrauli preys on its own in numerous other ways, from poisoned land to toxic waters—all in the name of economic development.

As an industrial hub, Singrauli may be an extreme example of nature's desecration caused by corporate impunity and governmental abetment, but it's also a microcosm of the widespread and unchecked environmental abuse in India, where according to a report by the Global Alliance on Health and Pollution, 2.3 million people die every year because of pollution. Singrauli is a sooty specimen of how wanton human despoliation of the planet lays to waste the most basic elements of social life—land, water, and air. The result is a carnage of human lives and a spiral of inequity that makes a mockery of the principle that democracy stands for the equal integrity of human bodies. After all, can people be said to have the same right to vote and enjoy equal social dignity if they don't have the same right to breathe or have equal access to water?

Nearly a third of India's land area has been degraded through deforestation, over-cultivation, soil erosion, and depletion of wetlands. Reckless industrialization, mining, and urbanization, as well as deeply flawed agricultural policies and skewed land distribution, have reaped a bitter harvest of dislocation and deprivation. This dispossession adds to India's historically unequal land holdings. Along with the poisoning of life-giving water and air, land alienation and destruction create a hierarchy of citizens suffering unequal access to the fundamental ingredients of social life. In this systematic evisceration of democracy-defining social equality, Singrauli typifies the destruction of the elements by the collusion of poligarchs—the entanglement of the state and big business—and the priority given to private profit over public good.

Land

The bustling Singrauli of today is a vastly different place from the assorted sleepy hamlets nestled among green-topped mountains before the mining boom in the 1960s. Lives are lost, but livelihoods are made, too. But not for the hundreds of thousands like Nandlal Baiga (Baiga is how his tribe is called locally, and used generically as a surname) who have been robbed of their habitats and traditional occupations to make way for mines and factories, then left to rot on a pittance. The millions who live amidst Singrauli's toxins have been sentenced to slow death. But for those like Baiga, sacrificed at the altar of the shiny monsters of Singrauli, death is more palpable.

Baiga's is the usual story in these parts. He was promised a home, a job, compensation, and perfect living standards to vacate his abode in a forest for a 'company' coal project, but received precious little. In Singrauli, people use the generic 'company' to denote the nearest corporate oppressor rather than specify it by name. In the eyes of the locals, they are all the same, united in their quest for profit, identical in their appetite for ruthless exploitation. Like the 'government'—or 'sasan', as it is called in Hindi here—'company' is a composite, only more powerful than 'sasan'. The identity of the 'company' varies from one part of Singrauli to another, but in casual conversations people identify which particular company is being referred to depending on where the conversation is taking place. There's no part of Singrauli that hasn't been laid to waste by one company or another.

Apart from the false promises of emoluments, Baiga also faced violence, as often happens with people who refuse to heed the company's requests to go quietly. In 2012, he left his ancestral habitat in the forest and moved to an area near the city where the company was building a colony for the displaced. He hated it. The tiny, stuffy, two-room apartment felt like a prison cell compared with his breezy mud home by the hills in the forest. In the unforgiving urban patch that housed the colony, the sun beat down on the thin roof during the day and the open drains sent mosquitos to feast on his body at night.

There was no forest to go to for a living either. He's from a tribal community—an Adivasi, considered India's indigenous people whose ancestry predate the Dravidians and the Indo-Aryans. Adivasis comprise about 8 per cent of India's population. A creature of the forest,

Baiga used to till his three acres of land there and collect leaves, medicinal herbs, timber, firewood, vegetables, and honey to sell in the city. With all that gone, without a forest and without the livelihood he was promised for leaving the forest, he saw no reason to hang on to this new life of misery, and went back to the forest after six months.

The company let him be for a few years. Then it struck back. In early 2019, a large contingent of company people along with police and local administrative officials arrived at the forest settlement inhabited by him and others holding on to their land. They flattened the homes with bulldozers. They threatened the community with dire consequences if they tried to protest, bundled them into vans, and brought them back to the company colony.

Baiga, 36, never got the job he and hundreds of others at this colony were promised. Those whom the company wouldn't employ were promised the equivalent of the minimum wage as dole. After years of petitioning, a handful of the displaced are now given less than half that amount. Baiga is among the lucky few (Figure 11). The money doesn't go far. Unused to manual labour and unskilled for the modern economy, some have managed to find casual work as agricultural labourers, porters, or construction workers. But as the milling crowd of able-bodied men in the colony lazing about in the sun on a weekday afternoon showed, steady work was in short supply.

The companies provide homes, such as they are, but not the property deeds. If and when they give jobs, it is low-level manual work outsourced to intermediary firms that do the hiring. This way, the companies get to hire informally even though they promised formal, permanent jobs to make people give away their land. Companies in Singrauli, as in the rest of India, are averse to hiring locals. Outsiders with no local networks are considered safer and more productive. Hence, migrant workers get preference over those from local communities. Social life in Singrauli feeds on these resentments. 'Even the English didn't torture us as much. People have been reduced to semi-bonded labourers, with no property rights or job security. Private companies are simply taking up more and more government land

Figure 11. Nandlal Baiga and his son, displaced by 'development'

with the connivance of the local administration. 'It's total Company Raj', said lawyer Avnish Dubey, who is fighting several companies in court, alluding to the British East India Company's reign in the sub-continent till the mid-nineteenth century.

In Deosar, on the western side of the Singrauli district, where a company was trying to start a coal mine, angry locals were pushing back. They said the project was being railroaded through deceit and coercion. Local officials, allegedly, staged a fake village council meeting to give an appearance of the community's consent to the project. Thousands of villagers protested. At grave risk to themselves. Typically, whenever there's organized resistance, the company tries to break it up by isolating the leaders. Some are bought off, some intimidated with violence, while others are slapped with fake charges with the help of government functionaries. Complaints of such fraudulent corporate takeover of tribal land abound in mineral-rich states. An enquiry report on similar allegations in the eastern state of Odisha concluded: 'There is no rule of law, but law is what the mighty mining lessees decide.'[1]

Columbus Redux

What emerges from Singrauli and elsewhere in India is a pattern of intensifying land grabs in the guise of industrial activity. A 2009 government report said India has been witnessing 'the biggest grab of tribal lands after Columbus'. It noted landlessness in the country had spiked to about 52 per cent in 2004–5, up from 40 per cent in 1991, when India started liberalizing its economy.[2]

Land inequity goes back much further. Widespread landlessness has long trapped millions of Indians in cross-generational poverty and damaged social lives in a country where 60 per cent of the population is involved in agriculture. Land in India is not just a unit of production that generates livelihoods. It provides dignity and creates opportunities for people to live as social equals. Its absence has ruinous social consequences. According to government data, 42 per cent of households don't own land other than their tiny homestead patch. While one-third of households are landless, those 'near to landlessness' make up another one-third. The next 20 per cent hold less than 1 hectare.

The constitution makers' grand socialist dream of distributive justice through land redistribution didn't succeed, as big landholders were allowed by the political and bureaucratic class—drawn from the same dominant landed classes—to game the new rules. Some big estates were broken up, trimming the holdings of the old landed gentry and helping wealthy tenants to become substantial landowners. But not much changed for the landless labourers who actually tilled the soil. Land reform in the '50s and the '60s in states like Uttar Pradesh and Bihar was a far cry from the slogan of 'land to the tiller'. It merely installed a broad base of wealthier peasants who were 'expected to support and be part of the Congress Party'.[3] For several more decades, land reforms continued to feature as fertile political rhetoric. But it began to wane in the popular imagination with the onset of market reforms, when economic redemption began to be associated more with industry and enterprise than land ownership.

Extremely skewed landholding is the consequence. Some 10 per cent of the population controls over 55 per cent of the land; 60 per cent has rights over only 5 per cent of the land.[4] The 2011 Census estimated that 56 per cent of rural households, or about 500 million people, were landless. There are additional dimensions to land inequity: caste and gender. As the pattern of land distribution broadly reflects the Hindu caste hierarchy, large landowners tend to be upper castes, while medium-sized landowners, who cultivate their own lands, belong to the middle castes. Dalits and Adivasis own little or no land, and even when they do, it is often appropriated by those higher up the caste structure. A government study from 1997 concluded that 77 per cent of the Dalits and 90 per cent of the Adivasis were either *de jure* or *de facto* landless. Two decades later, another government report on landless families noted that large parts of India resembled a 'feudal society'.[5] Women are similarly deprived, owning less than 13 per cent of the land even though they do about two-thirds of all farm work.

Large-scale development projects for urbanization, industries, dams, and mines only add to this prevalent land deprivation, disproportionately hurting Adivasis and the lowest castes who toil as landless agricultural workers. The pattern is especially striking in mineral-rich regions, where Adivasis are concentrated. Governments since independence have for the most part shied away from taking responsibility for the development-displaced. There wasn't even a policy for the displaced till the 1980s. A rehabilitation and resettlement policy was first introduced in 1985 and was debated for two decades. Although by the year 2000 an estimated 60 million people had been forcibly displaced, the National Policy on Resettlement and Rehabilitation was formulated only in 2004, but couldn't clear the Parliament. Finally, a law called the Right to Fair Compensation and Transparency in Land Acquisition, Rehabilitation and Resettlement Act, or LARR, came into effect in January 2014. Replacing a colonial-era land acquisition law, LARR increased compensation for landowners and made the process of obtaining landowners' consent more rigorous. It also made it mandatory for projects to first study the social impact of land acquisition. But the new Modi BJP-led government that came to power five months later saw the law as a hindrance to economic growth, and allowed states to bypass it and carry on with the colonial law for acquiring project land. It had taken independent India nearly seven decades to replace a 120-year British-era draconian land acquisition law with one that was more just, only to kill it in a matter of months.

The result of the indiscriminate land grabbing by state and corporate poligarchs is that in the last seventy years India has deforested about 57,300 square kilometres—thirty-eight times the size of Delhi.[6] Modi's government wants more. While most countries are moving away from coal-powered plants, or claim to be doing so, India is doubling down on coal. In June 2020, with much fanfare, Modi launched the auction of forty-one coal mines for commercial mining. His environment minister prides himself on not allowing his department to 'obstruct' industry. As the country entered lockdown in March 2020, the environment ministry pushed through a new law that radically diluted existing environmental norms for industry and cleared a raft of new mega-projects. These included a hydropower plant that would involve clearing a rainforest and felling 270,000 trees, exploration of uranium in a tiger reserve, and coal mining inside an elephant reserve.

As millions more Baigas are being readied for the slaughter, the impunity with which they are dispossessed without compensation, or even consultation, is justified by the mantra of 'national interest'. It is suitably aided by antiquated laws like the Coal Bearing Areas Act that allow government to take over land without consent if it is 'satisfied' that there's no alternative. The blueprints for 'development' are drawn up by 'experts' who know best. Democratic accountability counts for little, or nothing. The top-down decision-making template was wired into policymaking from the early days by Nehru. Kicking off the construction of India's first major river-valley project, the Hirakud Dam in Orissa, a few months after Independence, he said in his speech to those facing displacement: 'If you have to suffer, you should suffer in the interest of the country.'

And suffer they have. In Singrauli's case, repeatedly. First by the Rihand Dam in the 1960s, then by thermal power plants, coal mines, railways, heavy industry, and urbanization. Even when resettled, the poor living conditions and lack of economic opportunities eventually force people to leave, as rows of empty apartments in any company colony reveal. Many move to nearby areas in search of livelihood, but most travel further to big urban clusters, where they encounter yet more social decay. There's still no accounting for a fifth of the 200,000 people who were displaced in the mid-'50s when construction began on the Rihand Dam that flooded 146 villages. It remains one of Singrauli's biggest mysteries.

If the evictees of the Rihand Dam were the victims of Nehru's so-called 'socialist' model of development, Baiga is a victim of a new kind of 'neoliberal' state capitalism in which the blurring of the boundary between the state and private capital works to the benefit of rich and powerful poligarchs. It also results in democracy failure. The global rule is that nine out of ten megaprojects exceed their projected costs and incur delays and suffer outright failures unless those in charge of their complex design and operation are subject to lengthy public scrutiny and democratic accountability. If there's little or no monitory democracy in this sense, megaprojects typically produce disasters. The nuclear meltdown at Fukushima, the massive oil spill caused by the failure of BP's Deepwater Horizon, and the 1984 Bhopal gas tragedy were examples of how badly things can go wrong in the absence of monitory democracy. These were not accidents, but political disasters, large-scale democracy failures caused by the absence of watchdog mechanisms that could have prevented the destruction of whole eco-systems by powerful corporations and the state.[7]

Baiga is a victim of the same democracy failure. Displaced from his land and plunged into a world where his land-related expertise is rendered redundant, he will be forced to migrate. He said he'd been thinking about it a lot. If he ended up in a big city, he would join millions of other villagers in India forced by the shrinking opportunities at home to seek a dignified life in the cities' informal economy of low-end jobs. Most of the injustices Baiga would be trying to leave behind will follow him to the city, however. A World Bank survey in 2004 found that, in rural Maharashtra, nearly 80 per cent of landless Adivasis like him migrated to cities for four to six months every year, and that most of them worked under semi-slavery conditions in stone quarries, brick kilns, salt pans, excavations, and construction sites. With no skills and no social networks in the city, Baiga will end up in the city's fringes like other migrants, with or without a roof above his head, sleeping under a flyover or on a pavement. If luckier, he will find a place in a slum, where one in every six city people lives, in conditions that the 2011 Census calls 'unfit for human habitation'. As things stand, Baiga's best-case scenario is to swap rural indignity for urban indignity.

Water

One of the first things a visitor is taught in Singrauli is the art of drinking water. When you pour a glass, never drink it right away. Let the water rest for a while so that the small metal particles whirling in it can settle. 'If you boil the water, you will get a strange white residue. And there's something else. I have never seen this before—if you leave a glass of water overnight, it sets like curd', said Baiga. In Singrauli, water curdles.

People, Baiga said, have been dying like flies since moving to the colony from the forest. And it's because of the water. He feels unwell all day. His two children complain of stomach cramps and often get rashes. It's a standard symptom in the area, where people regularly talk about neighbours who died for reasons unknown. Unknown, because they were never diagnosed or treated. The 'company' had promised free health services and has built a clinic, but all it does is hand out pain killers or paracetamols, and refers patients to a hospital, the nearest one being 200 kilometres away in Varanasi. In the forest, the Adivasis knew which herbs cured what. Here in the city, they neither have access to herbs nor modern healthcare.

Local journalists who have covered past spates of what the media calls 'mystery fever' blame a combination of hunger, pollution, and toxic water. Proper filtration might have helped, but it's beyond the reach of the poor. Baiga has heard of water filters, but has never seen one. He can't afford one anyway, even though water purifiers are inexpensive and widely used by India's middle classes.

He bathes once a week with the water from the hand pump near his home. By bathing, he means pouring a couple of mugs of water over his body. If he could help it, he wouldn't touch this water at all. He once did try a stream nearby to escape the rush at the hand-pump. It was so dirty that it gave him boils and itches. The greyish stream, which gathers coal dirt from a nearby mine, flows into the local Kachan river, which in turn meets the Rihand Dam's reservoir, Govind Ballabh Pant Sagar, India's largest artificial lake, before flowing downstream. The condition of waterbodies in this coal belt is alarming. Many ponds and ditches have turned jet black. There's so much coal dust around that some have even begun to cake into dark, semi-solid clay. The toxic water seeps deep into the soil and poisons crops.

The Democracy of Water

In India, per capita water availability has dropped 70 per cent since the early 1950s. The World Resources Institute now ranks India thirteenth in the list of seventeen countries facing 'extremely high' levels of water stress, with more than three times the population of the other sixteen combined. According to the World Health Organization

(WHO), a person needs 50 to 100 litres of water a day to meet their most basic needs. Baiga is on about 20 litres, on a good day.

There are 600 million Indians like him, according to the government's own reckoning, who face high to extreme levels of water stress. The stress is not *all* caused by climate change and droughts, as is commonly believed. As in healthcare and food supply, neglect and poor planning by successive governments at national and state levels have for decades failed to ensure clean freshwater, check groundwater depletion and water wastage, preserve water sources, and foster sustainable agriculture. River basins, without exception, have been over-exploited. This has drastically reduced the amount of water in major rivers and reinforced the growing aridity.

A quarter of India is undergoing desertification. Excessive mining, deforestation, and increasing use of borewells to extract water are just as responsible as climate-change factors such as reduced rainfall. Inefficient crop patterns and lopsided geographical concentration of agriculture haven't helped. Government crop procurement for subsidized public distribution is skewed in favour of water-intensive sugar cane, rice, and wheat grown in the most water-stressed parts of India. The central government, for example, buys most of the rice from the naturally parched northwestern states of Punjab and Haryana, even though it requires far less water to grow rice in the wetter, eastern states like Bengal and Assam. Subsidized—and often free—electricity for the electorally all-important farmers makes matters worse as it results in reckless water extraction. Little wonder that the groundwater levels in the northwestern states are dropping rapidly. In the western state of Maharashtra, too, water use has been similarly distorted. In the state's Marathwada region, which has been experiencing droughts, spiralling farmer indebtedness and suicides, poligarchs tied to the powerful cotton and sugarcane lobbies have used policy incentives to steer agriculture towards these very water-guzzling cash crops, replacing traditional crops.

Little has been done to check water pollution. India relies heavily on groundwater, yet an estimated 60 per cent of its groundwater reserves are polluted. The overdependence on groundwater, in turn, stems from the virtual destruction of surface water, 80 per cent of which is polluted. Rampant dumping of untreated sewage along with industrial waste has made major rivers unusable. According to the country's Central Pollution Control Board, eighteen of India's major rivers are unfit for domestic and industrial water usage. Take the 2,500 kilometre Ganga, which flows through eleven states of India and provides water to more than 500 million people. Considered holy by Hindus, who dip in the river to cleanse their sins, Ganga is also the final destination of much of India's industrial effluents and domestic waste. Reuters estimates that if just one day's wastewater that is pumped into the Ganga were packed into half-litre soda bottles, they would stretch to the moon and back nearly four times. For decades, Indian leaders have been promising to clean this arterial river. Yet little has changed.

Three quarters of Indian households lack direct water supply in their premises, fewer than half have access to tap water, while under a third enjoy treated tap water. Villages are far worse served than cities. As of 2017, only 17 per cent of India's rural homes had piped water. The inequity of water distribution has both gender and class dimensions. It's the women who bear the burden of collecting water, be it queuing up at roadside taps in cities or travelling long distances to obtain water in the countryside. The water treks keep women away from productive labour, expose them to musculoskeletal disorders, physical injury, degenerative fatigue damage, as well as higher risks of infections because of frequent contact with unsanitary water. For young girls, this chore can mean falling back in studies and eventually dropping out, resulting in the denial of education and irreversible damage to their life outcomes (Figure 12).

Water injustice has in part been caused by agricultural policies and practices. Governments through the years have done poorly at conserving water. It's yet another instance of democracy failure with ruinous social consequences. The country has a per capita storage capacity of just 213 cubic metres, compared with 1,964 in the United States and 1,111 in China. When land is irrigated, it's done mostly by

Figure 12. Girls fall behind in their studies because of chores such as fetching water

groundwater, because the surface water is unusable. As a result of over-exploitation of this precious resource, India now uses more groundwater than the United States and China combined.[8] The reckless run on groundwater has begun to take its toll, as water tables drop alarmingly across the country, triggering farming crises in rural areas. By 2025, farmers in the northern states of Punjab, Rajasthan, and Haryana face the prospect of having no groundwater for irrigation.

Legally, landowners control the groundwater under their land. Decades of debates to regulate groundwater as a public good have gone nowhere because the federal and state governments haven't been able to come to a consensus on how to do so (water comes within the ambit of state laws). The bigger landlords, from higher castes, disproportionately control more groundwater. This reality, coupled with financial resources that allow them to invest in more advanced water extraction systems than smaller farmers, gives them a competitive advantage in controlling the means of irrigation. These powerful groups also try to corner the community hand pumps and wells in water-stressed areas. Clashes over access to water are commonplace.

Connivance between higher-caste government officials and local villagers when crafting water policy also often results in the diversion of water resources to suit the needs of upper-caste households. As a result, lower-caste women usually have less access to water and are forced to travel further to fetch it. As upper-caste men often use sexual violence as a power tool to assert domination and control—with the female body treated as the hostage of community honour—the strenuous chore of collecting water can be fraught with risks of violence as well. Water, in its scarcity, thus becomes a medium of political patronage and social degradation. At the Chuni village in the mountains of water-abundant Uttarakhand, where upper-caste Kshtariya women take pride in controlling the water that flows around the year from springs and in irrigation canals, ecologist Deepa Joshi recounts a Dalit woman's experience of water scarcity:

> Ask us what water scarcity is—it is to not bathe in the summer heat, after toiling in the fields. It is to reuse water used in washing vegetables and rice to wash utensils, to use this water again to wash clothes and then to feed the buffaloes this soapy water. Water scarcity is to sit up the whole night filling a container glass by glass as it trickles into our one small spring. We often don't wash the utensils and just wipe them with a cloth. We feel so dirty and unclean in the summer. We do not wash our clothes for weeks, just rinsing them with a little water. These people [upper castes] say we are dirty and smell. But how can we be clean without water?[9]

Race to the Bottom

In cities, where groundwater has been falling drastically, water injustice takes a different form. From Assam's Guwahati in the east to Bangalore in the south, poor city planning means the water distribution system has failed to keep pace with urban expansion. Bangalore, for example, has seen its population nearly double to over 11 million in two decades, in which time most of its lakes have either vanished, been paved over, or severely contaminated with sewage. Elected representatives entrusted with managing the city have been an active agent of this destruction through their profiteering from the real estate boom that urbanization brought. Plunder by colluding poligarchs at every level of the state and business power pyramid is more or less the story of every Indian city. The upshot is that water in most cities, beyond a small core area blessed with the original piped network meant for a smaller city, has to be procured independently. This is where access to water becomes intricately linked with individual and group power. Borewells get more and more expensive as the groundwater level drops, so giving those with deeper pockets a huge advantage in accessing water, leaving the poor to struggle to meet their daily water needs.

Water disparities are a way of life in Indian cities. Safi-ul Rahman, an executive at a construction company in Guwahati, lives in an apartment block in the city's upmarket 'Survey' area, where the residents have changed the borewell four times since 2013. Beginning with one that went 800 ft deep, the current bore reaches 1,500 ft underground. The next time the bloc runs out of water and needs to bore deeper, it will cost 'serious money' to upgrade, he said. Rahman and others in the gated community, all white-collar professionals, could afford the additional cost. Their less prosperous neighbours, who've been living in the area for much longer, cannot, and they hate the moneyed newcomers for stealing their water. Anupam Saikia, who drives a car for a cab-hailing company, had a borewell of 350 feet at his modest two-room home. Thanks to gated blocs that sucked out all the water at that level, his borewell is now obsolete. He knows there's no point buying a deeper borewell because he can never outspend 'those rich people', who can always dig much deeper than him. So, Saikia has abandoned the borewell race and gets his water from a private supplier instead. He pays about 200 rupees for a 750 litre canister that comes in an auto rickshaw and lasts his five-member family about five days. He's doing far better than Baiga but is way short of the WHO estimate of 50 to 100 litres of minimum daily water requirement.

Since municipal governments fail to ensure equal access to water, private providers such as Saikia's supplier flourish in an unregulated market. They profit by turning a universal right into a commodified privilege. In Bangalore, for example, the armadas of private tankers that criss-cross the city keep its swimming pools full and toilets flushing. But they do so without any trade licence. As the gleaming office towers in India's Silicon Valley and the condominiums housing the city's ever-increasing population have sucked up most of Bangalore's groundwater, the tankers now meet the shortfall by sourcing their water from Bangalore's outlying areas. This effectively transfers water to the city from the outlying areas, depriving villagers at the urban periphery of their water in favour of richer city dwellers.

Water transfers from the less privileged to better-off groups is part of a much bigger diversion of water 'from food crops to cash crops; livelihoods to lifestyles; [from] rural to urban', notes Palagummi Sainath, author of *Everybody Loves a Good Drought*.[10] In parched Marathwada's Aurangabad city, for example, the beer industry has been flourishing, just like its water-guzzling sugar cane crop. As if to reinforce the scandalous water use asymmetry, the city was picked to run a water privatization pilot project designed to hand over all water supply responsibilities to private players. Aurangabad is part of a broader trend in which foreign companies, in partnership with local firms, control municipal water distribution. The emerging model of privatizing municipal water supplies is of a piece with the commodification of water evident in the moderately priced and ubiquitous bottled water and water filters throughout India. These forms of sanitized water are widely used by the upper and middle classes but are out of reach of poorer Indians, even though—given the state of the country's water shortages and toxicity—they are a necessity rather than a luxury. That a few can buy their way to water safety while many are left to their fate adds to the social injustices of India's democracy. By allowing water to be commodified, the Indian state has not only washed its hands of the responsibility for ensuring the democratic provisioning of clean water. It has shifted control over water from elected representatives into private hands protected by government officials. The public has no say in this naturally available and vital public good anymore.

Back in Singrauli, people know this trend well. From their experience, elected officials tend to represent corporate interests more than the people anyway. As companies happily go about ravaging lakes, rivers, and groundwater, the people's representatives at all levels are seen as the agents who do their corporate masters' bidding. In Singrauli, in matters of land and water, poligarchs reign supreme.

Air

The government think tank Niti Aayog (formerly the Planning Commission, rechristened and repurposed under Modi, as India has done away with five-year plans) records that 70 per cent of India's water supply is contaminated, resulting in nearly 200,000 deaths a year. Arsenic contamination, for example, alone affects some 250 million people.[11] Fish farms produce hazardous levels of lead and cadmium, resulting in diseased produce and toxic waste.[12] Water-related diseases and deformities are on the rise across the country.[13] Tap water is safe for drinking in just one city, Mumbai, according to government tests. Twenty other state capitals fail the same test. But even by India's water pollution standards, Singrauli stands out. Mercury levels in some areas of Singrauli are twenty-six times higher than what the government deems safe. More than 84 per cent of blood samples contain mercury above the safe level.[14] Tests also find high levels of arsenic and other heavy metals. The fluoride content of water samples in many areas is twice the permissible limit, causing diseases like fluorosis, hyperacidity, peptic ulcers, kidney stones, and skin rashes.

Yet water is not Singrauli's biggest problem. The real killer is air.

In the post-mortem examinations he conducts as a government doctor, R.B. Singh at the District Hospital in Waidhan town invariably finds lungs severely blackened, even of those with no history of smoking. In his three decades in Singrauli as a doctor, every post-mortem examination has been a morbid reminder of how much poison he is forced to ingest and how little he can do about it. 'Our lot is to die silently, sacrificed in the service of the nation.'

The volume of coal dust from mining, combined with carbon dioxide, small particulate matter (called PM 2.5) that enters lungs and bloodstreams, heavy metals, sulphur, and nitrogen oxides pumped into the air by burning coal, are unimaginably high. Poor regulation and deficient public monitoring make it worse. India's emissions from thermal power plants are 14 per cent higher than China's, making Indian coal power plants the dirtiest in the world.

The coal is moved in and around Singrauli through giant dumpers, some of which consume 100 litres of diesel an hour. Thousands of such dumpers and trucks ply Singrauli's roads round the clock, belching smoke and spreading coal and soil dust in the air. Railway stations are wantonly used as coal yards. The sheer amount of ambient coal dust at the station is sometimes thick enough to hide an approaching train from sight. The impact of all this on cardiac and respiratory health is telling. Breathing complaints are common, as are asthma and chronic obstructive pulmonary disease (COPD).

The high pollution levels in Singrauli may seem unexceptional given the cluster of power plants and collieries, but the air isn't much better in the rest of the country either. A *Lancet* study estimates air pollution killed 1.7 million people—nearly one out of six deaths—in 2019 in India, where the concentration of PM 2.5 is eight times the World Health Organization's standards. People in India are exposed to the highest PM 2.5 concentrations globally, according to the State of Global Air 2020 report. Fourteen of the twenty most polluted cities in the world by PM 2.5 levels are in India, which has now decisively overtaken China as *the* most polluted country in the world. Even the gods are not safe from the omnipresence of particulate matters. Long

Figure 13. Hell descends on Delhi every winter as pollution levels spiral

before the coronavirus made face masks ubiquitous, priests in Varanasi have been covering their deities on bad-air days with masks.

Every winter, around November, Delhi is hit by a particularly nasty bout of smog (Figure 13). PM 2.5 levels go off the charts as farmers in neighbouring states burn crop residues in preparation for the next sowing season. The stubble burning is itself caused by late sowing of rice paddies. Decades of cultivating water-intensive rice in semi-arid states like Punjab and Haryana have driven down water tables there. The government has acted to protect groundwater, belatedly, by pushing back paddy sowing to June to coincide with the onset of monsoons. The aim is to force greater usage of rainwater to minimize the use of groundwater. But this leaves little room for farmers to sow the next crop, wheat, in November, forcing them to hurriedly clear the fields by burning the stubble of the previous harvest. When they do, black plumes envelop the capital. The city authorities declare a public health emergency, appeal to people to stay indoors if possible, and shut down schools. During such episodes, India's Delhi-centric media reports nothing else. But less reported is the fact that the air in the rest of the country for the rest of the year is often just as bad. The state of Bengal, for example, has the most number of polluted cities (36) in India, finds one study, but is seldom seen as a dirty-air hotspot. According to this Greenpeace study of PM 10 concentration in 287 Indian cities, just one, in the northeastern state of Mizoram, met the levels prescribed by the World Health Organization.

From diabetes and strokes to memory loss and anxiety, air pollution is increasingly linked to multiple health ailments. Research is exposing the magnitude of the organized destruction of social life caused by the failure to maintain clean air. But, as in other instances of democracy failure and social decay, India's 'airpocalypse' fails to stir elected governments into action. Before 2015, India had no specific emission standards for power plants. When it did finally get around to drafting one that year, it allowed much laxer official standards than Chinese plants. A deadline was set for coal based power plants to meet the new standards by 2017. Not much happened, so it was moved to 2022. Bending and bowing to lobbying by electricity producers, the power ministry again extended the deadline, this time indefinitely.

Gas Chambers

What kind of elected executive allows air to be poisoned with such abandon? Consider these figures. Air pollution kills a newborn every five minutes in India.[15] After neonatal disorder, lower respiratory tract infection (LRI) caused by air pollutants is the second most significant reason for child mortality in the country, killing 1.2 million children every year.[16] In Delhi, where residents inhale the equivalent of half a pack of cigarettes on an ordinary day, and two packs on a bad day, just by breathing, the number of lung cancer cases has surged. Compared to other countries, the incidence of lung cancer in non-smokers is increasing much more rapidly in India, where more than half of lung cancer patients now come with no history of smoking. Deaths from cardiovascular diseases more than doubled from 1.3 million to 2.8 million between 1990 and 2016. Chronic Obstructive Pulmonary Disease (COPD), which includes bronchitis and asthma, now kills 1 million Indians a year, according to the University of Washington's Global Burden of Disease study.

India's environment minister still tells Parliament—with a straight face—that there's no link between air pollution and shorter life spans. The 2021 national budget cut funds for reducing air pollution by half. It is tempting to draw historical parallels with past rulers who subjected some of their people to chambers of noxious air. Every year when hell descends on Delhi, at the time of stubble burning, political leaders squabble and trade charges rather than sit down and agree to a workable solution, even as 86 per cent of the residents report pollution-induced health problems.[17] In 2019, when Delhi was again enveloped in toxic haze and a parliamentary standing committee called a meeting on the crisis, twenty-five of the twenty-nine MPs on the committee didn't bother to turn up. The democratic norms of parliamentary deliberation and public accountability count for little. The result was evident the following winter, when Covid cases spiked as pollution smog hit Delhi again. As higher pollution levels tend to increase Covid incidence and mortality, with lungs weakened by long-term exposure to pollution unable to cope, the pestilence revealed the deadly fallout of yet another long-tolerated democracy failure of ensuring clean air.

Apart from industrial emissions, construction and road dust are also major, often underrated, components of air pollution, accounting for almost 45 per cent of air pollutants in major Indian cities. Piles of sand or cement lying by the road are a common sight in Indian urban centres. So is loose soil along the sides of streets. Poor municipal oversight, lax construction standards, and unplanned and incomplete roadworks contribute to the profusion of urban dust.

The overall result is evident. Less than 1 per cent of Indians enjoy air quality that meets the WHO benchmark. Enduring 18 per cent of the global population, says *The Lancet*, India accounts for 26 per cent of the world's premature mortality and health loss attributable to air pollution. The World Bank estimates that healthcare costs and productivity losses from pollution amount to 8.5 per cent of the gross domestic product.

But not all Indians are suffering. Sales of air purifiers are booming. They are the new tools of the privileged. When Barack Obama visited India in 2015, local media reported that the US president could lose six hours of his expected lifespan after his three days in Delhi, where the average annual PM 2.5 level was fifteen times higher than the WHO-prescribed levels at the time. To protect the president and his staff, the US embassy in Delhi reportedly installed 1,800 indoor air purifiers. Between 2014 and 2017, Modi's government itself reportedly spent 3.6 million rupees (about $55,000) to buy air purifiers for the prime minister's offices and at least six federal departments.[18] It's difficult to protect yourself from killer air unless you are the leader of the world's 'oldest democracy' or leader of its 'largest democracy'. Or at least have the dough to do so. For the rest, breathing poison is their lot. In Delhi, anyone who's riding an auto rickshaw or cycling is exposed to 2.5 times more PM 2.5 than a person travelling in an air-conditioned car or cab.[19] Out on the street, PM 2.5 exposure is heightened by vehicular pollution and the failure to provide adequate public transport. With rapid urbanization and rising purchasing power, the absence of democratic means of transport has caused a spike in private transport modes and a consequent increase in traffic fume levels, which now cause 350,000 new cases of childhood asthma every year in India. Each year, an estimated 74,000 deaths are caused by transport-related pollution, two-thirds of them linked to tailpipe emissions from diesel vehicles.[20] Even the air that Indians breathe is not equal for all. But fear not. Help is at hand. The brand new 'oxygen bar' in Delhi is where pure oxygen by the lungful is available in seven flavours, including lemongrass and peppermint, for just 300 rupees.

Motion Sickness

Moving Laboratories

Cities are often described as democratic laboratories, for good reasons. Cities are where the idea of democracy germinated and where its defenders have fought against its corruption by the rich and powerful. The ideals and customs of democracy, understood as self-government by assemblies, were born of ancient cities such as Nineveh, Byblos, Vaisali (the capital of a 6th century BCE city republic in northern India), and Athens.[1] Etymologists remind us that the vocabulary of democracy includes precious words such as citizen, drawn from civitas (the inhabitant of a city), and civis (a citizen of a town). But the connections between democracy and cities run deeper, to include important urban inventions. In the Atlantic region, towns like Naples, Nuremberg, Bruges, Amsterdam, and Edinburgh resembled levers used by citizens to turn the old Christian feudal world upside down, initially by raising basic political questions about who was entitled to get how much, when, and how. It's to their citizens that we owe some basic constitutional inventions that later fed the wellsprings of modern democracy. The right to resist tyranny, the abolition of monarchy, constitutional conventions, written constitutions, popular election, and limited terms of office: all these basic democratic procedures have roots in early modern urban life.

The towns of Europe had another democratic significance: they resembled tension-producing engines. Energetic motion through space was among their defining features. Town-dwellers were perpetually on the move. The constant rumble of wheeled carriages and the hubbub of the weekly or daily markets compounded the sense of motion through space. To Berlin-born scholar Georg Simmel, large metropolises were restless mosaics of dynamic social interactions. Motion machines, he called them. In the late nineteenth and early twentieth centuries, not surprisingly, cities felt pressures for a new round of democratization. The development went by names like the 'reorganization of local government', 'gas and water socialism', 'local democracy', and 'municipal socialism'. In each case, the provision of cheap gas and water and electricity to all citizens and improved sanitation and land-use planning were seen to be the responsibility and duty of publicly elected city governments. Public schools, public parks, public drinking fountains and public libraries, mechanics and literary institutes were to be made available. They were reckoned to be public goods that should be available to all citizens, usually on a free of charge or limited-charge basis, paid for through general taxation of the wealthy classes. In this new universe of widened access to public goods, public transport was considered essential. Streetcars, also called trams, trolleys, or electric streetcars, became regular fixtures of urban life. There were public bridges and steam-driven river boats, funiculars, and electric and underground railways.

For the first time in the history of democracy, the working principle was that urban transportation was a matter of the highest public concern, not principally a technical issue or engineering challenge to be managed and decided by a few, for the few. The formula implied that more rapid movement of human bodies and luggage through space was a political matter. It was linked to the unavoidable, if difficult question of who was to benefit from the new motion machines. Champions of local government were firm in their reply: the means of transportation should be owned publicly, a punctual and affordable means of public use and enjoyment by all city dwellers. A democracy was not just written constitutions, votes for all, uncorrupted elections, and liberty of the press. Democracy demanded that citizens are practically entitled to equal freedom of social movement through the streets and neighbourhoods of the cities in which they dwell. The enjoyment of public space shouldn't be the luxury of the rich but the entitlement of each and every city inhabitant. Motion was not charity. Hereon it had to be democratic.

In the abstract, that meant that the local social world was to become larger for everybody. A democracy required a way of life and type of government in which the poor had as much right of movement as the rich. Not only the rich but also the poor could take advantage of the unhampered daily opportunities afforded by public transport. Class-biased geography was to lose its social significance. The tram and the omnibus were to be a journey within a journey: for the poor, physically indisposed, and other socially disadvantaged people, public transport was to be a journey upwards, a notch or two up the class hierarchy, an elevation for the downtrodden, a step towards closing the gap between the well-dressed and sweet-smelling rich and poor folk dressed in dirt and degradation. Motion was to be the great equalizer. It was to be a great vehicle of democracy, transporting societies, furthering freedom. Motion was meant to be an epiphany. A seat gained would be a soul saved.

Written in Blood

Or a seat denied, a journey to hell. Commuters packed like livestock into beaten-up trains and buses in badly administered public transport systems are commonplace in India. If cities are democratic laboratories that nurture free and equal motion then India fails the test every day. Motion is meant to alter and enhance lives. Not take them. But in Mumbai, one of the greatest metropolises of modern day, democracy's failure is written on its train tracks in blood.

The arterial train lines connecting the seven islands that were fused by the East India Company to create the then Bombay, today keep the heart of Indian finance ticking. It was in this mighty western Indian city that Indian Railways, currently the seventh largest employer in the world, began its journey when the country's first passenger train ran from the city to the suburbs of Thane in 1853. The life-changing import of that opening day wasn't lost on anybody. Karl Marx even predicted that the advent of railways would eventually destroy the caste system. The day was declared a public holiday. The suburban train services have expanded manyfold since and are seen as the city's lifeline, connecting its constituent islands and the hinterland, and its people with their livelihoods, communities, and dreams. But a ride on a Mumbai train in rush hour is more the stuff of a nightmare than dream. It veers towards the deadly, with overcrowded coaches carrying people forced to hang out of open doors.

Traveling like animals, risking their lives for livelihood, has been the lot of Mumbai's daily commuters for as long as they can remember. So deadly are its trains, and so low the safety bar, that zero fatalities on one day (26 June 2019) was marked as a milestone. The very next day it was back to business, with nine deaths.[2] In 2017, eight people died every day on Mumbai's train tracks. Of the 3,014 casualties that year (the figure doesn't include train accidents such as derailment or collision), more than 650 people fell to their death from running trains. For many of them, death came when they hit an electric pole while hanging from the door of a speeding, overcrowded train. Others fell when they simply could not hold tight enough against the outward bulge in the coaches bursting with peak-time commuters.

As Indian Railways fails to provide enough trains and coaches, up to sixteen people can find themselves packed into one square metre of space, about the size of a phone box, inside a carriage during peak hours. There's a faintly respectable, technical-sounding official term for this inhuman clustering of humans: 'super-dense crush load'. Reached in peak hours, super-dense crush load can result in 5,000 people travelling in passenger cars meant for 1,700 people at most. But that's not the only way that blood is spilled on India's train tracks. About 15,000 people die across India every year just trying to cross the tracks. Thousands more get maimed and injured.

One rainy night in 1989, Samir Zaveri lost both his legs while crossing the tracks. The station had no footbridge. In the following years, while travelling in special coaches for the disabled, he kept meeting people like him who had lost their limbs in train accidents. A small-time businessman, Zaveri became an activist. He had previously accepted his own accident as misfortune. 'But this many people? This was clearly systemic injustice. It needs to be tackled systemically', said Zaveri, shuffling through the documents he'd prepared for the interview at his home office in the bustling Tamba Kanta market area of south Mumbai. Filing for information through the Right to Information Act, he dug up a mountain of official data and material, on the basis of which he routinely takes the Railways to court with public interest litigations.

In his time as an activist, Zaveri has made some startling discoveries. He busted a scam in which the railway police would fraudulently arrest and fine commuters crossing train tracks. The corrupt cops had even created a fake courtroom, in which a head constable acted as 'magistrate' and granted 'bail', issuing fake bonds. Zaveri unearthed internal reports on train derailments that show many of these accidents boiled down simply to the shortage of nuts and bolts necessary for connecting rail tracks. Every year he extracts a detailed breakdown of the deaths and accidents on the tracks. In 2019, his query revealed, 611 people fell to their death from running trains in Mumbai, 533 died of 'general illness' (read suffocation in the crowded carriages) and 1,455 died while crossing the tracks. The high number of deaths while walking across tracks happens because often there are no station footbridges. Yet more democracy failure. And even when there are footbridges, platforms are changed at the last minute, triggering a stampede across tracks. His persistent court cases forced the government to order fencing between train tracks across India. But the deaths haven't stopped.

A government review committee in 2012 called the deaths from track crossings a 'massacre' and urged the authorities urgently to replace all railroad crossings with bridges or overpasses in five years. Little was done. Five years later, a colonial-era railway footbridge collapsed under the weight of its users, killing twenty-two people and leaving dozens injured at the Elphinstone Road station. Dilapidated by age, the pedestrian bridge built by the British for a remote nineteenth-century mill area had long been rendered inadequate for a station serving a twenty-first-century buzzing neighbourhood now host to hundreds of trains and hundreds of thousands of people. The population had grown exponentially, but they were still left to the mercy of the slender bridge built by the British. The tragedy was not unexpected. Government inspection reports, social media posts by local commuters, and several letters from public representatives had been warning the railway ministry about the shoddy state of the bridge and the danger posed by the regular overcrowding during peak hours. All that the government did was change the colonial name of the Elphinstone Road station into a more Indian 'Prabhadevi' station. It didn't have the money for a new bridge, the railway minister hinted in internal communications, even while his department was clearing the decks for a fancy bullet train project. Just two weeks before the stampede, Prime Minister Modi and his Japanese counterpart Shinzo Abe laid the foundation stone for India's first bullet train project. At $17 billion, Modi's favourite project—connecting his home province of Gujarat with Mumbai—was to cost 70 per cent more than the entire country's budget to build national highways that year.[3]

Democracy Under the Bus

In the superficial administrative stunts like name changes and the gross misallocation of resources in prioritizing white elephants over essential services, the Elphinstone footbridge collapse is a parable of the daily damage done to social life by the arbitrary power of incompetent government. The daily indignities and inconveniences of travelling prevents citizens from freely accessing goods, services, and social networks that are key to the pursuit of their chosen life strategies. By hindering everyday mobility, hazardous and insufficient transport options have the anti-democratic effect of perpetuating social inequities and dispersing communities into isolated silos that

prevent collective assembly, deliberation and action. India's overcrowded buses have the same effects.

The country is woefully short of buses, even though buses and
democracy belong together. They are among the most democratic
means of mobility as they occupy far less road space per person than
cars and facilitate cheap mass movement rather than privileging the ease
of motion only to those with the means. That's why state-run buses
have been the key to public transport strategies when the most unequal
societies set out on the road to democracy. In post-apartheid South
Africa, city planners in Johannesburg set in motion a transport-led
urban programme to create a more inclusive city. They did so by col-
lapsing the distance between the wealthy, white core of business and
residential activity and the peripheral black townships synonymous
with urban poverty. The distance between the two had been carefully
nurtured in apartheid-era Johannesburg through discriminatory housing and transport policies. Projects such as a rapid bus transit system
with dedicated bus lanes—what its mayor Parks Tau called the 'Corridors
of Freedom'—broke down this distance and stitched together the
divided city. In Colombia, Bogotá's rapid bus system, called TransMilenio,
similarly democratized urban space in a country of extreme inequality
by providing easier everyday mobility through low-cost buses that its
mayor, Enrique Peñalosa, called 'symbols of equality'.

In India, experiments with rapid bus systems have by and large
failed. Densely packed neighbourhoods, uncoordinated transport
bureaucracies, and jurisdictional overlaps among competing city
agencies haven't been conducive to establishing and running dedicated, citywide bus lanes. More democracy failure. Only in Gujarat's
capital Ahmedabad, relatively less built-up, has rapid bus transportation gained some traction. But even there, the rapid bus system hasn't
much helped the bottom 30 per cent of the population, who find its
air-conditioned buses restrictively expensive.[4]

The absence of a robust bus infrastructure and shortages of buses
have been major hindrances to transitioning to rapid bus systems.
Delhi has 270 buses per million people and Mumbai has 180. Beijing,

on the other hand, has 1,710 buses per million people; Shanghai has 1,240; Seoul, 730; and São Paulo, 1,040. Overall, India has just 1.2 buses per 1,000 people. The corresponding number is 8.6 in Thailand and 6.5 in South Africa. Even this average number is misleading as it varies wildly among states. If it is 3.9 in rich Karnataka, it's just 0.02 in the much poorer state of Bihar, meaning one bus there serves 50,000 people.[5]

Few, except those who endure them, can imagine the shoddy state of bus services in India. That is, in places where there are buses. Only sixty-three of 458 Indian cities with a population of more than 100,000 have a formal bus system. According to the government's own calculations, India has less than a tenth of the number of buses it actually needs (Figure 14). The country requires 3 million buses but has only about 280,000. In big cities like Mumbai and Delhi, bus numbers have actually been falling because of underfunding. This has led to greater congestion as private vehicles surge. Four of the most congested cities in the world are in India, according to the TomTom 2019 Traffic Index, topped by Bangalore. In Mumbai, residents on average waste eleven days a year stuck in traffic.

Figure 14. Shortages of buses produce a surplus of everyday humiliations and dangers

India also does badly in train-based mass-transit systems. Only a handful of cities have metro networks, and they fare poorly by global comparisons. Bangalore, for example, with 8.4 million people, has a metro that covers just 42 kilometres. There are just 630 kilometres of metro rail in thirteen cities, with more than half of it in Delhi alone. Most of the metro lines, such as in Kolkata and Mumbai, are single-line metros and out of reach for 70–80 per cent of these cities' populations. Even Delhi, the most elaborate of the Indian metro networks, comes across as fairly underutilized when compared with, say, Shenzhen in China. Both metros started around the same time and have nearly similar track lengths, but Shenzhen carried about 10,000 more people per kilometre than Delhi in 2017–18, translating into 730 million more commuters a year.[6]

In smaller cities, towns, and villages, there are no mass transit systems at all and very little or no role for state-run buses. Commuters are left entirely to the mercy of unregulated private operators. Workers on private bus networks tend to be un-unionized and with no regular work contract or salary. Their pay is linked to the volume of passengers they carry. That results in heavy usage of dilapidated buses, overcrowding, rash driving in rush hours to pick up more passengers, and frequent accidents. With buses being rare, three-wheelers, or autorickshaws, the quintessential Indian mode of transport, offering shared rides, is often the only source of regular public transport beyond city limits, and in smaller towns and villages. Forty-two per cent of India's urban population lives in fifty-three cities with populations of more than 1 million, while the remaining 58 per cent live in about 8,000 'urban centres' with population ranging from 50,000 to 1 million people. Since the main focus of urban transportation has historically been geared towards big metropolitan cities, transportation in these smaller towns and villages suffers neglect. Practically devoid of public transport, these small towns and villages are entirely dependent on what is technically called intermediate public transport (IPT) modes, such as shared autorickshaws and vans. 'Autos', as they are called, are cheap, efficient, and generate employment (there are an estimated

5 million auto drivers), but they operate in a complete regulatory void as the government does not recognize them as a formal mode of transport and virtually treats them as illegal. This often results in dangerously expanded seating capacities by way of retrofitting to maximize profits, and the use of old vehicles and adulterated fuel, subjecting people outside cities to hazardous commutes as the state has by and large forsaken its transportation responsibilities. While there's some accounting of the deaths caused by trains, there's no data on the hundreds of thousands of people outside the cities who fall victim to the risky and unhealthy transport options they are forced to use.

A poor public transport system doesn't just cost lives and limbs, or lost time and missed personal opportunities. It imposes other social costs. Women, for example, hesitate to explore educational or employment opportunities too far away from home in the absence of guaranteed transport. The gruesome Delhi gang rape in 2012 occurred when a woman and her boyfriend couldn't find any transport after an evening film show. They were lulled into entering a private bus driven around by a gang of sexual predators hunting for their nightly prey. It was only 9.30 p.m., and it was India's capital.

The lack of safe and reliable public transport has caused an exponential growth in private cars and motorcycles, but these are out of reach for most Indians except for a section of the growing middle class. From fewer than 1 million vehicles on the road in 1961, India had more than 120 million by 2013,[7] nearly three-quarters of them motorcycles. Correspondingly, public transport has rapidly declined. Buses as a percentage of vehicles fell from 11 per cent in 1951 to 0.8 per cent by 2016. A study by the city authorities in Mumbai found that while ownership of private vehicles rose from 71 per 1,000 in 2001 to 248 per 1,000 in 2017, the share of public transport plunged during the same period from 78 per cent to 65 per cent. As a result, people have been forced into finding personal transport solutions. But denial of free movement has also amounted to the denial of a clean environment to all. A person travelling 10 kilometres on a two-wheeler in Delhi contributes sixteen times the amount of cancer-causing particulate matter to the city's air than a person covering the same distance on a bus, calculates the non-profit Centre for Science and Environment. It estimates that private vehicles contribute nearly 40 per cent of the capital's toxic air. The state's failure to provide efficient transportation creates an uneven playing field that not only deprives millions of equalizing life chances and forces them into life-threatening modes of travel; it also subjects them to toxic air created by those who have an anti-democratic advantage of mobility.

Death Traps

Other than poor public transport systems, elitist policies and poor government oversight hinder movement—and democracy—in various other ways. Pavements for pedestrians are either dangerously narrow or non-existent. Where they exist, pavements are broken and uneven, and either encroached as parking spaces or by hawkers or the homeless, so forcing pedestrians to walk on streets and putting them in the way of speeding vehicles. Rarely are there continuous, walkable pavements in the main cities. In smaller towns, often there aren't any at all. The neglect of pavements reflects poor city planning and design approaches that privilege motorized users over citizens on foot or bicycle. Some 45 per cent of Indian households own a bicycle, found the 2011 Census. The number can be assumed to have risen substantially since—not least because politicians love to distribute bicycles as poll-time handouts to the lowest income quintiles. But Indian cities are no-go zones for cyclists. The general approach to cycles borders on hostility.

In cities such as Copenhagen, Buenos Aires, and Barcelona, publicly subsidized and shared cycles are at the centre of zero-carbon urban planning. But in deeply hierarchical India, cycles represent poor people getting in the way of the higher classes. Take Kolkata. In 2012, bicycles were banned from 174 roads. They've since been restored on some roads, but most remain off-limits for cycles. The discrimination against walking and cycling adds to the social burdens and restrictions on the poor. The bias against the poor in public travel and the state of roads and pavements also highlight the democracy failure of elected executives who are as bad at building transport infrastructure as they are at maintaining it in good working order. It took, for example, about five years and seven missed deadlines to complete a 2.7 kilometre road connecting south Delhi with the capital's airport in 2019, in what the local media described as the world's slowest flyover project, at less than 400 metres a year. The quality of infrastructure built is equally dismal, as is evident from the broken pavements and the crater-filled roads throughout India. Poor standards of roads are among the many reasons why India has exceptionally high numbers of road accidents. The country witnesses nearly half a million road accidents every year, accounting for 6 per cent of the world's road traffic accidents with just 1 per cent of the world's vehicles. According to government data, about 150,000 people died in road accidents in India in 2018, a tenth of them in the national capital itself. The World Health Organization estimates the number at twice that figure.

The extraordinarily high number of road accidents also signifies the wider malaise of unenforced laws and deep-rooted corruption, a democracy failure that results in lost lives and blooded limbs. Overspeeding, drink-driving, lane-jumping, and signal-breaking are also among the common causes of accidents. Lack of sufficient police on the ground hinders enforcement, with some 72,000 traffic cops managing 200 million vehicles. The gleaming six-lane Agra–Lucknow Expressway in Uttar Pradesh claims about a thousand lives every year and is dubbed the 'Killer Road' by the media. Nationwide, drivers involved in a quarter of all road accidents don't have a valid licence, or drive with a learner's licence. The government itself admits that nearly a third of the driving licences in the country are fake.

Poor planning multiplies the body bags. The Delhi–Agra highway, for example, cuts through villages, without offering pedestrian crossings—again privileging the motorized. Farmers often get killed just trying to get to their fields on the other side of roads. In southern

India, a tiny village in Telengana, called Peddakunta, adjacent to the National Highway No 44 that connects northern and southern India, is in fact known as the 'village of highway widows'. That highway has claimed the lives of almost all its men. Even the village headquarters is on the other side, requiring villagers to cross the highway to complete the most basic government paperwork. Many of them, including a villager who went to petition officials over the high number of highway deaths, died on the highway.

Like many of India's other daily atrocities, the steady drip of blood on its highways has been normalized as unavoidable travel hazards, rather than as signs of democracy failure and the destruction of social life. In the insurgency-stricken, erstwhile state of Jammu and Kashmir, traffic accidents killed nearly 50 per cent more civilians than armed violence in the thirteen years to 2017, but didn't cause a fraction of the outrage over terror attacks.[8] Elsewhere in India, death and grief are similarly privatized, as if they are no longer avoidable public problems. With passing mentions in media reportage of individual accidents, the victims of pathetic transport infrastructure are quickly forgotten. The sufferings of the surviving victims and their friends and families are reduced to muted cries for help from a dying democracy.

Satyagraha

No one heard Prakash Bilhore's cry for help when a pothole claimed the life of the 16-year-old on his way to a college to apply for admission. It had rained all morning in Mumbai that August day in 2015. Like most Indian cities, Mumbai doesn't have what the Indus Valley city of Mohenjo Daro had in 2,500 BCE—a well-functioning drainage system. Yet another democracy failure. This means the roads tend to flood if it rains too hard, for too long. As it did that day. Prakash was riding pillion on his cousin's motorcycle, and neither he nor his cousin saw the 5-foot by 18-foot pothole that lay in wait for them under the ankle-deep water. There was no safety barricade marking the pothole, as is required under the law. There never are barricades or markers. His cousin survived the accident, but Prakash died of internal bleeding soon after he was taken to hospital. The pothole was filled by the municipality after three days. 'Just three days. If only they had done it three days earlier, my son would still be alive. It was then that I thought, why not fill potholes myself if I can save lives', said Prakash's father Dadarao Bilhore, explaining how he launched one of the most unique non-profit projects in India. Within two weeks of his son's death, Bilhore, a vegetable vendor, started filling potholes all by himself, with plaster and cement. To his amazement, more and more people began to contact him, wanting to join him and contribute to the cause. His growing 'Prakash Foundation' team now fills twenty to twenty-five potholes a month (Figure 15).

Figure 15. Mumbai's 'Pothole Dada' Bilhore fills dangerous gaps left by government

Mumbai's 'Pothole Dada', as people call him now, uses more advanced material these days—an instant asphalt mix. It's more expensive than plaster and cement but far more effective. The foundation has even devised a 'pothole kit' that it encourages people to buy as a gift item to help people save lives. It's calling it the 'Gift a Pothole' campaign. Engineering students, meanwhile, helped him build a 'Spot a Pothole' app to crowdsource the location of potholes. People who download the app can simply take a photo of a pothole with geotagging, and it automatically enters a central map. The foundation then decides whether or when to fill it up. In Bangalore, Prathaap Bhimasena Rao, a former fighter pilot turned corporate honcho, has been running a similar start-up project called 'Pothole Raja'. He counts among his clients several big companies that chip in via their corporate social responsibility budget. A WhatsApp distress message away, Pothole Raja dispatches a team and gets it done for a small fee.

By official estimates, potholes killed ten people every day in India in 2017, a considerably understated figure given the technical definition of pothole deaths (if people die in an abrupt car swerve to avoid a pothole, for example, they aren't counted as pothole casualties). Bangalore's Rao, like Bilhore in Mumbai, has concluded that if the government cannot or won't step up to the plate then someone must. Citizens do step in where elected governments fail—or simply don't bother—sometimes with herculean strength. Dashrath Manjhi, an agricultural labourer in Bihar, carved out a 360-foot road through a mountain all by himself, during a twenty-two-year period, after his wife died crossing a narrow path around the mountain to fetch water. Manjhi resolved that the villagers would never again have to go around the mountain to get to the other side. In Orissa, Jalandhar Nayak single-handedly built a 15-kilometre road through hillocks in two years, using just a hammer, digging bar, and chisel, to connect his village to a town road so that his children could go to school. Daitari Nayak, a 75-year-old armed with just a hoe and crowbar, carved out a 3-kilometre canal through a mountain, to get water to his village, so that crops didn't die. Gangadhar Rout spent all his retirement savings to complete a river bridge that the government had started building but abandoned midway. These may seem like individual acts of heroism (Manjhi inspired a full-length Bollywood film, 'Manjhi—The Mountain Man'), but these tales of epic fortitude signify more than triumph of will power. They are social coping mechanisms in a failing democracy.

Popular protests that rocked Brazil, Chile, and France in recent years were all sparked by anger over poor quality public transport and deep discontent over the state of democracy in these countries. At its heart, France's Yellow Vest protests against tax increases on fuel, especially diesel, were expressions of the growing resentment in small towns and rural areas. Unlike big cities with 'eco-friendly' public transport systems, French villages and small towns lack decent public transport, and diesel is widely used as the least expensive way to fuel the only means of movement, the family car. In 2013, the massive protests that erupted in Brazil quickly morphed from grievances against the high price of public transportation to a nationwide cry against corruption and lack of democracy. In Chile, students launched a civil disobedience resistance in the capital in 2019 in response to a 30-peso rise in subway fares. It mobilized the widespread anger felt in an obscenely unequal country after decades of apartheid-like public services, oligarchic rule, and poverty wages. That in turn led to a referendum that strongly favoured the writing of a new constitution.

In India, local protests break out after road or train accidents. Stones are thrown, slogans are shouted, roads are blocked, cops rush in to disperse the crowds and 'control the situation'. Life then goes back to 'normal'. In earlier decades, increases in fares sometimes triggered political protests. Since most Indian citizens have given up on public transport by now, organized resistance has become rare. The society is tired. Short of catastrophes such as the collapse of flyovers or footbridges, with heavy losses of life, transport-failure events seldom become political rallying points. Quiet resignation is more the norm. Like most Indians, the Bilhores and the Manjhis have understood the inevitability of state inaction. They have recognized the breakdown of governing institutions. But they haven't made peace with it. They did not picket or riot, but instead stepped in to do what government failed to do, as an act of passive resistance. It is their own satyagraha, a muted cry of protest against the atrocities of their cloth-eared governing institutions.

Writing on the Wall

Downward Filtration

During the course of the nineteenth century, for the first time, peoples of the subcontinent were confronted with the style and substance of formal British education. Education has always been a contested word, but for the English-speaking masters it was most definitely an imperial thing. Education meant the privately funded independent or 'public' schools of England tasked with teaching ideals designed for dominance at home and abroad, throughout the colonies. Meant for the few, education was cultivation of civilized white-skinned gentlemen with a strong sense of worldly mission who were expected to become administrators, teachers, and missionaries. They served as the model of new institutions in India such as Mayo College, founded in Rajasthan in the 1870s and known as the Eton of the East. Education signified Oxford, led by men of distinction such as Sir Cyril Norwood, Master of St John's College, and the classics scholar Benjamin Jowitt, Master of Balliol. For them, education was synonymous with the cultivation of the highest English traditions through preparatory schools, public schools, and elite universities run by the elite, for the elite. Education meant the formation of a community of wealthy men of rugged, rugby-playing character, shared Christian and patriotic values, and codes of honour. The educated were men of arrogant self-assurance. They fancied themselves as naturally superior to creatures they called commoners. They were sure they were fit to rule the world, 'a breed of "philosopher-kings" in the Platonic model, prepared for public service and the running of an Empire'.[1]

In India, the jewel in the Empire's crown, there was even a theory for it. 'Downward filtration', they called it. Thomas Babington Macaulay, appointed president of the general committee on public instruction by Governor General William Bentinck, explained it clearly in his famous 1835 treatise *Minute on Education*:

> It would be more suitable to provide higher education to higher classes than to give elementary education to the mass . . . At present we should create such a group of people who may work as a mediator between us and the common people, a class of persons, Indian in blood and colour but English in tastes and opinions, in morals and intellect . . . who among their countrymen distribute some of the knowledge we gave . . . Drop by drop, the education should go to the common public.

Macaulay was grappling with the issue of education because the East India Company suddenly found itself in uncharted waters in 1813, when the British government tasked it with drawing up a policy for the instruction of Indians as a condition of extending its charter to rule over India for another twenty years. The colonial interest of shaping 'government servants' rather than citizens meant the reach of education was limited. In the thirty-five years between 1858 and 1893, for example, the five existing Indian universities produced around 15,000 college graduates, or less than 430 a year, in a country of (then) about 300 million people. In the latter half of the nineteenth and early twentieth centuries, local rulers of Indian states in fact spent twice as much per capita on education than British India, which had the lowest public expenditure on education in the world between 1860 and 1912.[2]

British education, both among Hindus and Muslims, was an upper-class affair. The methods and aims were Platonic. The ideal of educating 'philosopher kings' fit for running an empire suited the British as education in the imperial style was dead opposed to power-sharing democracy of any kind. The Athenian philosopher had warned that education must teach that *demokratia* was a gimcrack invention: a corrupt form of rule by the lowest and most misguided section of the population, the *demos*. Not surprisingly, later democratic thinkers struck back against Plato and the whole idea of education as the cultivation of a minority ruling class. The foremost thinker of this persuasion remains John Dewey (1859–1952), a teacher and mentor of B.R. Ambedkar, the life-long campaigner against social discrimination and principal architect of the Indian Constitution. An 'untouchable' Dalit rescued by education, Ambedkar found a natural intellectual ally in Dewey, who taught him for three years (1913–16) at New York's Columbia University. Dewey's *Democracy and Education* (1916) is still considered a classic.[3] It makes a case for thinking afresh about democracy as a whole way of life based on the principle of the equal value of individuals and groups joined together through various social bonds, and education as a process of enabling members of any given democratic society to communicate as equals with others their interests, concerns, fears, and hopes. In its broadest sense, Dewey saw education as the foundation of social reforms and democratic equality. He regarded education as much more than what happens in schools, universities, and other formal institutions. Education shouldn't be reduced to learning that is 'remote and dead—abstract and bookish', or learning that produces 'sharps' or 'egoistic specialists'. Education in both the formal and wider senses involves the cultivation among people, beginning with the young, of a 'social sense of their own powers'. Education is the antithesis of what goes on in 'despotically governed' states that 'educate some into masters, others into slaves'. Education and democracy properly belong together, both are against hierarchy and social confinement. They refuse masters and resist 'barriers of class, race, and national territory'. For Dewey, education has a moral purpose because for democracy to work, it requires a robust society of informed and wise citizens.

A New Dawn?

The elitist education policy of the British meant that by the time they left there was very little schooling in India. The adult literacy rate was just 12 per cent. The colonial policy had pushed India down a dark abyss of illiteracy just as more and more people in other parts of the world were attending school in the late nineteenth and early twentieth century. As of 1931, fewer than one in five Indian men and one in ten women could read and write. The gap between India and early leaders in schooling, such as the United States and Germany, had jumped from less than two years in 1870 to 7.8 years by 1950.[4]

As India gained independence and formally committed itself to democracy, the new state might have been expected to focus on education, especially because the independence movement had espoused the goal of universal, free, and compulsory education as the path to political emancipation. Soon after independence, a government report laid down the goal of achieving universal education for the 6–11 age group by 1960 and for the 11–14 age group by 1965. This recommendation shaped Article 45 of the 'Directive Principles' of the Constitution, mandating universal education up to the age of 14 years within a decade. But, in what has been called 'a homegrown folly reflecting an upper class and upper caste bias against the education of the masses', the young nation made little effort to universalize school education to make good on its pledge for democracy.[5]

The first Five-Year Plan, initiated in 1951, argued against opening new primary schools, and instead pushed a so-called 'basic education system' that was built on the backward-looking principle that children should learn through self-financing handicraft. This was actually the Gandhian view of education, as opposed to Ambedkar's, who believed literacy should be the prime objective of primary education and advocated free and compulsory primary education for all. The early ambivalence towards universal education later became a pattern. Successive governments made pious statements about the need to universalize education but pursued the task half-heartedly. The increasing role of private capital in later decades further deepened the class differences in access to quality education.

The next Five-Year Plan, starting in 1956, again laid down that 'the whole of elementary education has to be reoriented on basic lines.' This only deepened the confusion over the means and purpose of elementary education and reinforced the under-allocation of public money for a proper school system. As has been pointed out, even though this phase in India's economic life defined by Soviet-styled five-year plans is often called 'socialist', there was nothing remotely socialist about the way India was going about building basic services such as public health and education. While Indian policymakers were struggling to draw up a coherent elementary education policy and implement it, the Soviet Union was investing heavily in universal school education.

After dismally low investment in education became the norm, various government bodies began to stress the need to spend at least 6 per cent of GDP on education, most famously in the report by the Kothari Commission on Education in 1967. The proposal was passed into law by the Parliament soon after. Since then, political parties have dutifully promised increased education spending in their election manifestos. Yet spending still hovers around 3 per cent of GDP. The Modi government promised to increase spending on education to 20 per cent of government expenditure by 2030, but his years in office since 2014 inspire little hope. As a percentage of government expenditure, total education expenditure in fact fell from 4.14 per cent in 2014–15 to 3.4 per cent in 2019–20. Much of the allotted money was not even spent on education per se. A pet project of the government aimed at educating girls, called *Beti Bachao, Beti Padhao* (Save the daughter, educate the daughter), spent 56 per cent of its budget on advertisements, mostly featuring Modi himself.

Making adequate provision for education—enabling people to pursue better economic opportunities and lead a dignified life, widening their social horizons and nurturing their sense of worldly wonder—is among the most basic responsibilities of any democracy, especially in a country with a median age of about 28 years, with two-thirds of its 1.3 billion people in the working age of 15 to 64 years. India's dismal handling of its education policy sharply contrasts with the other big economies of Asia, many of whom don't lay claim to any democratic credentials, yet have done a far better job. Inspired by early twentieth-century Japan's example of virtually eliminating illiteracy in three decades, after a vigorous overhaul of its education system, a feat that formed the bedrock of its later industrial and social transformation, all major Asian economies have since considered education an indispensable instrument of development. India has done the same on paper, but telling is the way the lofty goal of providing 'free and compulsory education for all children' within ten years of the adoption of the 1949 Constitution took fifty-two years to become a Fundamental Right. It took six more years before the Right of Children to Free and Compulsory Education (RTE) Act became actionable law, that too after a protracted movement for universal education by social activists.

Progress, but...

The result of this feet-dragging is that India is now home to 313 million illiterate people, or 40 per cent of the world's unlettered population. Nearly 60 per cent of them are women, a gender gap—twice the global average—that has persisted for seven decades of so-called democratic rule. When examining these figures, some caveats must be borne in mind. One of them has to do with wide regional disparities. Education is on the 'Concurrent List' of the Constitution, meaning it comes under the ambit of both the federal and state governments, and some states have pursued the goal of universalizing education with far more sincerity than others, with impressive results. But the overall, India-wide trend is alarming. Out of every one hundred students who enrol, for example, only seventy finish school.[6] The exceptions are still worth noting as they offer ready evidence of how better basic services can work as a sustainable poverty-reduction strategy with democratizing effects.

Take Kerala, which at Independence was a state with an exceptionally high literacy rate because of the pro-education policies of its past kings and, later, the work of missionaries. Predictably, its human development standards continued to improve in the subsequent decades. Taking the cue from Kerala, Himachal Pradesh undertook a vigorous drive towards universal elementary education in the early 1970s, when it was still poor. Within four decades, it transformed itself from severe social backwardness and deprivation to an advanced state freed from abject poverty Tamil Nadu, which in the 1970s was as poor as Bihar, also followed a similar path of breaking out of poverty through universalist education policies, thanks to the political mobilization of the traditionally dispossessed lower castes. Services like health and education that had been denied to the lower castes earlier were made universally accessible. Tamil Nadu was the first state to introduce free and universal midday meals in primary schools as well as free early childcare to increase school attendance, both of which have now become the national template.

There's another qualification to be made when considering education trends in India. Unsatisfactory as they are, the country has actually made progress from the pre-Independence days. From just 12 per cent in 1947, the adult literacy rate jumped to 65 per cent in 2001 and 74 per cent by the time of the 2011 Census. The enrolment ratio of children in the age group of 6–11 years was 43 per cent in 1951. It has now crossed 97 per cent. The number of schools and colleges has similarly increased manifold.

The figures must be handled with care. When it comes to education, India's struggles with access and quality are far from over. With the gradual privatization of education and sustained underfunding of government schools, the pathways to good education are becoming inextricably linked to purchasing power. The vast majority of students who are too poor and disadvantaged to pay for education are forced to opt for free but broken government schools. As a result, while school enrolment is increasing on paper, the overall quality of public education for the poor is actually dropping, so deepening the country's grave social inequalities.

Global and national surveys report alarming learning deficits. A nationwide household survey found that after five years of schooling just 51 per cent of students aged 10–11 could read a text appropriate for 7–8-year-olds, worse than the 56 per cent who could do the same ten years ago. Just 28 per cent of this cohort/group could do simple divisions, compared with 37 per cent in 2008. 'It has to be understood that we are struggling even with basic literacy and numeracy', noted the Annual Status of Education Report (ASER) 2018 prepared by educational non-profit organization Pratham. 'This means that not only are we not creating a sufficiently literate population, but that most of our population is functionally illiterate', it says.

Poor infrastructure, such as lack of proper building or restrooms, lack of teachers, rampant teacher absenteeism, absence of midday meals that are designed to retain students, and poor government monitoring, are some of the reasons why standards have fallen. Separate surveys have found that a fifth of the government schools have just one teacher. With a teacher absentee rate of 21 per cent and a student absentee rate of 33 per cent, the probability of any one teacher and student being present at a school on the same day is about 50 per cent, which translates into an effective number of school days per annum of one hundred. Since any given government school is bereft of any teaching activity about half the time, a student actually receives, on average, only fifty days of teaching—a quarter of what she would get in a properly run schooling system.[7] Some surveys estimate this average figure to be even lower, at about forty days.

The probability of a chance encounter between students and teachers is further constrained by a severe shortage of teachers in government schools. The government's own think tank, Niti Aayog, estimates a shortage of 1 million teachers. Governments try to leave vacancies unfilled. When they do hire, they opt for cheap, short-term contracts, settling for less qualified and untrained teachers willing to work for a fraction of a steady government salary. Minimum effort goes into training teachers, funds for which have plunged. Even when qualified teachers are hired at full pay, they are forced to spend most of their time in non-teaching activities, such as handling other government duties and such administrative chores as maintaining midday meal registers, even supervising the cooking. Often, 'regular' teachers, or those hired on the government's pay scale and terms of service, don't bother attending classes, or even visiting their schools. One government teacher in Uttar Pradesh was recently found to be minting money by simultaneously 'working' in twenty-five schools. It's not uncommon for teachers who have 'regular' government jobs simply to subcontract others to show up on their behalf for a small fee while they make money elsewhere privately coaching students of means

Pinangwan's Class Struggles

The four 'regular' teachers for the 850 students at the 'Government Girls' Senior Secondary School' in Haryana's Pinangwan town have no such luxury. The official 'allotment' for the school is twenty-four teachers. It's been a hellish couple of years for both teachers and students since the school was demolished and they had to move to a junior school across the road. There are a few temporary teachers, but the total of thirteen still falls woefully short of the requirement. 'All of us take extra classes, including subjects that we don't know ourselves. We are overworked beyond imagination', said Mukesh Kumar, a History teacher. The principal's post hadn't been filled for nearly a decade, and senior teachers take turns to share the administrative burden. There are no specialist teachers for English, Physics, Chemistry, and Biology. There is no science laboratory. There are no computers or, rather, no working computers. The school did buy twenty PCs, but since there was no computer lab, they were never unboxed. Computing as a subject is taught from a textbook. None of the students studying computing has ever touched a computer.

The word 'senior' in Hindi on the school signboard at the gate has been freshly painted—over 'junior', the original school that had to make room for the extra students. In their new school complex, the 850 students from senior classes were crammed into the four allotted classrooms. Only one of these rooms had desks. Six to seven girls shared desks meant for four. In the other rooms, they just sat on the floor. Classes were also held in the corridors and on dusty, unpaved grounds outside because of the lack of classrooms. During monsoons and peak summer, when it is impossible to hold classes outdoors, many classes have to be cancelled.

The school has no non-teaching staff. The girls have to 'man' the gates, sweep the floors, and serve water and tea when guests drop by. But they drew the line at the toilets, which had become much too ugly for them to clean. 'They are clogged, horrible, we have to go outside', said Muskan Alvi of Standard XII, while listing the problems the girls face at the school. There are some pretty obvious challenges. The classroom was meant for forty with desks, but more than a hundred were sitting on the floor (Figure 16). With rats running

Figure 16. Government Girls' Senior Secondary School in Haryana's Pinangwan doesn't have desks, sometimes not even classrooms

around. But what really angered Muskan was the lack of science teachers. 'Seems the government has decided that since we are girls, we should all just study arts', she said, to a strong murmur of support from her classmates.

Standard XII is the final high school year. College entrance is determined by the results in the final public examination after Class XII. Basically, the trajectory of the rest of a student's life hangs on these two crucial years. Parents who can afford it arrange external tutoring to supplement school learning. 'Coaching classes' prepping students for medical and engineering entrances are among the biggest industries in India. But then, parents who can afford it don't send their children to government schools. The Pinangwan girls' school is located in the Mewat area of Haryana, adjoining Delhi. It is predominantly inhabited by Muslim Rajputs, a Hindu ethnic group associated with warriorhood who once converted to Islam. It is among the poorer districts of the state, which is one reason there are so many students in this free government school, rather than in the couple of private schools in the area.

A two-hour drive from Pinangwan, a world away, offers a glimpse of what government schools can be. The Rouse Avenue SBV Senior Secondary School (RASSS) located in the heart of Delhi could any day give some of the top private schools in the country a run for their money. Delhi's Aam Admi Party (Common Man's Party) government likes to showcase schools like these as testimony to its commitment to basic services such as education. It has spic and span classrooms, a well-stocked and air-conditioned library, a gym, state of the art laboratories, spacious auditoriums, well-appointed lavatories, and ample teachers. The sprawling, air-conditioned office of its principal—it has a full-time principal—comes with an antechamber and a built-in conference space with seats for all of its forty-eight teachers. There are two 'vocational classes' for Class XI students—one themed 'security' and the other, 'tour and travel', to familiarize students with these professions. The one on security comes complete with metal detector machines and alarm systems. It even has replicas of various gun models, which look slightly out of place in a school, but make for a far more exciting ambience than the 'tour and travel' room, with its maps and currencies.

The Delhi government spent a year renovating the school, founded in the early '50s, and evidently spent a lot of money. Fifteen million rupees ($15.3 million), cheerfully reported the principal, Dr Davindera (who prefers to use this shortened version of his full name). Several teachers were sent to Singapore for training, among the many things it has done that is unthinkable for government schools elsewhere in India. All Standard XI and XII classes are taught through computer projection. There are 'happiness classes' for students—a unique initiative that features meditation, exercises, group discussions, skits, story-telling, indoor games, and role-play, all designed to ease anxiety. The classes were clearly working for Laksh Rastogi. The commerce student said he was crestfallen when his parents told him they were sending him to a government school. 'Now I wouldn't go to any private school even if they asked me to.'

RASSS has achieved a rare feat. Even Indians who aren't well off try not to send their children to government schools. Scrimp and save if they must, they still prefer private schools, even though low-end private schools are barely a shade better than low-grade government schools. The pathetic state of government schools has made private schools, once limited to urban upper and upper middle classes, increasingly popular in rural areas as well. Low-cost private schools have thus mushroomed. The number of students enrolling in public elementary schools fell by 23.9 million between 2010–11 and 2017–18, while that in private elementary schools rose by 21.2 million. The government estimates that one out of four schoolgoing children in rural India are now in a private school. Overall, more than 50 per cent of Indian school students are estimated to be paying for primary education, as the state has reneged on its commitment to B.R. Ambedkar's democratic vision of universal school education. Even beyond school, considering students up to 35 years of age, 53 per cent of the students pay for their education.[8] The result is a widening learning gap between social groups, separated purely by their income brackets. Among the poorest 10 per cent of Indians, for every person who is a graduate or above, there are 127 who cannot read. The proportion of people with at least secondary-level education among the highest expenditure class is eight times that of the lowest expenditure class.[9] Education squarely belongs to those who can pay for it. The trend has been reinforced by the economic reforms since the 1990s that have seen the state progressively retreat from education, leaving it more and more to market forces. The damage to the social foundations of Indian democracy is palpable, with the gap between students in government and private schools widening. In 2008, the percentage of grade 5 children able to read a grade 2 level text in government schools was 53 per cent, compared to 68 per cent of children in private schools. This 15 percentage point gap had increased to 21 percentage points in favour of private school students by 2018.[10]

Class, Classroom, Caste

From the early days after Independence, higher education was given a far greater priority than creating a level playing field by spreading elementary education, as other Asian major economies did. The idea was to indigenize high technology in support of the state-led heavy industrialization programme to break out of poverty. While this led to the creation of centres of excellence, such as the famed Indian Institutes of Technology (IIT), the growth of primary education was severely constrained. That basic policy orientation continues to this day. While government funding for higher education rose 28 per cent in real terms in the six years to 2019, that for school education fell 3 per cent. The growing preponderance of private schools and colleges, along with steadfast policy emphasis on higher education, has created an unusually graded, hierarchical educational system. Many Indian colleges and universities and specialized professional institutes offer education comparable to the very best in the world. Much of Silicon Valley is run by graduates from the famed IITs and Indian Institutes of Management (IIMs). Indian medical colleges have over the decades supplied a steady flow of doctors to the UK's National Health Service. Faculties of other disciplines in colleges and universities across the world draw on talented products of the Indian education system. Merit-based competitive examinations do offer a degree of social mobility, and it isn't uncommon for brilliant children from poor backgrounds to make their way into coveted centres of learning. Newspapers often report uplifting stories of poor students making it to top institutions by dint of sheer hard work, but these are more exceptions than the norm. The bar for these achievers is far higher than for the rest simply because there is no level playing field in the early years, despite much talk of 'merit'. In the absence of state-driven equalizing opportunities, 'merit' is mostly correlated with the social class of students. With their educational resources and social networks, the privileged are far better placed to ace a system of 'testocracy', a 'twenty-first century cult of standardized, quantifiable merit'.[11] It's fairly safe to assume that no one from the Pinangwan girls' school is ever going to run a tech conglomerate in Silicon Valley. A profit-driven education system is in reality a contraption to keep the poor in their place. It's an offence to any political system that is premised on and professes equality.

Studies in the 'world's oldest democracy' of the United States show that children whose parents are in the top 1 per cent of the income distribution are seventy-seven times more likely to attend an Ivy League college than children whose parents are in the bottom 20 per cent. The most extreme case is Princeton, where 72 per cent are from the top quintile of income distribution and just 2.2 per cent are from the bottom. SAT college admissions records show that since 1998, the scores of students whose parents are well educated have increased by five points, while those of students whose parents have only an associate's (two-year college) degree have dropped by 27 points.[12]

In India, paid-for education similarly reproduces economic disparities. Despite government funding of primary education, residual caste discrimination and caste-related poverty continue to lock many future citizens out of the classroom. Oxfam estimates that 75 per cent of the more than 6 million children out of school are either Dalits (32.4 per cent), Muslims (25.7 per cent), or Adivasis (16.6 per cent). Enrolment data from other surveys indicate that it's primarily the children of the poorest and low-caste families who fill the rosters of government elementary schools as private school enrolment remains biased towards upper castes, the rich, and urban children. Government schools, the last option for families with higher levels of education and wealth, mostly cater for those who can't afford private education. It's not a surprise that 83 per cent of the children of Dalits, 78 per cent of Adivasis, and 83 per cent of the poor are enrolled in government schools.[13] Class and caste are almost co-terminous: 50 per cent of India's tribal population are classified as 'multidimensionally poor' (based on income as well as other indicators such as health, education, nutrition, assets, and living standards), as are 33 per cent of the Dalits and 33 per cent of Muslims. In contrast, only 15 per cent of upper-caste Hindus are multidimensionally poor.[14] Dalit and tribal households respectively earn 21 per cent and 34 per cent less than the national average annual household income, while upper-caste households earn nearly 47 per cent more than the average.[15] An education system mediated by the market is bound to be skewed against those who are socially marginalized. It's no coincidence that toppers of public examinations, a supposedly meritocratic exercise, are almost never Adivasis or Dalits.[16]

Though caste-based exclusion in today's India is far less intense than what existed pre-Independence, some 27 per cent of Indian households still practise untouchability. The figure crosses 40 per cent in northern and central India,[17] where caste-related violence, especially sexual assaults on women from lower castes, is commonplace. These wider social injustices are carried over into the classroom, which are often the site of reproduction of damaged social lives. Driven to government schools by poverty, the poor and the marginalized are often driven out by poverty and discrimination. Dalit and

Adivasi students seldom make it to the front rows. They are often forced to do menial work at school, such as cleaning the toilets, and are subject to humiliation from both teachers and other students. It's not unusual for lower-caste children to be made to sit separately at midday meals, eating leftovers off plates they bring from home because they are forbidden to touch school utensils. The impressive school enrolments achieved in recent years are thus undone by the vicious cycle of poverty, poor-quality state schooling, democracy failure, and persistent social divisions. Roughly half the students of state schools drop out before eighth grade. Most of them are from the disesteemed communities. As a result, the class and caste divisions between the education haves and have-nots are replicated in higher levels of education, which become ever more tilted in favour of richer, urban, and higher caste students, at the expense of potential students from rural, poorer, and lower caste backgrounds.

Upstairs, Downstairs

If the state's failure to provide equal access to elementary education sets this disparity in motion, it is entrenched firmly by the increasingly important role of private capital in higher education. About 40 per cent of universities and 78 per cent of colleges are now privately managed. The result is that privileged groups reproduce their grip on high-value service jobs such as business managers, professionals, and IT innovators. The marginalized are relegated to the lower ends of the economic value chain. Social immobility—a threat to any democracy—is the result.

The figures are telling. In urban India, only 6 per cent of young people from the bottom quintile of the population attend educational levels above higher secondary, compared with 31 per cent from the richest quintile. Students from the richest 20 per cent of the society are seventeen times more likely to be studying law than those from the poorest 20 per cent.[18] Dalits comprise just 12 per cent of India's college-going population, and Adivasis merely 4 per cent. Around 70 per cent of education loans for higher studies disbursed by the government go to upper-caste students, while just 3 per cent go to Adivasis. This is not because the government actively discriminates against lower castes. It's because those in the higher tiers of the social hierarchy are more likely to be able to invest the time and money, and have the requisite skills, to pursue higher studies.

Unsurprisingly, Indians are the least likely among peer countries to break out of the education and income bracket into which they are born. The World Bank reports that India offers the least educational mobility among the six large developing economies, including Brazil, China, Egypt, Indonesia, and Nigeria. A separate study by the World Economic Forum ranks India at a lowly seventy-two out of eighty-two countries in its Global Social Mobility Report. It takes seven generations for a member of a poor Indian family to reach the average income level, compared with Denmark, where it takes just one generation.

The most immediate fallout of the maldistribution and poor quality of education is felt in the job prospects of millions of Indians, who are forced to take up low-paying jobs that leave them with few resources to ensure good nutrition, decent health, and educational security for their children. Cross-generational cycles of deprivation eat away at the social foundations of Indian democracy. According to the data from the Global Business Coalition for Education, the Education Commission, and UNICEF, more than half (53 per cent) of Indian school students are not on track to have the education and skills necessary for employment in 2030. The World Bank puts India among the countries facing a learning crisis, noting that India has the highest percentage of Grade 2 students in the world who can't perform a simple two-digit subtraction, and comes second after Malawi in a list of twelve countries with the highest percentage of Grade 2 students who can't read a single word of a short text (Figure 17).

As in public health, India's poor performance in education raises serious doubts about studies that find a strong factual correlation

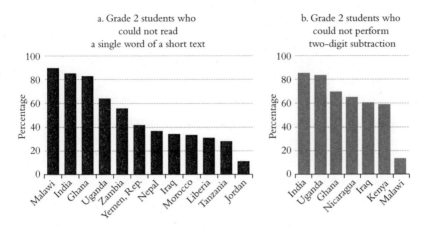

Figure 17. Percentage of Grade 2 students unable to perform simple reading or mathematics tasks

between education and democracy.[19] Chinese students now fare the best (among seventy-nine countries and regions) in the triennial Programme for International Student Assessment (PISA) conducted by the Economic Cooperation and Development (OECD). India participated only once in the survey, in 2009, when it ranked seventy-second out of seventy-three countries, outperforming only Kyrgyzstan.

Graded Classrooms

India's damaged social foundations mean that there are millions of students who are the first learners in their families. Remedying the complete lack of supervision at home, and the obvious financial hurdles to paying for external guidance in such families, would require the state to play a much more proactive role. Poorly funded and organized state schooling does the very opposite. Government schools account for 72 per cent of all schools, but poor funding and management mean they are best avoided. There are high-quality, federally funded government schools, but they're reserved for specific target groups, such as children of government employees or those in the armed forces. The reality is that classroom inequalities are worsened by policies designed to encourage the growth of a multiplicity of schools: government-run, government-aided but privately run, special federally aided, religious, low-cost private, middle-rung private, high-end private, and international schools.

This graded educational system mirrors the country's stubbornly rigid social hierarchies. The poorest children attend the free government-run schools and those from the highest echelons of Indian society increasingly attend international and other elite schools, with the rest of the society caught in between. After graduating from good schools, those with better education (generally the better off, higher castes, and living in cities) have a head start in gaining entrance to good public-funded institutions of higher studies, especially for professional degrees such as medicine and engineering. If they still can't make it to public colleges and universities, they can simply buy themselves into a preferred course at one of the many private institutions at home and abroad, where they study subjects from law and medicine to management and liberal arts. By contrast, the products of free state-run schools (mostly from poor, lower caste, and rural households) settle for menial or lower-order jobs, if they're available, or gravitate towards humanities degrees in low-ranking colleges with low entry bar and poor job prospects. Studies show that students from rural backgrounds, who by necessity mostly come from government schools, have low chances of getting into engineering colleges. Multiple simultaneous handicaps, such as being poor and rural, or Adivasi and rural, or Dalit and rural, reduce these chances to virtually zero.[20]

An additional constraint in rural Indian society is the relatively poor provision of physical infrastructure such as electricity, road connectivity, and Internet penetration. India's digital divide was palpably felt during the Covid lockdown, when educational institutions in many parts of the country switched to distance teaching to avoid physical assembly. Surveys found that 60 per cent of the students in government schools couldn't participate in these online classes.[21] Suicides were reported from across the country as students with limited or no access to digital devices or steady Internet connection were pushed into despair for failing to keep up. In November 2020, Aishwarya Reddy, a 19-year-old student at Delhi's prestigious Lady Shri Ram College, hanged herself at her home in the southern state of Telangana. Daughter of a tailor mother and a motor mechanic father, she had scored 98.5 per cent in her pre-college exams and broke through considerable social barriers to make it to the degree course for a major in Mathematics at one of India's top colleges. But the lockdown ended her dream. The family sank deeper into poverty, a promised government scholarship never materialized, and she fell behind in her studies as she could not afford the laptop and stable Internet connection she so desperately needed for online classes. Her family had already mortgaged their home to finance her studies and her younger sister had pulled out of school to save the limited family resources for Aishwarya. The guilt and the anxiety became too much to bear. In her suicide note, she wrote that she couldn't bear being a burden on the family any more.

The competitive environment that breeds such tragedies is exacerbated by an educational system dominated by top-down instructional designs. Dewey was an early critic of such textbook-driven systems oriented towards competitive tests that do not enhance individuality or community participation. In India, Rabindranath Tagore similarly experimented with broad-based education aimed at the holistic development of students in harmony with nature and society. Like elsewhere in the world, the curriculum-based mass education system that was eventually adopted in India—the kind that Dewey and Tagore rebelled against—is an elaborate system of picking winners and losers based on 'merit', measured by skills in mastering a centralized curriculum. As is typical of every 'meritocratic' system, India's elaborate process of educational ranking fails to alleviate social inequality.[22] Hiding behind the cloak of supposed competitiveness of public examinations that hold the key to college and university places, the schooling system privileges the socially advantaged and replicates the existing class and caste hierarchies, in a phenomenon that *The Economist* calls 'hereditary meritocracy'.

Aggressive affirmative action and greater spread of education enable more students from socially marginalized groups to access higher education than before. But they face hostility from higher-caste teachers and classmates who see them as undeserving occupants of precious college and university seats through reservations at the expense of more meritorious 'general category' (higher-caste) students. Students who come through reserved quotas for marginalized groups struggle to bridge the gap between the standards of the humble high schools they come from and those demanded at elite institutions. The harassment and stress can push students over the edge. Students from low-caste and low-income backgrounds often drop out and have been found to be disproportionately high in suicide cases at top engineering and medical institutions.[23] Those who complete higher education against all odds continue to be dogged by the inequities of social life. Studies of private-sector companies show that they use 'cosmopolitan attitudes' and 'family background' as hiring criteria, which are loaded against poor and lower-caste candidates. Dalit applicants to private-sector jobs are found to be 33 per cent less likely to get a call back from a company, while Muslims are 66 per cent less likely.[24] 'Fluency in English' is among the most elementary of these coded filtering mechanisms.

For college students from government or low-grade private schools, one of the highest hurdles is the English-centric nature of the higher education system. The primacy of the English language in a linguistically diverse country with no natural lingua franca, its role as both a marker and booster of status, deepens hereditary social divisions. Low-end, state-run schools usually impart education in the vernacular medium while private schools and elite government schools tend to teach in the medium of English. Since English proficiency is a must for entry into both state-funded and private elite institutions of higher education, and commands a premium in the job market and generally determines one's life chances, there is intense demand for English language education. The dynamic is captured in *Hindi Medium*, a Bollywood comedy-drama that portrays the desperation of non-English-speaking parents aspiring to get their children admitted to prestigious English-medium schools. With elaborate selection mechanisms that screen parents even more rigorously than the children, the richer and the upper castes are more likely to gain entrance into English-medium schools. As are students in richer states. National Statistical Office data show that while just 6 per cent of students in Bihar receive English language education, it is 63 per cent in Telangana. Those who make it to top English-medium schools—usually children of the affluent, middle-, and upper-middle-class parents who also went to similar schools—typically go on to corner seats in coveted state and private colleges and universities. They also travel abroad for higher studies. Their facility with the English language helps them navigate these opportunities at home and abroad. Thus is created and sustained India's very own 'English caste', the highest of Indian castes that monopolizes the pathways to a world of power, hereditary privilege, and comfort (Figure 18).

Ham-handed government measures to level the educational field and admit others to this exclusive club haven't ended well. Deep-seated

Figure 18. The 'English Caste' corners the pathways to power and prestige

prejudice against poorer classes burst out in the open after the Right to Education (RTE) Act stipulated that 25 per cent of places in private schools should be reserved for children from economically disadvantaged classes. Court cases, resistance, and protests by angry parents, elite school administrators, and teachers resulted in limited implementation of the rule. It didn't help that governments often failed to reimburse private schools for expenses towards fees, uniforms, books, and other activities (like tours) borne by poor students. That led to many private schools boycotting the RTE programme altogether. Very few elite schools in India now abide by it. Even when they do, disadvantaged students suddenly implanted in the midst of rich kids are often cruelly reminded of their disadvantage and undesirability in these upper-class settings. Unsurprisingly, RTE provisions have caused a spurt of dropouts and have hardly made a dent in the persistent pattern of inequalities.

India issued a 'New Education Policy' in July 2020, which vowed to break down the English caste barrier by discarding English as the medium of instruction in junior school, and replace it with regional languages 'wherever possible'. It sounds radical, but it isn't. Government schools already mostly teach in the vernacular, and private schools are unlikely to stop teaching in English. Parents prefer private education over government schools precisely because they teach in English. So, nothing will change. A highly graded schooling system fundamentally stacked against less powerful, rural, poor, and marginalized people will continue to tear the fabric of Indian social life. The educated, English-speaking elite will remain the elite. The stratified classroom will breed and protect the social privileges of the dominant classes.

As if the British had never left.

A New Slavery

Exodus

The night Santosh Kumar and his two friends decided to hit the road to flee Chandigarh city and return to their village in Uttar Pradesh's Gorakhpur district, they joined millions of migrant workers trekking across the country as the 2020 lockdown kicked in. Modi's announcement of the lockdown, with just four hours' notice, triggered a social catastrophe. Losing their livelihoods overnight, desperate casual wage earners began to flee the cities for their families and communities in the hinterland—hitch-hiking and cycling, but mostly just walking hundreds of kilometres to get home, often in faraway states. Balancing children in their arms and meagre possessions on their heads, they evoked comparisons with the mass migrations last seen in 1947, when people fled sectarian riots that accompanied the subcontinent's Independence and Partition.

Santosh and his friends Rakesh Kumar and Bhagwan Das, all in their early thirties and from the same village of Rohua in Gorakhpur, didn't join the first wave of the epic reverse migration. They hoped things would get better. They stayed put in Chandigarh, cooped up in the one-room slum home they shared, making do with half-meals. But within weeks, Modi announced an extension of the lockdown. The iron factory where they worked on a casual basis had already closed and stopped paying wages. An estimated 96 per cent of the migrant workers like Santosh received no government rations while 90 per cent had stopped receiving wages.[1] Reserve cash was drying up.

Sole bread winners for their families, they began to panic. From the conversations with his wife, Santosh could already tell she was worried for their two young daughters, aged 6 and 4. There was just enough money and food stocks to last another month, at best. Then what? The three decided that their best bet was to head home and be with their families, save on the city rent, and look for local work in the village. So, one April night, adequately stocking up on biscuits and water, they set out for Rohua.

They walked for nine days, and nights, with short breaks in between, to make it back to their village. Santosh and his friends survived the journey, but many didn't. Some collapsed on the way and died from exhaustion. Many were run over. Santosh was also lucky that he didn't encounter police brutality on the way for defying the lockdown, as many migrants did. Sixteen migrant labourers were crushed to death by a goods train. They were trying to avoid the zealous cops enforcing the lockdown on the highway and, instead, chose to walk along the tracks to get home. As night fell, exhausted, they fell asleep on the tracks, assuming that trains weren't running because of the lockdown. All that remained next morning on the train tracks were their bloodstained slippers and uneaten rotis.

Suddenly flushed from the slums by the coronavirus and spilling out on to the highways, hitherto-invisible migrant workers stared out of prime-time news at adequately stocked Indians wrestling with the monotony of watching Netflix and working from home in lockdown. The distress of India's informal labour had never been this visible (Figure 19).

The harsh realities of work in India run deep but are invisibilized by the headlines that celebrate million-dollar corporate hires. These stories from another India and its upwardly mobile middle classes hide the inescapable reality of work life for the vast majority of its population. The reality, brutally exposed by the migrant crisis in the lockdown, is that there is an acute shortage of paid work that is safe, meaningful, and offers remuneration sufficient for citizens and their dependants to live a decent social life. Child labour is common, as is

Figure 19. Migrant workers fleeing Delhi after the sudden lockdown announcement, March 2020

bonded labour. Huge numbers of women have either been pushed out of the labour market or still cling in desperation to paid menial work. There's a vast pool of poorly paid unskilled workers who suffer debt bondage and casual work. Joblessness is pervasive. Millions of adults are condemned to idleness that is officially classified as 'Not in Education, Employment or Training (NEET)', the highest rates of which are found in Rwanda and India.[2] Overall levels of joblessness had been rising steadily well before the pestilence and the lockdown. Even before the expected global wave of automation, the estimated number of people each year who began searching for full-time work (8 million) in India was four times greater than available job vacancies.[3] In 2019, some 3,500 people, including engineering graduates and MBAs, applied for street-sweeper jobs advertised by the municipality of the southern city of Coimbatore. The year before, 93,000, including 3,500 PhDs and 50,000 college graduates, applied for sixty-two positions of orderlies in Uttar Pradesh police, a role that merely required schooling up to Standard 5.

Making overall sense of the role that paid work, or the lack of it, plays in the social foundations of India is a challenge, not least because there's no proper language for capturing its dynamics. Words like unemployment and casual labour don't sufficiently capture the ugly realities. Three decades of steady economic growth opened up new opportunities and delivered unprecedented prosperity for a section of the middle and higher classes, who are well equipped for the demands of the global economy. Globally competitive salary packages, luxury condominiums, top-drawer health coverage, foreign holidays, and top-class education for children are the norms for these upwardly mobile classes. But for the overwhelming majority of the Indian workforce, it's a different story. It's a story of the 90 per cent of the economy that operates in the shadows of informality, where labour laws don't apply and administrative corruption and legal quagmires and lawlessness prevail. The story chronicles the steady decline of trade unionism and the erosion of worker rights, the rapid pace of informalization of even the formal sectors of the economy, and ingenious methods of legalizing temporary and contractual work in the name of making the labour market 'flexible'. All these practices have conspired to produce a giant mass of wage slaves. The estimated 100 million migrant workers who perform cheap and strenuous informal work are only the most telling face of this degraded labour.

The Indian Constitution recognizes the right to a living wage. India enacted the Minimum Wages Act as early as 1948. The Supreme Court has in various rulings since stressed the need to ensure the minimum conditions for dignified work and ruled that paying work- ers less than the minimum wage amounted to 'forced labour'. The minimum wage, accordingly, is regarded not just as an indicative remuneration for work. It is in effect an estimate of the monetary needs of a wage earner to meet their family expenditure, preserve good health, live in dignity, provide for children's education, and meet other contingencies. In short, the minimum wage is the money value earned through work for a decent social life. Conversely, the lack of a minimum wage is seen by the Court as degraded work, which reinforces the humiliation faced in other aspects of a worker's social life.

In 2019, the federal government set a daily 'indicative' minimum wage at Rs 178 ($2.5, compared to the international poverty line of $1.9) for states. It was less than half of what a government panel itself had recommended as a decent living wage, and didn't take into account the agreed principle of factoring in basic consumption needs for a decent social life. Yet even this paltry subsistence wage figure has little chance of being adopted because the high percentage of informally contracted workers makes state-set minimum wages largely irrelevant and difficult to enforce. Earlier studies found a third of wage workers weren't covered by minimum wage legislation. Recent ILO figures show that Indians are among the most overworked workers globally and earn the lowest minimum statutory wage in the Asia-Pacific region, barring Bangladesh.

If the lack of minimum or decent wages amounts to 'forced labour', or slavery, then Indian slaves are everywhere. But slavery in India goes well beyond the lack of minimum wages. The new slavery is work done because the only alternative is starvation. Slavery is forced hysterectomy to increase productivity, no toilet breaks, fifteen-hour work shifts, whole families in wage-less work, and sexual predation by masters. It is back-breaking work in brick kilns, spinning mills, granite quarries, and tin-shed factories. At other times, in other places, the new slavery is shit work like cleaning night soil, sifting through garbage for metal scraps, odd jobs for a pittance, prostituting in red light areas, or casual work with no rights to collective bargaining. Their ubiquity notwithstanding, the new slaves are mostly invisible and aren't even considered bit players in India's growth story. That story is more about its software engineers, consumers, and billionaires. In the marathon homeward journeys of distressed migrant workers lay the other story of extreme labour inequities. A story of wage slaves toiling in a so-called democracy where nearly three-quarters of the national wealth generated every year goes to the richest 1 per cent, who also own four times the combined wealth of the bottom 70 per cent.[4]

Democracy and Slavery

The relationship between democracy and slavery has always been fraught. Ancient Greek assembly democracies led by Athens stood for the dignified equality of citizens, yet they fed upon slavery. All-purpose slavery was typical in the households of citizens. But the daily life of slaves in Athens was moderated by the practice of democracy. The ambivalence surfaced in laws against hubris and the custom of treating certain types of slaves as worthy of a wage and entitled to earn their freedom by saving part of their earnings. Still, ancient Greek assembly democracies failed to resolve the contradiction between slavery and democracy. It was left to modern representative democracies like the United States to deal with the contradiction, using more drastic means.

A trans-Atlantic anti-slavery movement and a civil war ended the legitimacy of institutionalized slavery. The moral victory against what had been called Slave Power sharpened democratic sentiments and began the process of destroying slave-based customs and institutions. The combined effect of these changes was to push representative democracy in new and challenging directions. Despite many setbacks, the spread of anti-slavery sentiments in the field of labour markets was striking. From the mid-1800s, and for the next century, political demands to abolish 'wage slavery' were to convulse democracies everywhere. The distinguished historian of this period Karl Polanyi summed up the reasons. 'To allow the market mechanism to be sole director of the fate of human beings and their natural environment even of the amount and use of purchasing power, would result in the demolition of society', he wrote.

> For the alleged commodity 'labour power' cannot be shoved about, used indiscriminately, or even left unused, without affecting also the human individual who happens to be the bearer of this peculiar com- modity . . . Robbed of the protective covering of cultural institutions, human beings would perish from the effects of social exposure; they

would die as the victims of acute social dislocation through vice, perversion, crime, and starvation.[5]

This was a way of saying that representative democracy was cursed by a new form of slavery for which no quick or easy remedy was found: the challenge of reconciling the democratic vision of equality of persons with the maltreatment of workers by the creative destruction and greed of profit-hungry capitalist economies. Greek assembly democracies placed restrictions on commodity production and exchange; when adult, male citizens met in public, they saw themselves as the higher-order beneficiaries of the production by women and slaves of the necessaries of life in the lower sphere of the *oikos*. Politics trumped economics. Assembly democrats didn't believe there was such a thing as an 'economy', whose independent laws of accumulation had to be respected and valued for the sake of unending economic growth. In various parts of the world, modern representative democracy similarly took a stand against the fetish of economic life. The quest of equality and 'one person, one vote' triggered struggles for the abolition of slavery and the enfranchisement of women as the equals of men. Property qualifications for elected representatives were abolished. Representative democracy helped begin the still-unfinished process of liberating children from workhouses and factories. It made room for independent trade unions, peaceful picketing and political parties committed to ending wage slavery and reckless accumulation. Factory safety inspectorates and boards of health were established. Local governments were pressured to provide sewers, rubbish removal, and clean running water.

The experience of these innovations in the northern Atlantic region, in countries such as France, Germany, and Sweden, is well-documented. Much less well known are the exemplary welfare state reforms championed in the early years of the twentieth century by the Uruguayan governments led by José Batlle y Ordóñez. They proved for the first time anywhere in Spanish America that it was possible to use the institutions of representative government to create a more egalitarian society—in effect, to produce a type of representative democracy that rested on democratic social foundations. Against fierce opposition from hostile employers, Batlle fought tooth and nail, with considerable success, for the eight-hour working day, unemployment insurance, night work restrictions, retirement pensions, and enforceable occupational safety standards. The point was to ensure that the fictitious commodity of 'labour power' wasn't shoved about, abused, or left unused. The aim was to prevent death by social exposure by weakening the grip of market forces in favour of democratic equality. Under Batlle's direction, government became heavily involved in the field of education. Free and universal high school education and unlimited access of women to university were approved. Batlle said repeatedly that education was the right of 'all, without distinction of social class'.[6]

Lost Years

Sweeping reforms of the labour market and stronger social protections of this kind never happened in the Indian republic. And unlike most Atlantic-region states that rebuilt their democracies after the Second World War by providing universal healthcare, education, and other welfare entitlements, India set out on the path to electoral democracy devoid of welfare state protections of the social lives of its citizens. Unlike in the Atlantic and East Asia regions, the Indian welfare state hence exists largely as a fine promise in the 'Directive Principles of State Policy' of the Constitution. Different from fundamental rights, the directive principles—a set of governing guidelines—are not enforceable in courts of law. And it shows. Unactionable, these 'principles' are reduced to being lofty instructions to the state that exist only on paper. They include the right to just and humane conditions of work, 'adequate' means of livelihood, and the right to public assistance in case of unemployment. The panic over food and work within less than a week of the lockdown, and the frantic reverse migration that India witnessed for months thereafter, were not a great advertisement for the seven decades of Directive Principles.

In contrast to countries where the universal franchise and electoral democracy followed the rise of capitalism—where democratic preferences of voters for redistribution of wealth and labour unions moderated capitalist institutions and practices—the Indian adventure with democracy coincided with bureaucratic, state-led industrialization. For the first two decades after Independence, the emphasis was on capital accumulation (increasing the stock of productive capital), embracing machine-age technologies, import substitution (making at home rather than buying abroad) and using the Reserve Bank of India to fund budget deficits, if they occurred. The strategy of privileging the state as the leading entrepreneur resulted in the first growth since the end of the Mughal Empire (from a small base, the economy grew on average 4.09 per cent between 1952 and 1965), but striking was the absence of social subsidies and welfare entitlements to liberate the society from poverty. There was no Keynesian welfare state. Only millions of citizens living in heartbreaking poverty and dependent on scarce, low-paying jobs that amounted to a new form of enslavement, not helped by an economy that crawled along at no more than 3.5 per cent in the first three decades up to 1980.

Some part of the new slavery can be traced back to the historical concentration of land in a small gentry and the process of deindustrialization that happened during the colonial era. The country's artisan classes paid heavily for Britain's industrialization as a flood of cheap British imports aided by mercantilist trade duties destroyed village economies. The consequent deindustrialization of India mightily added to the numbers of impoverished, landless agricultural workers. Half-hearted land reforms after Independence did little to alleviate the condition of the landless. For all the political rhetoric associated with land reforms, about 500 million Indians are now landless and some 96 per cent of farmers who own land only hold tiny parcels.[7] The inheritance-related fragmentation of holdings and declining productivity of land over time have resulted in stagnating wages and pushed both small landholders and landless labourers deeper into debt. This debt is contracted mainly from the landed classes in the absence of organized credit for asset-poor households, creating a fertile ground for bonded and distressed labour. The level of indebtedness has been rising through the decades. A farming household in 2013 had more than 630 per cent higher debt to asset ratio than one in 1992, and professional moneylenders charging usurious rates are holding more of this rural debt than ever before (from 19.6 per cent of total debt in 2002 to 28.2 per cent by 2013).[8] Factors such as water stress have pushed agricultural labour further into distress. With less farm work around, inflation-adjusted agricultural wages barely rising, and debts piling up, the armies of cheap and desperate workers have swelled.

India never saw the kind of state-driven but outward-looking strategic industrialization backed by private capital and social redistribution that resulted in the so-named East Asian miracles and later, China's global ascendancy. Large supplies of low-cost surplus labour extruded from the unproductive farm sector plus the urban informal sector fed the process of sustained industrialization, which helped transform these economies by generating jobs and spreading prosperity. India was deprived of this type of transition to a manufacturing-led economy. Instead, it chased a failed policy of autarky combined with state-led heavy industrialization. A bureaucracy-driven industrial policy was combined with nepotistic local private capital into a highly corrupt and inefficient 'Licence Raj' that ensured that manufacturing was limited and sluggish. When in the early 1990s governments opted to liberalize the economy, going straight from an agricultural economy to an economy led by services, the impact on jobs was underwhelming.

The services sector now accounts for 63 per cent of the GDP but contributes only about 25 per cent of employment. Since the services sector demands higher educational and skill levels—scarce in the absence of welfare mechanisms such as decent universal education—services can accommodate only a small portion of the overall labour force. For the rest of the working population, for whom factory work could have been a source of gainful employment, there isn't much on offer. The historically small role of manufacturing in India remains unchanged nearly three decades after liberalization. Manufacturing now contributes about 16 per cent of the GDP (compared to 29 per cent in China and South Korea), unchanged since 1991, and employs only about 12 per cent of the labour force (compared to 28 per cent in China and 25 per cent in South Korea).[9] As a result, the major part of the labour force remains trapped in less productive agricultural activity, casual jobs, and outright or disguised unemployment.

To make up for widespread joblessness, and to protect the right to meaningful work, India in 2005 enacted a law that ensured a minimum of one hundred days of manual work to at least one member of every rural household. Modi has been a long-time critic of the programme, known as the Mahatma Gandhi National Rural Employment Guarantee Act (MGNREGA). It is for him a 'living monument to Congress failure to eradicate poverty in 60 years'. Mocking the Congress in Parliament, during his first year in office, he said: 'You had to send people to dig ditches and pay them.' But even he has had to fall back on this public works programme, as paid jobs have continued to be in short supply, even before millions of migrant villagers fled back home during the pestilence lockdown.

Social Foundations

Recent initiatives by successive governments have failed to produce new jobs on a significant scale. In 2014, Modi's government launched an ambitious 'Make in India' drive to attract foreign manufacturers to open plants in the country in pursuit of the goal of making manufacturing account for 25 per cent of the GDP. That hasn't happened as planned. Old patterns are unchanged. India's elected governments have failed to build the social conditions necessary both for democracy and significant advances in state-of-the-art manufacturing.

This democracy failure threatens to hobble the Indian economy even more in the coming decades, especially as automation picks up and demand rises for educated workers. The point needs emphasis: the industrial success of countries like Japan, Korea, and Malaysia was accompanied by land reforms, which boosted domestic demand and redistributed income to foster the political stability sought by domestic and foreign investments. To encourage technology transfers from foreign investors, those economies also made enormous state investments in education, health, roads, and electricity. Policies ensuring universal literacy increased productivity and promoted social equality. An emphasis on female education led to reduced fertility, reduced population pressure, and an increased supply of educated labour. The export focus of manufacturing growth also helped those countries to increase productivity and acquire competitive advantage, on a global scale. These carefully synchronized social and industrial policies led to high rates of economic growth. In turn, they provided the state with the fiscal resources to promote equality that then helped them avoid the gross inequities that typically accompany market-based capital accumulation.[10]

Chronic underspending on health, education, and physical capital is instead the Indian pattern. Not only are the bulk of Indian workers comparatively underequipped to adapt to complex new technologies. They work for only 6.5 years at peak productivity compared to twenty years in China, sixteen in Brazil and thirteen in Sri Lanka. Poor physical infrastructure adds to the hurdles for expanding marketable skills. Children in rural areas often drop out of school because of the lack of electricity, proper roads, easy public transport and Internet access. Girls drop out more than boys, who can still migrate and continue their studies. Social customs prevent girls from travelling too far from home for education.

As the pace of automation through artificial intelligence picks up, in what's being called a new industrial revolution, already vulnerable groups face great social risks, calcified by seven decades of poor policy choices and general democracy failure. Not only are fewer Indians likely to escape the new slavery by finding jobs good enough to make meaningful progress in life. Such jobs are more likely to go to the more privileged groups in the labour force. Work, rather than acting as a vector for spreading prosperity and equalizing life chances, will thus become an agent for reproducing slavery because of the state's failure to mitigate birth-related disadvantages and promote the democratization of social life.

The impact of automation on labour has already been evident for some time. In the early 1980s, 10 million rupees of investment created around eighty jobs in the organized manufacturing sector. By 2015, allowing for inflation, this figure had fallen to fewer than ten jobs.[11] As productivity rises even more in the coming wave of automation, unskilled manufacturing jobs will shrink further in importance, even if overall manufacturing increases. New studies on employment are already beginning to reveal this labour market trend. For the first time in India's history, total employment between 2011–12 and 2017–18 fell, by 9 million.[12]

Agriculture also contributes to this decline. Some 37 million workers left agriculture during that six-year period. But they weren't absorbed into meaningful forms of labour in great numbers in a weak manufacturing sector. Women have been hit harder, as the social pressures of male dominance and relatively lower education levels of women make it difficult for them to compete for the limited opportunities in the manufacturing sector. In a complete departure from global trends, about 25 million women left the workforce during this period. Only seven countries—Yemen, Syria, Iraq, Jordan, Algeria, Iran, and Egypt—have a lower female labour force participation rate than India, where the participation rate for women has fallen to an historic low of 21 per cent. In some states like Bihar, it's as low as 9 per cent. Squeezed out of agriculture and bereft of opportunities in manufacturing, women are forced to find low-end informal work, such as domestic help in middle-class city homes, whose women increasingly pursue their careers and outsource the drudgery of house work to new arrivals in the city.

Desperation

There's never a shortage of new arrivals from the decaying country-side: agricultural refugees fleeing a decades-long social emergency marked by poor healthcare, inadequate and inequal education, low-intensity famine, and environmental breakdowns. India lifted 271 million people out of poverty in the past decade, but statistically that still leaves about 365 million impoverished people. An estimated 111 million Indians, or about a tenth of the population, are considered chronically poor. For them, poverty is hereditary. Recent Niti Aayog data suggest that ever more people have been joining the ranks of the poor. This large-scale deprivation produces a vast pool of desperate, cheap, and unskilled workers preyed on by an unregulated informal sector with poorly enforced labour standards and laws. For the poor, this shadowy economy generates more than 90 per cent of jobs, the kind of casual factory gigs Santosh Kumar and his two friends found in Chandigarh.

According to the 2011 Census, 80 per cent of those registered as 'engaged in work activities' in Kumar's tiny Rohua village are actually involved in 'marginal activity providing livelihood for less than six months'. Rohua and Kumar are examples of the denial of well-rewarded work and slave-like work conditions. The factory where he last worked used to make iron gates and grills. A school dropout who couldn't finish his studies because of poverty, he was required to do everything from working the moulding machines and welding to grinding and portering in hectic six-day weeks. He earned about 8,000 rupees, or $100 a month, but had no job security because on paper neither his job nor his factory existed. Small units like his try to stay beneath official radars by remaining small, to avoid onerous labour laws that significantly add to business costs.

Informal work made available to the desperately poor is often a euphemism for slavery. The Global Slavery Index estimates that 8 million Indians are living in modern slavery, the highest in the world.

More than 18 million, it says, have lived in modern slavery at some point in the last five years. Even going by the Supreme Court's definition of bonded labour as any work rendered below the minimum wage, this can only be a massive underestimation.

Slave labour is a criminal offence, but prevalent. Reports of slaves being rescued appear in newspapers frequently, but they're not considered a major scandal. Like the 10.1 million child labourers, they seem too ubiquitous to evoke outrage. A long history of caste-based labour bondage in feudal India (now outlawed) and the continued financial distress of the landless poor temper outrage as *any* work is an improvement on the alternative. Typically herded into their enslavement by 'labour contractors' preying on their abject poverty, India's modern slaves are often short-term migrants whose lack of social support networks renders them vulnerable to submission to exploitative working conditions. The poor, landless, lower castes, and Adivasis are over-represented among the millions who undertake these migrations every year. In the brick kiln industry that mostly runs on migrant labour, for example, debt bondage and child slavery are endemic. Rather than daily wages, workers are hired as a family unit and compensated on the basis of what they produce. The families are paid an advance at the beginning of their tenure. The final payment, adjusted for their output against the advance paid earlier, is withheld till the end of the contract, which usually runs for eight to ten months. Little or nothing is paid in between. Workers are thus reduced to chattels, at the mercy of kiln owners, begging for a decent final pay. Adults on average work at least fourteen-hour days. The children also chip in to help the family reach the target, their soft little bodies hardening along with the bricks in the infernal heat from the baking furnaces in peak summer, the prime brick-making season.

Brick kiln workers are the emblems of Indian slavery. They make far less than the minimum wage and are forced to live in subhuman conditions, in cramped and unhygienic spaces, with limited or no access to electricity, clean water, or toilets. Their children have no access to schooling. Women are at high risk of sexual assaults. Yet such is the extent of rural joblessness that brick kilns, estimated to employ about 23 million people, are the last resort of sustenance for many of India's landless and marginal farmers.

Brutal, slave-like work settings are prevalent in other industries as well, from textile mills to agriculture and construction (Figure 20). In Maharashtra's Marathwada region, migrant workers who harvest sugarcane have been found to undergo en masse hysterectomies as they cannot afford to lose pay in the event of menstrual cramps and vaginal discharge. Lack of sanitary facilities at work in the parched land and the unhygienic and inhuman working conditions—up to sixteen hours of non-stop work—can also lead to genital infections, entailing income losses. Women in village after village thus prefer to have their uterus removed altogether. As in brick kilns, entire families are hired by labour contractors who pay them in advance, and demand to be compensated for any loss of work. The acceptance of an advance payment essentially locks these families into bonded labour, pushing them into a state where they will do anything to pre-empt the likelihood of having to return the advance.[13]

Figure 20. Hazardous work and wage slavery are rampant in the construction industry

When Work Kills

Slavery is life-threatening work. The colourful nineteenth-century Marxian description of wage slavery in India as a predator 'drinking nectar from the skulls of slain workers' may sound exaggerated today, but the killing of degraded labour, active or passive, for reasons of profiteering, is widespread.[14] Brutal enslavement is found not only in brick kilns but in such industries as spinning mills in Tamil Nadu and sugar cane farms in Maharashtra. Employers minimize liabilities through contractual work, often by outsourcing rather than direct hiring. They cut corners on both worker and environmental safety. As a result, even in the better regulated and supposedly better super-vised industrial units, occupational deaths are common. In just one state, Gujarat, industrial accidents killed 989 people between 2013 and 2018, mostly at the factories run by some of the country's biggest companies. Smaller factories and workplaces, ubiquitous yet unseen and unregulated by government authorities, are killing fields. When a fire in an unregistered paper factory on the second floor of a building in Delhi snuffed out forty-three lives in December 2019, the city's chief fire officer told media that 'half of Delhi is like this.'[15]

According to government data, between 2014 and 2016 more than 3,500 people died and 51,000 were injured in factory accidents across India. Global labour organizations estimate a much higher annual toll of 48,000 victims. The British Safety Council calculates that only a fifth of India's workforce are covered under the existing health and safety legal framework. Separate studies estimate 37 million occu-pational accidents a year in India.[16] India's $140 billion construction sector, the country's second largest job generator after agriculture, contributes nearly a tenth of the GDP and employs 44 million people. But it is the deadliest, with an average of thirty-eight fatal accidents a day.[17] Falls from heights, electrocution, and collapsing walls and scaf-folding cause one out of four deaths in this sector, where a third of the country's seasonal migrants work, for slave wages.

Given the way Indian construction sites, factories, and other industrial units operate, all such estimates of industrial deaths can safely be assumed to be grossly understated. The scale of social harm and injury is much greater. There's simply no available accurate data tracking these accidents. A fraction of the actual number of factories is registered and even the government has no complete or consistent data on the exact size of the unorganized sector of poorly waged slavery. When accidents occur, managers 'settle' the matter by paying off victims' kin, government officials, and the police. This stifles possible media attention that might force an occupational safety investigation. Yet another democracy failure as a result of a malfunctioning watchdog mechanism. Police cases, if they happen, are registered only in cases of deaths. There's no way of ascertaining the number of victims who die later from injury. Neither is there a method of accounting for the deaths caused by diseases in hazardous workplaces. As the International Labour Organization puts it, 'enforcement is so weak that there is a huge gap between the estimated fatal and non-fatal accidents reported by ILO for India, and the figures reported to ILO by the Indian government.' By the ILO's estimates, just the *reported* fatality rates in Indian factories is twenty times greater than that in Europe.[18]

The Indian Precariat

The dangerous work environment of Indian workers is symptomatic of the global decline of organized labour and the corresponding rise of what's now widely called the 'precariat'.[19] India's new slavery is an egregious version of this trend. A global class of labour that lives perpetually in economic uncertainty and moves in and out of jobs that give little meaning to their lives, the precariat are characterized by volatile earnings, chronic debt, and a lack of non-wage and rights-based state benefits. In the global hierarchy of labour, they come below the traditional working class, for whom welfare states were built and trade unions acted. In India, where welfare provisions are poor and more than 90 per cent of workers are in the informal sector, the social foundations of working life have historically been degraded. The shrinking space for unionization has further degraded social life and working conditions. Like elsewhere, the power of organized industrial workers, among the most potent modern agents of social dignity and democratization, has been systematically eroded in India. During the post-1945 years, in advanced West European economies, trade unionism helped narrow pay gaps. The power of organized labour in India may have had the same effect, but since the mid-1970s, trade union membership has been shrinking and unions have lost power to their parent parties (Indian unions are all linked to political parties).[20] Since the onset of economic liberalization, the power and social influence of trade unionism has waned precipitously. Trade union density (defined as the percentage of union members and associations in the total workforce) in India plunged by nearly a fifth between 1993–94 and 2011–12 to 28.8 per cent. It currently stands at just 13.4 per cent.[21] The labour income share as a percentage of the GDP has been falling, much more steeply than in the rest of the world. While internationally, it has declined modestly from 52.2 per cent to 51.4 per cent in the seven years to 2017, in India it has plunged from 56.8 per cent to 49 per cent over the same period.[22]

With even the tiny formal sector increasingly using informal labour, collective bargaining is fast becoming a relic from the past. In just one decade between 1999 and 2011–12, the percentage of casualized workers in the formal sector jumped from 38 per cent to 51 per cent.[23] A recent government labour force survey shows that less than half of the working age population is employed. Among them, only about 25 per cent get a regular salary or wage. Of those who do, more than 70 per cent don't have a job contract, while more than half aren't eligible for paid leave or social security benefits.[24] The state itself increasingly hires informally, thus compounding the new slavery.

Back to Gorakhpur

The 2020 pestilence provided the powerful with an opportunity to trample what remains of labour rights. Amid widespread job losses (a fifth of salaried jobs in one year[25]), the federal government in September 2020 introduced new labour codes that make it easy for companies to convert permanent jobs into fixed-term contracts. Companies no longer need to outsource contract jobs to other companies; they can directly hire temporary workers themselves. Several state governments have chosen to do away with pesky labour laws to help businesses shake off the economic slump. Businesses in those states were legally allowed to force workers to do twelve-hour shifts, and to abolish minimum wages and obligations to provide ventilation, toilets, rest breaks, lighting, protective equipment, canteens, and first aid. The 'boldest' measures were taken by Uttar Pradesh, which suspended thirty-five of its thirty-eight labour laws and even decreed that other states would need permission to hire people hailing from Uttar Pradesh.

Uttar Pradesh and Bihar, two of the most underdeveloped states, are among the biggest exporters of migrant workers. Migration, especially long-distance migration, is never an easy decision, as people are naturally reluctant to leave their communities for work. Distress migrations for slave wages are a symptom of the despair stemming from the bleakness of opportunities at home. There's always been plenty to despair about in Uttar Pradesh's Gorakhpur city, where sixty-three children died in a hospital in 2017 because the government failed to pay the bills for oxygen supplies. 'There's no village in Gorakhpur that doesn't have families whose members are working elsewhere because there's zero work here, apart from crime,' said Sunil Singh, who once headed the Hindu Yuva Vahini (Hindu Youth Army), a right-wing youth militia, before he fell out with the Vahini's founder, Yogi Adityanath, the BJP's rabble-rousing priest-politician from Gorakhpur and now the chief minister of Uttar Pradesh.

The degradation of social life in Gorakhpur isn't such a bad thing for politicians like Adityanath and Singh. There are always enough angry young men around with nothing much to do, and waiting for just the sort of muscular action that types like them offer. The saffron-draped Vahini cadre, armed with swords and sticks, made their name with vigilante violence aimed at Muslims. Its leaders were regularly charged with rioting and arson, but that only helped raise the profile of Adityanath and his Vahini, high enough to force the BJP to make him the chief minister of India's biggest state, which has the same population as Brazil's. At its peak, the Vahini had more than 1.5 million members. When Adityanath became chief minister in 2017, the application for membership passed 5,000 a day. As the new chief minister needed to underplay the violent ways of his past, the Vahini began easing off on enlisting new volunteers.

There are 3 million people in the Gorakhpur district, yet it has just one engineering college and university. This is how joblessness and angry disaffection are nurtured, Sunil Singh pointed out. Unemployment helped swell the ranks of Hindu Yuva Vahini, he said. 'If you start a show in Gorakhpur, you'll find a crowd because no one has anything better to do here.' That's why Singh has started his own show. It's called Hindu Yuva Vahini Bharat, a brand-new militia that will take up where Adityanath's private army left off. Just like its predecessor, Hindu Yuva Vahini Bharat hasn't had problems filling its ranks. There aren't, after all, that many recruiters in town.

Persistent unemployment leads to a drop in labour force participation rates as more and more people who are unable to find work simply stop looking for it. The consequence of this has wider socioeconomic implications beyond the job market, as youths in the 15–29 age bracket are basically reduced to idleness. The trend isn't confined to Uttar Pradesh. The number of India's NEET, or 'Not in Employment, Education and Training', rose from 70 million in 2004–5 to over 115 million by 2017–18. This is more than 30 per cent of the youths in this age group, compared with China's NEET of 11.6 per cent and Brazil's 20 per cent. Growing at about 2 million a year

in the decade to 2011–12, India's NEET has since been increasing by
about 5 million a year.[26] The UN puts the percentage of NEET youths
in India even higher, at 40 per cent. Those are all-India estimates. For
backward states such as Uttar Pradesh, the problem of NEET is much
grimmer.

Give Me a Despot

Studies by historians and statisticians armed with large country samples show that personal joblessness experience often translates into
political cynicism and yearnings for strong-armed leadership.[27] When
promised equality but given slavery, people are tempted to conclude
that democracies are indecisive and breed too much quibbling, and
that a leader who doesn't bother with the niceties of Parliament and
elections is preferable. It should come as no surprise that this popular
yearning for despotic rulers and a strong state is alive and well in India.
At all levels of government, the corrosive sense of bitterness felt by the
victims of social degradation is fodder for despots looking to prey on
popular resentments, such as the antipathy towards Muslims tapped by
the various avatars of Hindu Vahini.

Political recruitment is an escape from a life of slave wages and
social degradation. For the disesteemed, the remedy for indignity is a
party bike, money, and the indulgence of law enforcers. It's the protection of local power networks, the licence to extract protection money
from small businesses, and the power to inflict indignity onto others.
Political enlistment offers reassurance, a whiff of power. The educated
are especially vulnerable. Raised to be more aspirational and resistant
to a life of modern servitude, they are more likely to fall prey to disap-
pointment and disaffection. Jobless figures in India show that, compared with other groups, people with a graduate degree are more than
twice as likely to be unemployed, as they are more resistant to slave
labour and can afford to wait for more suitable career openings.[28] An
ever-bulging number of educated unemployed youths is raw material
for political parties and private armies of politicians (Figure 21).

Figure 21. Political parties find it easy to recruit jobless young men

Bike and car cavalcades of young men brandishing weapons and party flags are common sights in India, especially around the time of elections. The thousands of young people who mill about in the middle of work days easily become the hired hands and foot soldiers of despotic politics. They are the ones who make Indian elections the greatest show on earth—rallying, canvassing, fighting, killing, and getting killed for leaders who give them ready access to cash and power, rather than manifesto promises of a rich future. The recruitment of disaffected youth certainly brings energy to politics. It serves as a proxy for gainful employment. It raises hopes and expectations of betterment. But it also hands razor sharp weapons to local and national despots— political demagogues like Adityanath who prove by their deeds that shortages of meaningful work are deep gashes on the body of a democracy already suffering a thousand social cuts.

Democide

Vote, or Else

'Life of Contradictions'

In his last speech to the Constituent Assembly drafting independent India's Constitution, in November 1949, B.R. Ambedkar dwelt at length on the dangers that confronted the new sovereign state. Democracy, he pointed out, was not entirely a new phenomenon for India. He cited ancient kingdoms with established checks on power and Buddhist councils in the third century BCE that were drawn from regional representatives to settle philosophical disputes with Parliament-like voting procedures. India, he rued, lost that golden democratic tradition once, and risked losing it again. 'It is quite possible for this new-born democracy to retain its form but give place to dictatorship', he warned, because what India was entering was a 'life of contradictions' caught between a newly minted system of political democracy and deeply embedded social injustice. 'Political democracy cannot last unless there lies at the base of it, social democracy', he cautioned. To protect political democracy, India would have to quickly erase the 'graded inequality' of its social and economic life.

Seven decades on, massive social injustices threaten the old story of India as the world's largest and most successful new democracy. It has become a fairy tale that hides ugly social realities. It camouflages the fact that India has been suffering an undeclared, decades-long social emergency that should serve as a warning to democrats and democracies everywhere about what happens when governments fail to nurture the equality and social dignity of their citizens. Even before his last speech, Ambedkar had been warning that democracy in India was only a 'top-dressing on an Indian soil, which is essentially undemocratic'. But he was still optimistic that constitutional democracy in India would work to narrow its historical inequities. Facing a blistering attack from Hindu conservatives for trying to reform and codify Hindu personal law, his optimism didn't last long. In a 1953 interview with the BBC, when asked if he thought that democracy was going to work in India, his prompt reply was: 'No.' Democracy, he said, would not work 'for the simple reason that we have got a social structure which is totally incompatible with parliamentary democracy.'[1]

Showstopper

Through ill-planned and half-hearted welfare policies, successive governments of independent India first failed to provide social support for many millions of voting citizens, then went on to embrace neoliberal policies that forced socially unequal people into the unforgiving competition of markets, setting them up for failure. As the social foundations of Indian democracy continue to crumble, its governing institutions are being torn and twisted, cut and carved into a strange kind of despotic government led by corrupt and cunning rulers who, in the name of 'democracy' and 'the people', prey on their privations, destroy democratic institutions, and yet manage to win their quiet resignation, or their active support, through the legitimacy bestowed by elections.

Elections are considered the heart and soul of democracy. At their best, elections are moments of public excitement and uplift. Voters previously unaware of their strength or excluded from government suddenly get a whiff of political power. They sense that they can change things. The powerless prepare to swap places with the powerful. All that was once solid and taken for granted begins to melt away into thin air. Expectations mount. Rumour mills work overtime. Everybody speculates about what will or will not happen. Nobody actually knows what the future will bring, which is why all eyes are on the polls, turnout figures, and the final results. A popularly elected government is then formed, so confirming in practice the principle, as incoming American president John Quincy Adams famously put it, that 'the best security for the beneficence, and the best guarantee against the abuse of power, consists in the freedom, the purity, and the frequency of popular elections.'[2]

Elections captured Indians' imaginations from the moment of Independence. The tone was set in the first parliamentary elections that began in October 1951 and took six months to complete. Since that first ever voting extravaganza, elections have come to dominate public life, to the point where some observers speak of India as a psephocracy, a political system in which elections become the end-all. Political analysis is focused on voting trends, swings, intrigues, and the cut and thrust of campaigns. The vibrant colour and the noisy gaiety of the world's biggest exercise of universal adult franchise is a show-stopper. Voter turnout is high and, unusually by global standards, the most marginal parts of the society show up at the polls more often than the wealthier middle and upper classes. Votes count. Votes are dignity. Indian elections have even spawned a whole new business stream of 'election tourism' that draw visitors from around the world keen to partake of the festivities—like 'wedding tourists' who come to witness first-hand the big fat Indian wedding. Indian and foreign journalists marvel at their intensity. They like to fetishize the country's elections as the greatest show on earth.

One drawback of this obsession with elections as the supposed defining marker of democracy is that it doesn't acknowledge that during the past half-generation, voting has ceased to be the preserve of democratic systems. In countries such as Belarus, Iran, Russia, and Vietnam, as well as states in the Gulf region, central Asia, and elsewhere, the ruling oligarchs have a definite fondness for elections. These new despotisms don't do away with elections. They embrace heavily rigged and corrupted 'phantom elections'.[3] Elections serve important functions for the rulers. They offer approved candidates the

chance of higher office, and allow a measure of multiparty competition. The rulers buy votes and intimidate opponents. They fiddle the
results. Sensational media events are concocted, constituency bound-
aries are gerrymandered, voter rolls are altered, votes are miscounted,
and ballots are made to disappear magically. Elections nevertheless
lend a 'democratic' feel to the political system. And elections do sometimes result in the felt improvement of the lives of people. Elections
have other politically useful functions. They enable dissenters in the
governing hierarchy some room for manoeuvre. Electoral contests
can help settle old scores, resolve disputes, and offer low-cost exit
options for discontented regime politicians. Elections can create
opportunities for spotting new political talent willing to serve the
ruling power. They distribute patronage to supporters and potential
supporters, and serve as early warning detectors of public disaffection
and opposition. Elections can as well be powerful means of placing
opponents in a quandary: since they almost certainly lose the election,
opposition political parties suffer bitter division and demoralization.
Most importantly, the rulers of the new despotisms use elections to
toy with their subjects. Elections are exercises in winning the voluntary servitude of their subjects. When citizens vote under these conditions, they do more than cast their votes. They give themselves away.
They license their political masters. They grant them authority. The
razzamatazz of elections is an awesome celebration of the mighty
power of the regime, which in effect offers its subjects a chance to
behave as if they believe in the regime, through something like an
'election contract'. The new despotisms show that elections *without*
democracy are possible.

Worlds Turned Upside Down

The belief that Indian elections are the greatest show on earth,
and that they are proof positive of democracy as a living reality, is
challenged by a second consideration. There's an ugly, corrupted, and

violent side to elections in India that is relatively less reported and understood. Not every election is corrupted, or tainted by thuggery, guns, and bombs. But not every election is about the peaceful canvassing of votes, public debates, or the building of governing coalitions either. Not every election ensures a peaceful transfer of power. Elections can be and are distorted by money and violence, robbing them of their function as a fair means of democratic representation and accountability. The intensity of electoral corruption and violence varies from state to state. But in some, like the eastern state of Bengal, they've long been bloody affairs.

For Hema Parvin, the 2019 national elections were no different. Trouble started with a few gunshots outside her hutment. Within minutes, a dozen young men, pistols in hand, came running into the narrow alley running through the slum, randomly hurling small bombs at the homes lining the lane and shooting in the air. They kicked open the gates of the homes, shouting at the top of their voice, threatening people to leave. Most ran inside in panic; those unfortunate enough to get in their way were mercilessly beaten. For the next fifteen minutes or so, the gang went through every home on the lane, forcing out the residents, pointing guns at their heads. Parvin's world was turned upside down that afternoon of June 2019.

In her mid-twenties, Parvin is a dressmaker by profession. She lives in one of the slum settlements adjoining Kankinara Jute Mills, about 30 km from Kolkata, the capital of Bengal. That day, when violence descended on her slum, her family had about five minutes to grab whatever they could, and run. They took refuge for a week at a nearby school, which had turned into a makeshift shelter home for people similarly evicted in this new spate of post-election violence. Nobody dared to sneak back to the slum. The whole area had turned into a battlefield ever since inter-party clashes erupted during the national elections the previous month. Every day, there was fresh news of deaths and injuries of friends and acquaintances in street fights and neighbourhood battles. News also reached those hiding at the school that their homes were being systematically looted. As the school had by now filled up with people fleeing the violence, Parvin and her family left for the neighbouring state of Bihar. Aeons ago, her grandfather had come from Bihar to work in Kankinara Jute Mills. That was a different time. West Bengal (born of the Partition of undivided Bengal into Hindu-majority West and Muslim-majority East, the latter going to Pakistan) was India's industrial powerhouse. Jute was not yet a dying industry. Kolkata was Calcutta, the former capital of the British Raj, still undimmed in the afterglow of the Empire.

When Parvin's family finally managed to return to their home three months later, there was nothing left inside. The attackers took whatever they could, and destroyed everything that was left. Parvin was to marry in a few months, and she and her mother had painstakingly hoarded the modest trousseau in all of two bags. They were gone, as were the mattress, the TV, the fridge, the rice, even the utensils, the lights, and the fan. Parvin knew the rioters. 'They are Hindu boys who live nearby. Some of them work part-time at the mill, some are unemployed. They wanted to terrify us and loot.' Lane after lane, it was the same story. Hazrat Khatoon, 60, who works as a migrant domestic worker in Jaipur for much of the year since her husband lost his job at the mill a decade ago, said the attackers even took the fourteen sarees she owned. 'I wear borrowed sarees now.' Shabana Begum's son, Sahil, had stopped going to school. They burnt his books.

The electoral violence of June 2019 had erupted as the BJP was beginning to make inroads as a new political force into a state ruled by the local Trinamool Congress party, or TMC. Thanks to the BJP's Hindu voter mobilization strategy, the violent political battles in the area had taken on a communal colour in a state where nearly a third of the population is Muslim.

Across the main road, in a different bloc about ten minutes from Parvin's lane, was a different story, of Hindus forced to flee by Muslim attackers. Anil Kumar Gupta's small electronics shop was raided and destroyed on the day of the election. His is among the one-storeyed houses in a small cluster of thirty-two 'Hindu homes' in a Muslim neighbourhood. A group of Muslim men barged into the common courtyard the houses share. They threatened them against casting their vote, forced their way into each home, and ransacked them systematically. 'They assumed Hindus would vote for the BJP', said Gupta. But here too, the attackers were motivated by communal and political fervour as much as by the incentive to steal. After forcing the Hindu residents to flee, they came back later that night and took whatever they could find. Many of the residents never returned. Gupta, who couldn't afford to rent another place, came back after a month. His wife, a heart patient, died from the trauma two days after the election.

Battlefield Bengal

Parvin and Gupta found themselves trapped in the hellish crossfire of Bengal's latest political turmoil. Since 2011, the state had been ruled by Mamata Banerjee, a popular local leader who broke away from the Congress in the late 1990s to float the TMC. Credited with ending a thirty-four-year reign of a Leftist coalition in the state headed by the Communist Party of India (Marxist), or CPI(M), she came to power on a wave of popular resentment against the Left government's move to acquire cultivable land for industrial purposes. Heading a party and government that are essentially centred on her, she has created a personality cult rarely seen in the state. Giant pictures of her adorn highways and street corners; her smiling visage flashes in government ads in newspapers; special municipality tax breaks are given to houses that are painted in white and blue, her party colours (matching the signature blue-bordered white sarees she wears) and all government buildings and public infrastructure, such as hospitals and bridges, are painted in white and blue (Figure 22). Popularly known as 'Didi', or elder sister in Bengali, fawning party leaders fall over one other to demonstrate their loyalty to her. But her iron grip on power had begun to be threatened by the BJP. The emergence of a viable challenger to the existing order had sparked

Figure 22. Giant cut-outs of Mamata Banerjee are part of her personality cult

a bloody conflict. The Bhatpara-Kankinara area had become one of many battle grounds in the violent contest for power.

Violent political collisions in Bengal date back to the time before Mahatma Gandhi and his followers transformed India's Independence struggle into a predominantly non-violent mass movement. Undivided Bengal was the epicentre of militant resistance to British rule. Home to several armed rebellions and attacks aimed at the Raj, and youth organizations professing militant nationalism, Bengal also witnessed, from the mid-1940s, sustained peasant movements led by Leftist forces. The cycle of armed conflicts between the state and the landed classes on the one hand and political activists on the other created a legacy in which bombs, guns, and private armies, rather than paper rocks and democratic persuasion, became the weapons of choice in political turf wars.

For two decades after Independence, Congress governed unchallenged in Bengal, but in 1967 an alliance of Left forces and a breakaway faction of the Congress ended the party's monopoly over power. That year was a turning point in the history of modern India. The Congress's national grip on power began to slip. Of the sixteen states at the time (India now has twenty-nine), just eight returned the Congress to power with absolute majorities in the state legislatures. After several years of political turmoil, the Congress returned to power in the state in 1972. The election was marked by large-scale rigging of votes and intimidation of voters by the Congress, 'ousting thousands of opposition party workers from their localities, creating a reign of terror by using both police and goons'.[4]

Violence had begun to be mainstreamed in Bengal's political life. The biggest threat to the Congress was the ultra-radical 'Naxalites'. Inspired by Mao Zedong (one of their popular slogans was, 'China's chairman is our chairman'), they had split from the communists, who chose to participate in elections. The Naxalites derived their name from a Bengal village called Naxalbari, where they attempted an armed peasant uprising in 1967, with the aim of redistributing land to the landless and overthrowing the government. A large-scale, ruthless crackdown on the Naxalites was launched in 1971. So, when the Congress returned to power in 1972, its ranks had filled with thuggish elements that had helped it restore the party's political supremacy by force. Under the leadership of the new Congress chief minister, Siddhartha Shankar Ray, an ace lawyer, these violent elements played an important role in neutralizing, in concert with the police, not just the Naxalites but the rest of the Left forces as well. Murders, midnight knocks, forced disappearances, custodial tortures, and killings by 'liquidation squads' became the norm. Political opposition was met with intimidation, street violence, and unlawful arrests. '*Goonda*' (hired thugs) became the mainstay of Bengal politics.

Close to Indira Gandhi, Ray represented a much broader, countrywide trend of criminalization of politics. The Congress, enfeebled by a raging factional feud between Indira Gandhi and the old bosses, finally split in 1969. What remained of the Grand Old Party was quickly transformed into Indira Gandhi's personal fief, with a handful of people close to her calling the shots. Internal party democracy collapsed. Sycophants began to replace mass leaders. An organizationally weakened Congress without its familiar ability to stitch together broad social coalitions could no longer enlist support in the traditional way, especially because party competition had set in as long-suppressed social groups started to assert their concerns and interests. And so it became necessary to enlist bad actors, who could recruit followers armed with knives and guns. They delivered electoral victories without the open-minded rigour of democratic persuasion. Simultaneously, the local governing structures, especially the police forces, began to be bent to the party's will. This in turn served as an incentive for criminal elements to collaborate more closely with politicians: creeping political control of the police produced a safe haven for criminals, shielding them from the law. The apogee of this criminalization of politics was the 1975 Emergency, which was Ray's brainchild.

Ray's rule in Bengal ended in the backlash against the Congress when elections were called in 1977, after twenty-one months of Emergency. But the legacy of his blood-soaked years in power lingered. Violence became an integral part of elections. After the Congress lost in the state and, for the first time, in Delhi in 1977, the Leftist coalition headed by the Communist Party of India (Marxist) swept to power in Bengal. It went on to rule the state for thirty-four years. In the early years, successful measures like land reforms and decentralization of power through a three-tiered panchayat system of local government helped them consolidate power. But the grassroots reforms polarized the state along party lines and spawned cut-throat competition for the limited available basic services. In rural Bengal, elections became fiercely-fought contests among political parties operating as monopolists of patronage. Association with a party can make the difference between citizens' access to a borewell, or a hospital bed. These contests for basic social services were accentuated during the communist years by the gradual deindustrialization of the state, as businesses left to escape government-backed militant trade unionism. In 1960, Bengal and Maharashtra were two of the richest states in India. But by 1993, per capita output in Bengal had fallen by more than a third compared to Maharashtra. Bengal's contribution to India's total factory output shrank from 6.2 per cent in 1990 to 2.45 per cent in 2011–12.[5] The jute industry was one of the biggest sufferers. Hundreds of mills closed. Lack of economic opportunities and prospects for social advancement made the stakes even higher for electoral access to basic services provided by the state.

The long-term consequence, said a district TMC leader who must remain unnamed, is that 'from birth certificate to death certificate, everything depends on the panchayats, making political contests in rural Bengal a matter of life and death.' People kill and die for their parties because politics has become a matter of survival. Come election time, parts of Bengal turn into veritable war zones, especially whenever a new challenger emerges to threaten the status quo. Decades of economic decline and damage to the social fabric have spawned armies of young, unemployed men with low prospects of advancement and willing to be weaponized as hired muscle.

When the communists' winning streak was finally broken by Banerjee in 2011, she tried to monopolize power by replicating her communist predecessors' technique of rewarding the faithful and ravaging the rest. Banerjee hardly pioneered the art of hijacking elections through force. She merely took it to new heights. Lacking a dedicated cadre base like her communist predecessors, she chose to depend less on political mobilization and more on patronage tinged with brute force. Violence within the state's politics spread. According to the National Crime Records Bureau statistics, Bengal on average saw twenty political murders a year between 1999 and 2016. Using brazen displays of force, Banerjee's TMC 'won' 90 per cent of the seats in the 2018 local panchayat elections. More than twenty-five people were

killed and scores injured in election-related violence that saw ruling
party cadres openly parading the streets, wielding guns and swords.
They attacked with impunity opposition rallies and anybody who
dared even to file nomination against TMC candidates. The TMC
'won' a third of the 60,000-odd panchayat seats uncontested simply
because the opposition wasn't even allowed to field candidates.

Just as the Left met its match in Banerjee, she too met hers, in the
shape of the BJP. Modi's party proved it could fight fire with fire. But
the battles subjected Bengal to a kind of political contest it hadn't
known before—one fought on religious lines, rather than along party
political divisions. Debasish Pal, a schoolteacher in Kankinara, said
he'd never seen this kind of violence. 'There used to be the usual gang
wars between party men. But it didn't touch us, the common people.
This is different.'

Different it certainly was. Devoid of an established political base in
Bengal, the BJP draws from the support system formed by the myriad
arms of the party's giant Hindu nationalist parent organization, the
Rashtriya Swayamsevak Sangh (translated as National Volunteer
Organization). The RSS, as it is commonly known, was founded in
1925 on the principles of Hindutva (loosely, Hindu-ness) that seeks a
homogenized, majoritarian Hindu cultural and political order in
which Hindus are more equal than others. The existing pluralistic
democratic model has allowed 'appeasement of Muslims' and the
treatment of Hindus as 'second-order citizens', says its mission statement. In Modi (who was a long-time RSS 'preacher') and his sweeping majority, the RSS today sees the best chance to correct this
historical 'injustice' and achieve its goal of remaking India's secular
republic into a Hindu state. Its vast network of volunteers and allied
organizations in almost all walks of life—from trading bodies and
cooperative organizations to labour and student unions—especially
in the northern and western states, is a major factor in the BJP's growing reach. *Sakhas* (camps) are the RSS's most elementary organizational units for ideological induction. Volunteers meet daily at *sakhas*
for early-morning physical drills, to begin a lifelong association with

the Hindutva project. There are about 60,000 *sakhas* across India. In Bengal, there are about 1,800. Decades of dedicated grassroots volunteering through *sakhas*, informal schools, health camps, self-help groups, professional training programmes, and religious and cultural gatherings, have yielded a rich network of community organizers and followers aligned with the Hindutva worldview.[6] Leveraging this right-wing ecosystem, the BJP has emerged as the only alternative to Banerjee. As the Congress and the communists and other political parties in the state have withered, many of the workers and leaders from these parties have migrated to the BJP, with Modi's popularity and the party's seemingly infinite spending capacity adding to its attractiveness. Recharged, the state BJP's strategy of Hindu mobilization by aggressively targeting Muslims has been politically effective, but socially destructive. Arguing that Banerjee had pandered to the Muslim vote and disregarded Hindu voters, the BJP transformed a battle for political power into an everyday religious war. In Kankinara, as Parvin and Gupta found, both Hindus and Muslims who previously had nothing to do with politics suddenly felt the heating hand of a new kind of violently schismatic electoral politics.

Violence Unseen

Bengal's problem of political thuggery and violence is acute, but by no means exceptional. It mirrors the gradual bloodying of Indian electoral politics. But the decadence doesn't end there. A wide range of innovative, cunning, ground-level practices stand at right angles to the highest principles of 'free and fair' elections seen as a 'timeless' and non-negotiable feature of the good political life. One of the most common tactics, popular for a long time, was 'booth capturing'. It involved party toughs physically taking over polling stations and stamping ballot papers in their favour. It used to be a common electoral strategy until 2004, when electronic voting machines were introduced, so making ballot papers redundant. In-booth vote tampering, by smuggling into booths people who will press the right button, still happens but is far less prominent simply because its utility is limited by the precision of the covert behaviour required to pull it off.

More subtle tricks have been at play. One is blocking access to school and college buildings, the places widely used for voting. In most Indian villages, schools tend to be located in upper-caste areas because the dominant groups that control the local institutions of power corner public goods such as schools. During elections, not allowing lower-caste voters to traverse through upper-caste areas— difficult even in ordinary times—has been a common ploy. It amounts to 'silent booth capturing'. Practices such as these faced a major challenge in 1989, when a fresh round of affirmative action, proposed by the now-famous Mandal Commission, was initiated for backward castes that set in motion a process of breaking down upper-caste dominance of electoral politics. The transition wasn't peaceful. The strategic use of violence and open patronage granted to criminals by emerging backward caste leaders, such as Lalu Prasad Yadav in Bihar and Mulayam Singh Yadav in Uttar Pradesh, to combat the upper-caste stranglehold over power structures, meant that older tactics of silent booth capturing were replaced by violent booth capturing and fierce clashes. As the structural injustice within the social foundations of Indian democracy began to be physically resisted, elections became louder, rowdier, and more violent.

Many of the drivers of electoral violence have changed over time. Some states once particularly prone to violence, such as Bihar and Uttar Pradesh, have become less so with the introduction of new electronic voting technologies that render older strategies of ballot theft redundant. The violence hasn't disappeared, however. It's just become less overt. For the 2019 national elections, between 10 March and 25 May, the Armed Conflict Location & Event Data project (ACLED) recorded 327 reported fatalities across India. The number, collated from media reports and volunteer networks, is significantly understated given the scale of unreported electoral violence. Official figures such as these that focus on actual physical violence also don't

Figure 23. Voting at West Bengal's Birbhum has always been fraught with violence

reveal the true extent of intimidation and threatened violence, much of it taking place away from sight of polling stations (Figure 23).

Bloodless Coups

The usual focus on visible forms of violence hides much more insidious forms of coercion. There are two particularly effective strategies that political parties employ. One is using fear to stop potential supporters of rival parties from reaching the polling booth. Creating a climate of terror in the neighbourhood helps in deterring voters from stepping out. This doesn't necessarily lead to any loss of life and happens far away from voting booths. The second, and the more effective tactic, is scaring away the polling agents fielded by rival parties. The polling agents representing their parties inside the booths are key to ensuring free and fair elections, along with the presiding officer, who manages and monitors the election. The presiding officer, a government employee from another district, whose details are available to the government, may be susceptible to ruling-party pressures, especially if she or he senses a risk of physical threat. Polling agents of multiple parties ensure that a dominant party doesn't subvert the voting process by infiltrating the booth with its representatives and take over the voting machine, or, previously, the ballot papers and boxes. The toughest task for a political party trying to break the stranglehold of the ruling party—if the latter is not averse to playing dirty—is to find polling agents, ensure they show up on the election day, stay put at the booth and not blink in the face of terror tactics used by opponents. This isn't easy. Dominant parties not only send their own polling agents into the booth. Because they also tend to prop up 'dummy candidates', either as independents or candidates from smaller parties they fund, the dominant parties also get to send in their own dummy polling agents on the day of the vote. On a particularly fraught polling day, with the sound of gunfire shots interspersed with bombing in the distance, a dedicated opposition-party polling agent and an honest presiding officer may find themselves surrounded inside the booth by ruling party men disguised as voters and half a dozen or more polling agents who claim officially to be from other parties, but who are actually doing the ruling party's bidding. How they respond to this threat—not registered in official statistics as 'violence'—can swing a seat and make or break governments.

Then there is off-booth voter intimidation. The practice can range from a simple home visit by bike-borne party workers, with a friendly reminder to vote for the 'right' party, to more direct threats to fall in line. Electronic voting has eliminated some forms of violence such as booth capture but has increased the scope of voter intimidation as it increases the risk of exposing a voter's party preference. When votes used to be cast by paper ballot, all ballots would be mixed up before being counted. This would eliminate the scope of parties finding out who voted for them at individual booth levels. In electronic voting, the same could be done using a 'totalizer' machine that electronically mixes up votes registered in different voting machines before they are counted. But despite repeated public demands and court petitions, electoral authorities have refused to use totalizers. Hence it is easy for local party workers to guess from the numbers who may have, or not, voted for the party. 'We'll know who you voted for' is not an empty threat.

A tour of the volatile Bolpur parliamentary area of Bengal's Birbhum district during the 2019 elections showed that heavy policing fails to overcome these instruments of electoral fraud. Local leaders of the CPI(M) in Birbhum, now out of office and subject to the same terror tactics they once wielded against their opponents, complained how difficult it was to field polling agents. An ascendant BJP was putting up a better fight. That in turn sparked raids by TMC men on neighbourhoods that the party felt were shifting to the BJP. At the TMC's plush district headquarters in Bolpur city, the party's regional boss, Anubrata Mandal, monitored the situation—on live television. Journalists had started mobbing the party office from the night before the election, when the Election Commission put him under surveillance, ordering the federal police to watch him till the end of the elections, and to confiscate his mobile phone to prevent him from influencing polling (Figure 24).

Mandal has been a long-time party lieutenant of Banerjee. Once the poster boy of courageous anti-establishment resistance against

Figure 24. Bengal ruling party strongman Anubrata Mandal the night before the 2019 national elections

communist rule, he had now become the face of the ruling TMC's brute power and organizational prowess. In the past, he tried to hide the arrogance bestowed by the invincibility of power. On this election day, surrounded by journalists at the sprawling conference room at his party office, he wasn't even trying. He pointedly called his booth-level workers on a mobile phone (not his own, so technically not flouting the rules) to find out if the presiding officer was 'allowing' the votes to be cast 'fast enough'. It was a loaded question, and he did it on camera. The message was not lost on anybody. Just a few days earlier, bragging that he 'gets elections done', he had stirred a controversy by openly declaring that his party would help maintain peace during the elections if polling officials allowed the TMC to 'manage' 500–600 votes every booth. Mandal was not unaware of the risks of official reprisal or the potential for public outrage at such open declarations of vote theft. The fact was, the rewards far outweighed the risks Mandal's public advertisements of his coercive power may appear foolhardy, but it was actually a conscious signal to his constituency that he and his party meant business.

Muscle Power

As the political scientist Milan Vaishnav has explained, criminality is a valuable asset in Indian politics. It's an indicator of the capacity to bend rules.[7] Crumbling social foundations and the Indian state's failure to deliver basic services create conditions in which voters have little hope of accessing justice or public goods in a rule-based manner. Rules are, in fact, seen as a hindrance. Rules are regarded as a failure of institutions that don't work. A candidate's disregard for the law and the ability to get away with it is a sign of their ability to get things done. By flaunting his disregard for rules on live TV, Mandal was advertising his ability to deliver the constituency the promised goods. For the same reason, the BJP's state leader, Dilip Ghosh, openly threatens to break the limbs of TMC workers and kill them. When social life is degraded and governing institutions are floundering, democratic accountability goes missing. Politics becomes a protection racket. Election campaigns resemble street fights.

Surveys find that 50 per cent of Indians seek the help of elected representatives in panchayats or municipal wards to gain access to public services, or to get official work done, such as secure a water connection or guarantee hospital and school admission.[8] Among so-called democracies, India has the highest rate of people using personal connections to access public services (46 per cent), finds Transparency International's Global Corruption Barometer. As the state fails to provide adequate social services, the electorate looks for strongmen who are substitutes for the state, people who can fill the gap in government welfare capacity and deliver some measure of social justice. Since voters see a lack of probity as competence, bad behaviour becomes good politics.

The lack of basic social services and the consequent criminalization of politics are sources of voter disagreement about criminal politicians and their ability to deliver basic services. Middle- and upper-class folks, with better access and greater resources to procure basic services, even when they are not well provided, express outrage at crime in politics. The not-so-fortunate are less agitated by criminal politicians, which helps explain why the number of crooked politicians keeps swelling and why democracy failures and despotic rule flourish in the subsoil of a crumbling society. In 2004, some 24 per cent of Members of Parliament (MPs) in the directly elected Lower House had declared criminal cases against them (self-declaration is an election rule). That rose to 30 per cent in 2009, 34 per cent in 2014, and to 43 per cent in 2019. The numbers are starker when it comes to 'serious' criminal cases, which include charges related to murder, attempted murder, kidnapping, rape, and other crimes against women. Some 29 per cent of winners in the 2019 national elections had declared serious cases against them, their number doubling since 2009. One Kerala MP, from the Congress, faced 204 criminal charges, including cases related to culpable homicide, house trespass, robbery, and criminal intimidation. In Kerala, 90 per cent of the MPs had criminal cases, followed by 82 per cent in Bihar.

Faced with criminality on this scale, efforts by the Election Commission and other bodies to clean up elections and raise their level of integrity are an uphill battle. The Supreme Court in February 2019 made it mandatory for political parties to publish the names of candidates saddled with criminal charges. It observed that 'winnability' couldn't be adequate justification for allowing a tainted politician to run for office. A year later, the Election Commission told the Supreme Court that its directive hadn't helped curb criminalization of politics, and that political parties should be asked not to field candidates with criminal backgrounds. Given the cold calculus of elections, this was sheer wishful thinking.

Apart from the appeal of strongmen and their ability to get things done in an inefficient and corruption-plagued governing system, the brutal truth is that it pays to have criminals in politics. They bring money to the table. Lots of it, in quick time. Indian political parties, most of which have long ceased to function as mass-based organizations and operate as oligarchies, and hence unable to raise money from organized cadres and followers, find the appeal of hard cash difficult to resist, especially as elections grow more expensive. Hence criminals have become part and parcel of Indian political life. Gangsters increasingly push politicians aside by linking their criminal enterprise with political office. Come elections, prisons often turn into party offices for incarcerated dons. There can be other grim farces, as when police raided a grand event hosted by the notorious gangster 'Red Hills' Surya, who joined the BJP in Tamil Nadu in August 2020. Surya, who fled the scene, was only the latest in a long list of celebrity toughs to join the party. A sheepish state spokesperson for the BJP later explained things by saying that other parties too had leaders with criminal cases against them.

Criminal connections bring additional benefits, such as access to large masses of idle young men. Big money pours into politics. Dark money, corruption, and cronyism flourish. Candidates who have to hand, at short notice, a large pool of personal cash, tend to be more active in rent-thick industries, such as land, where their regulatory power of issuing licences—once elected—can be traded for financial favours. Politicians have hence become key players in the construction industry, where they do more than just dole out favours to builders in return for money. Their stakes in the industry may be hidden through the usual proxies of friends and relatives or more innovative quid pro quos, but from the smallest towns to the biggest cities, the politician as part-time builder and builder as a part-time politician is now normal. The end result is the convergence of the criminal, the political and the entrepreneurial—the formation of a new class of politicians who bear more than a passing resemblance to the poligarchs of new despotisms such as Russia and Turkey.

Studying almost 60,000 candidates over six years, Vaishnav found significant correlation between money and political muscle. He found that candidates facing serious criminal charges have a significant wealth advantage and are thus three times more likely than 'clean' candidates to win at the national level, and twice as likely in state elections.[9] The evidence is also borne out by the rapid rise in number of 'crorepati' candidates (those worth more than 10 million rupees). While 43 per cent of the MPs who were elected in 2019 had criminal charges against them, 83 per cent were fat-cat crorepatis, up from 58 per cent in 2009, calculated by the election watchdog the Association for Democratic Reforms (ADR). The criminality feeds government policy failures, mismanagement, and corruption. The process is unmistakably despotic: people who run for office and go on to wield political power over others are both increasingly criminal and rich. In the country famous for its election extravaganzas, wealthy poligarchs with muscle power are winning hands down.

Chremacracy

Quiet Battles

April 2019: the candidate Tamanna Simhadri was resting at home, a windowless sliver of brick and cement that doubled as the war room of her election campaign. Situated in a narrow lane off the busy Labbipet area of Andhra Pradesh's Vijayawada city, Tamanna's campaign headquarters wore an oddly deserted look. Not many people like to venture out in Vijayawada's April noontime heat—when temperature can reach 45 degrees centigrade—but it was after all election season and she wasn't just any candidate. Tamanna was taking on the crown prince of Andhra Pradesh, Nara Lokesh, in the southern city's Mangalagiri constituency. Son of the chief minister and one of the leading members of the opposition, Chandrababu Naidu, Lokesh is as blue-blooded as it gets in India's firmament of political dynasties. Apart from being the son of the longest serving chief minister of Andhra Pradesh, who ruled the state for fourteen years, he's also the grandson of three-time chief minister and founder of the ruling Telugu Desam Party, N.T. Rama Rao.

And this wasn't just another day. The campaign had just ended. The election was two days away. The 'cooling off period' of forty-eight hours had kicked in. This is when candidates are by law barred from campaigning. They are supposed to put up their feet and recuperate from the final campaign slog before the votes are cast. But it doesn't quite work like that. This is when the most important campaign work begins—reaching out to voters with gifts and money. Since it is punishable by law, it needs to be done in subtle ways and channelled through people who can be trusted to deliver the goodies to the voters, as well as extract from them a promise of loyalty. Parties hold this off till the very end so that the memory of the candidate's munificence is still fresh when they cast their vote. Most election managers have come to believe that this is the most crucial part of the campaign. They say that since Indians consider all politicians crooks, voters will go with whoever gives them the biggest cut of the loot. It sounds cynical, but millions of people and most parties have come to consider the practice axiomatic. As the refrain in campaign circles goes: if you pay, you may not get the vote, but if you don't pay you will definitely not get the vote.

In this 2019 Legislative Assembly election, held alongside the national election, the two main parties in Andhra reportedly distributed between Rs 3,000 and Rs 4,000 to each voter. The phenomenon of vote-for-cash is variously interpreted by political scientists. Some see it as a sign of a crude form of clientelism, whereby votes are turned into a commodity and auctioned off to the highest bidder, with voters forfeiting expectations of proper representation. Others view votes-for-cash as a more complex and mutually enriching transaction aimed at winning and consolidating both the support of constituencies and key local community members, who act as political intermediaries through whom money and gifts are typically channelled in exchange for promised votes.[1] Whatever the case, the last-minute exercise has emerged in recent decades as one of the biggest election expenses in the business of targeted messaging. Feasts come in particularly handy. Voters enticed with copious offerings of alcohol in the final days are said to respond favourably.

The lack of buzz, or even a party worker, at Tamanna's one-room home-cum-office suggested she was unencumbered by the necessities of effective campaigning. 'I do not care if I win or lose,' she said, 'but people like me need to stand up and indicate that we want things to change.' People like her, who are not millionaires or children of

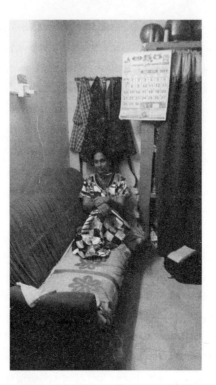

Figure 25. Tamanna Simhadri relaxes after a punishing campaign in peak
Vijayawada summer heat

powerful people, she explained, needed to run in elections, or nothing
ever would change. 'Are we going to live like animals, carry their flags
at their campaigns, so that they will rule us forever?' Tamanna did care,
a lot, but this was the best she could do. She could neither dole out
air-conditioners to voters nor did she have enough money to pay the
media to limelight her candidacy. She could only wage a quiet ethical
battle in India's raucously corrupted election extravaganza (Figure 25).

A transgender woman who ran away from her conservative family
to the city, and changed her religion, Tamanna's life has been one long
struggle. 'This is another injustice I had to fight.' She first tried to
work her way up the ladder at a local party but found that they were
only interested in fielding rich candidates. 'It's all a business for them.
They will spend a million to run for office, then make 10 million in
office.' Tamanna, who then started working for a small non-profit,

spent a modest Rs 50,000 (less than $700) to print leaflets. She campaigned by foot, door to door, with the help of some 200 friends and acquaintances who volunteered to work on her campaign. 'Sometimes, when it gets too hot and I can't walk, a friend lends me a car.'

Money, Money

In another part of Vijayawada, her opponent Lokesh had just concluded his campaign, awash in a sea of yellow, his party's colour. Thousands of his father's Telugu Desam Party came out to march in a final show of strength. Hundreds of bikes, trucks, and cars filled with party workers led the parade, bringing traffic to a standstill as it snaked its way through the city. Rallies like these cost a fortune. Elections mean patronage. 'Supporters' need to be compensated for their time and effort. In Vijayawada, the going rate is Rs 500 a pop. For their troubles, they expect refreshments and transport, too. Logistics, often including a helicopter for top leaders, and fuel expenses for campaign vehicles to ferry party workers and paid supporters, take up a chunk of the expenses. As does 'buzz creation' through media.

The working principle of media coverage is simple. 'A party pretending to be the most active and acting like the frontrunner, is enough to make people believe that it is most likely to win, which often translates into actual support and votes,' writes Shivam Shankar Singh, a member of a new breed of political animals called 'election consultants'.[2] Social media has added a whole new expense stream to campaigns, with the need to maintain dedicated party cells to stay on top of all digital platforms. India's data protection laws are weak. For a price, data brokers harvest vast quantities of phone numbers from sim-card dealers and telecom companies that the parties then buy to use for micro-targeted messaging on a scale and intensity not seen in any other democracy. WhatsApp groups are particularly important for building a band of dedicated followers and keeping them on message.

The BJP promotes its own app called the 'NarendraModi App', also called the 'NaMo App'. Even traditional media advertising has changed. Paid news is common. There are specialized media planners who arrange paid news 'packages' for candidates, handling their 'outreach'. They also help blank out negative reportage. The really good fixers even help minimize the coverage of rival candidates.

It's not for nothing that elections in India, like elsewhere, have become exponentially more expensive in recent decades. Not only has India trodden the path of what social scientists call psephocracy, a manic obsession with elections. The whole system of elections is becoming a chremacracy, a term derived from a rather ungainly and old-fashioned Greek word (*chrema*, money, 'to need', 'to use'; *kratos*, 'to rule') used to describe a type of politics in which money not only talks, but decides things. The cost of elections has increased for several reasons. The size of India's economy grew eight times since privatization and market competition began in 1991, making India richer. Its electorate has expanded by more than half. Electoral competition has increased, with many more parties and candidates joining the fray than ever before. Even the number of elected positions has risen exponentially, from around 4,500 to nearly 3 million as a result of the devolution of power to village and town levels. Since money makes the world of elections go round, it isn't surprising that the overall volume of money in Indian campaigns has grown astronomically too (Figure 26).

The Centre for Media Studies reports that the 2019 parliamentary elections were the 'most expensive election ever, anywhere'. At Rs 60,000 crore ($7.2 billion), it beat the $6.5 billion the US presidential and congressional races cost in 2016.[3] That means India spends more on elections than the US, but with just 3 per cent of its per capita income. On average, nearly Rs 100 crore, or Rs 1 trillion, was spent per seat. Up to a quarter of the total expenditure, Rs 12,000–15,000 crore, went directly to voters as cash and gifts. The estimates were based on the 'front end' costs and expenses that were traceable. 'It is only the tip of the iceberg', said its director,

Figure 26. Sky-high election campaign expenses narrow the field to rich candidates

General P.N. Vasanti. 'Imagine how deep and wide is this iceberg beneath, and how it can damage our democracy.'[4]

It's true every democracy on our planet is faced with the challenge of funding elections; a democracy without methods of campaign financing is both unthinkable and unworkable. Yet India is one of seven countries in a list of fifty-two so-called democracies that have no state funding for political parties or proper regulation of party finances—in the company of Senegal, Jamaica, Botswana, Mauritius, Switzerland, and Latvia. Measured in terms of a fifty-four-country study of the quality of the regulation and enforcement of dark money in elections, India scores 31 (out of 100) and is ranked twelfth from the bottom.[5] Shady dealings are the norm of campaign finances for cash-needy parties trying to finance mounting election costs. Despite strict limits on candidate spending on paper, money trails are impossible to verify, meaning there is effectively no cap on either raising or spending money for campaigns. Parties can spend unlimited amounts of money and get away with it, as there is no independent audit. Supposedly the guardian of Indian democracy, the Election

Commission has limited powers of scrutiny. In spite of its declarations and good work, and compared with sister institutions such as the Instituto Nacional Electoral (INE) in Mexico, it fosters democratic failure. It doesn't even have the right to deregister an errant political party.

Candidates and political parties find cunning ways to work around a loophole-ridden regulatory system. In the opening decades of the Indian republic, the Congress's absolute hold on power in both Delhi and the states, backed by an elaborate 'Licence Raj' system of business licensing and regulation in a heavily controlled economy, gave the party easy and ample access to corporate funding. But after the Congress began losing elections in several major states, Indira Gandhi, fearing rival pro-business parties would eat into the corporate funding pie, banned corporate donations altogether. No alternative, institutional funding model was adopted. The trend towards public funding of elections that happened in many democracies, especially in Europe, never took root. Though her son Rajiv, as prime minister, again legalized company donations in 1985, the nexus between politics and 'black' or undocumented money had by then become entrenched. Chremacracy became a fact of life. As the economy continued to be highly state-controlled and political competition increased, businesses had practical reasons for not declaring openly which party they were funding.

Since the mid-'90s, there have been stricter court-directed rules and administrative initiatives to enforce disclosure of party accounts. But anonymous donations have continued to constitute the bulk of party finances, with neither the Election Commission of India given any teeth to punish parties if they flout the rules nor the parties subjected to any government scrutiny of their books. More than 75 per cent of the funds raised by the six national political parties between 2004–5 and 2011–12 came from 'unknown' sources. The Congress, in power during this period, received 90 per cent of its income in cash donations, and the BJP, around 67 per cent.[6] As parties don't have to reveal their sources for donations under a certain amount, they fudge the accounts by breaking up large underhand donations into multiple small tranches to avoid disclosure.

Electoral Bonds

In 2018, the already shady party finances system took a quantum leap towards absolute chremacracy when the Modi government introduced electoral bonds, an instrument that allows individuals, corporations, and other legal entities such as trusts and associations anonymously to channel unlimited amounts of money to political parties. Under this new measure, anyone is allowed to buy tax-free bearer bonds for specified amounts via the state-owned State Bank of India (SBI) and then deposit them into the registered bank accounts of political parties. The donors aren't required to reveal their contributions, nor are the recipients asked to declare the identity of the donors. In the name of transparency, electoral bonds have made India's already murky campaign finance system infinitely more opaque. Through electoral bonds, Indian and foreign companies, even shell companies that do little else other than ferry money in and out of jurisdictions, can now route unlimited amounts of money to Indian political parties in complete anonymity. Even the anonymity feature sold to the public as a virtue of the bonds—supposedly allowing companies to fund parties not in power without attracting government reprisal—turned out to be false.[7] The government, it later transpired, can find out the identity of the bond buyer. Not surprisingly, 95 per cent of the money donated through these bonds went to the ruling BJP in the 2019 election. In the 2017–18 financial year, the BJP bagged almost 98 per cent of the total value of electoral bonds.

Just as access to moneyed sources once helped the Congress, links to such massive funds have now sharply tilted the playing field in favour of the BJP. The new political hegemon accounts for nearly three-quarters of the combined income of India's seven largest political parties. Just the donations it receives amount to more than 2.5 times the combined income, from all sources, of the next six largest parties put together. This gives the BJP the firepower to outspend massively its rivals in matters of organization, campaigning, and general outreach. The official BJP page on Facebook, with over 16 million followers, is Facebook's biggest advertising spender in India. Pro-BJP pages on Facebook accounted for 70 per cent of the total advertisement revenue in the run-up to the 2019 general election. The year before, as elections approached in four states, the BJP was India's leading brand in TV advertising. It aired its ads 22,099 times, 10,000 more than the next brand on the list of ten top advertisers—Netflix.[8]

More than 90 per cent of the money raised through electoral bonds comes through coupons with denominations of Rs 1 crore, or Rs 10 million ($140,000). Obviously, these donors are not your average party supporter. Mass-based parties were born of ninteenth-century struggles, when political parties waged campaigns to attract millions of active supporters by offering them literacy, jobs, and the right of men and women to stand together to vote as dignified equals. For the past generation, political parties everywhere have become shadows of their former selves.[9] One pressing consequence of the transformation of political parties into machines without souls is that they now have to find other sources of funding. In India, the principal donors are evidently rich political benefactors, often corporate entities or people in business seeking quid pro quos, and doing so in the shadows. It isn't that electoral bonds have for the first time brought together campaign financing and corporate lobbying. Businesses seeking favours from politicians have long found innovative ways to channel their investments as best bets, starting with cash-stuffed suitcases to more complicated but equally untraceable offerings. But electoral bonds have given influence-buying an institutional structure and have helped electoral financing scale up to unprecedented levels. A booster shot to chremacracy, electoral bonds are the playground of poligarchs, a shiny new medium of securing hidden cooperation between corporate oligarchs and political bosses. For businesses in India, where the state, even after decades of supposed economic liberalization, continues to wield enormous power through policy levers that can make or break companies, campaign contributions function as more than buyers of influence. They are insurance policies.

Such hedges against capricious state power are a necessity as even the biggest conglomerates are not immune to policy whims. Take the mighty Tatas. J.R.D. Tata, among the tallest figures in Indian business and the first person to obtain a pilot's licence issued in India, launched the country's first commercial airline, Tata Airlines, in 1932. A year before India's Independence it was renamed Air India. Six years later, the Nehru government decided to nationalize Air India but invited him to stay on as its chairman. For the next twenty-five years, JRD, as he was popularly known, nurtured Air India into a profit-making regional titan and inspiration for later airlines such as Cathay Pacific and Thai Airways. But in 1978, the government of Morarji Desai (who rose to power in the anti-Emergency vote in 1977) dropped JRD from the chairmanship of the company, without so much as informing him. In 1980, when Indira Gandhi returned to power, she reappointed JRD to the Air India board. In the 1990s, when markets were opened up, the House of Tata, now run by JRD's successor Ratan Tata, saw an opportunity to re-enter the group's long-cherished airline industry. It put together an alliance with Singapore Airlines to launch a domestic carrier. But the laws changed overnight and foreign airlines were barred from holding any stake in domestic carriers. Tata's dreams were dashed, but those of homegrown Jet Airways took wings. Jet started operations in 1993, the year JRD died. His dream of owning an airline was left unfulfilled. The Tatas were finally allowed to fly Vistara in alliance with Singapore Airlines only in December 2014—nearly two decades after JRD's death. Jet went out of business in 2019. The same year, the government announced it would sell the heavily loss-making Air India that JRD had pioneered, only to be taken over by the state and turned into a wreck.

The fortunes of men and businesses much smaller than JRD and Tata are made and unmade by state policy. A small tweak in regulation or a pithy file note can make or break a business. From the smallest contractor digging canals in the countryside to the country's biggest conglomerates building airports, bridges, and highways, every business person understands the importance of paying their fealty to the wielders of state power. State policy is suitably framed and applied— or not—to help business help politics. Electoral bonds are only the latest innovation to consolidate this symbiosis. Other, more elementary forms of donations also enable parties to raise money without any accountability. Apart from small cash donations that require no disclosure and are used to mask big campaign contributions, there's no cap on corporate donations anymore. Earlier, individual companies could contribute to parties up to 7.5 per cent of their average annual profits over three years, and were required to detail such contributions in their annual statements. The Modi government removed this cap and simultaneously scrapped the requirement of detailing corporate campaign contributions. Thanks to the Foreign Contribution Regulation Act (FCRA), foreign donations, once barred, have also been made easier, with a wide variety of foreign organizations now legally allowed to make political donations. The Lok Sabha in 2018 passed without debate a bill exempting political parties from scrutiny of funds received from abroad in previous decades. The amendment was supported by both the ruling BJP and the opposition Congress, both of them found guilty earlier by the Delhi High Court of illegally accepting foreign funds.

Like political violence, the organized secrecy over money irreversibly distorts the spirit and institutions of electoral democracy. The misallocation of resources that results from poorly regulated campaign spending ensures that elections and governments are captured by special interests. There's no way of knowing at whose behest policy decisions are made. This makes a mockery of the principle of 'one person, one vote'. Chremacracy cheats those millions of Indian voters who look upon elections as a chance to get even. Just as the poor and downtrodden of medieval Europe annually enjoyed religious carnivals when they were allowed to mock the powerful, fling flour and dirt at their masters, and generally turn the established world of morality upside down, many Indians think of voting as a synonym for dignity, a chance to get equal with their superiors. That's a key reason why women's participation in voting has increased at a much faster pace than men's during the past 60 years, why the poor vote more than the rich, and why voter turnout levels are highest at the local level.[10] But, when money buys elections, citizens' belief in the levelling effect of elections is eroded. They are confronted by the fact of growing political inequality—the realization that one-person, one-vote actually means things are decided by the rich.[11] Without adequate transparency and regulations, not only do voters have less say on policy matters than big contributors. They are left in the dark. They have no easy way of knowing why a policy is being framed in a particular way, with a particular set of beneficiaries. If an important general principle of democracy is the public allocation of resources through popular choice, a transparent and equitable system of campaign finance must be at the core of the exercise to translate people's will into executive action. A severely damaged electoral finance regime distorts and defeats the very purpose of elections. Democracy is the public ownership of the means of deciding who governs. Chremacracy turns public goods into private privileges. It helps kill democracy.

The grip of private money on electoral politics is detrimental to the quality of representation, as it skews the field of available choices. A system of free choice is gamed into one of prompted selection. Studying the data on nearly 22,000 parliamentary candidates for the three general elections of 2004, 2009, and 2014, political scientist Neelanjan Sircar finds wealthier competitive candidates are more likely to win (a competitive candidate is one who has a serious chance of winning). This creates strong incentives for parties to pick wealthy candidates over more talented but less-resourced aspirants. His study finds that competitive parties select candidates who are about twenty times wealthier than other candidates, and that wealthier candidates are about 10 percentage points more likely to win.[12] Another study of candidates in these three national elections shows the poorest

20 per cent of the candidates measured in terms of personal financial assets only had a 1 per cent chance of winning, while the richest quintile had a 23 per cent likelihood of winning.[13]

For reasons peculiar to the Indian context, chremacracy favours moneyed politicians, or candidates who possess greater *personal* resources, not just access to greater resources. This distinction is important because of the corrupting impact of a candidate's personal wealth on free choice and public policy. In democracies such as Canada, outside funding by individual sources or party volunteers is strictly capped (no individual or organization can contribute more than CA$1,625; no candidate running for office can contribute more than CA$5,000 to their own campaign). Forced to look for diverse sources of funding, candidates have to work with various interest groups, which in turn expands their support base, compels them to craft policies for a wider set of beneficiaries, increases the democratic accountability of candidates, and reduces the incentive for corrupt fundraising. In these regulated circumstances, self-funded candidates in fact tend to fare poorly because acting alone, or with a handful of donors, reflects a smaller support base.

In India, it is the opposite. As active party membership shrinks, the frequency and intensity of elections grows and campaigns become slicker, and elections become ever more expensive. The base of dedicated cadres (who these days expect to be paid rather than to contribute financially to the party) shrinks. The lack of internal party democracy reduces most parties to fiefs of dynasts (22 per cent of MPs elected in 2014 hailed from political families) and political bosses. They are the ones who take the final decision on who stands as a candidate. Their decision can be made just weeks before an election takes place, thus leaving a candidate no time to raise funds. Self-funded candidates who don't add to the party's financial strains, and who can begin campaigning early with their own money, and even help the party with cash to support other candidates, naturally stand a much better chance of winning party tickets and the election. The consequence: not only is the quality of representation impoverished by rich candidates with their own axes to grind and seeds to sow, but public office is privatized. It becomes the site of doing business, forging criminal connections and recouping personal investments with interest, rather than a process of publicly addressing and mediating the competing concerns and diverse interests of voters.

Neither a billionaire nor a criminal, neither dynast nor moneyed celebrity with instant brand recall, Tamanna Simhadri never really stood a chance in her joust with the rich crown prince Lokesh. The dice was loaded too heavily against her. The die was cast long before voting began. When the election results were finally declared, she found out that just a few hundred votes had come her way. But Lokesh didn't win either. It was the turn of another young dynast, Y.S. Jaganmohan Reddy, who had floated a party named after his late father, a popular chief minister who died in a helicopter crash. The new party swept the elections in the state and his candidate in Mangalagiri was re-elected. Jagan, as he is popularly known, with declared assets of Rs 375 crore ($30 million) and thirty-one criminal cases to his name, took over as the new chief minister, ending the reign of Lokesh's father. Yet another election, yet another triumph of money and muscle.

Elective Despotism

Resort Politics and Turncoats

The people's will must be protected, said the tallish man with greying temples, as he tried to push his way through the hotel entrance. He had only come to save India's democracy, he pleaded. As journalists jostled for his soundbites and party workers pushed against the police cordon, Mumbai's five-star Renaissance Hotel that turbulent July day in peak monsoon turned into an unlikely battle ground for the will of the people—of the neighbouring state of Karnataka.

At the centre of the fracas stood a dubious custodian of popular will, Doddalahalli Kempegowda Shivakumar. Popularly known as DKS, he'd yet again embarked on a mission to 'save' the Congress. On the morning of 10 July 2019, when DKS flew into Mumbai from Karnataka's capital Bangalore and was driven straight to the Renaissance, the fate of the ruling coalition government of his Congress party and regional ally Janata Dal (Secular) back home in Karnataka hung in the balance. A dozen of its lawmakers had earlier resigned and fled to Mumbai. Their defection threatened the coalition's slender majority in the state Assembly. Ten of them were lodged at the Renaissance. With the BJP determined to bring down the Karnataka government and form its own, the heavy-set man in a white shirt standing in front of the Renaissance Hotel was the only force standing in their way.

DKS has a reputation as a specialist in 'resort politics'. For the uninitiated, this is the Indian ritual of herding away lawmakers like rustled sheep to secure places, usually hotels and holiday resorts, to

'protect' them from rival parties. This usually occurs when no one
party or alliance of multiple parties has a clear majority in the legislature. At such moments, lawmakers are bought for billions of rupees
and promises of high office by the highest bidder. Their parties take
extraordinary steps to keep their flock together, such as taking away
their mobile phones and subjecting them to round-the-clock surveillance, lest they succumb to temptation. Robbing agency of people
who are in the business of representing people isn't easy. It takes a
certain skill, a delicate balance of coercion and persuasion, blackmail
and inducements.

DKS is among the most skilled practitioners of this very Indian
game of thrones. Several times in the past, he had displayed his skills
by herding party legislators away from the evil eye of the enemies.
Whip in hand, he proved himself to be a master shepherd in a political
system that has reduced many elected representatives to mere sheep,
parties to wolves, and voters to fodder. If electoral democracy is dis-
figured by criminality, organized violence, and chremacracy, 'resort
politics' marks the final stage of its decadence. As parties and legislatures kowtow to political bosses and executive supremacy, the drift
towards what Thomas Jefferson first called 'elective despotism'—
elected governments that concentrate power in a few cunning and
bossy hands—is unmistakable.[1] Resort politics is the death stage of
democracy in representative form (Figure 27).

DKS's consummate theatrics in Mumbai didn't work this time. The
BJP, amidst high drama, managed in the end to form a government in
Karnataka after the ruling coalition crumbled without the numbers it
needed to survive. In all, seventeen legislators switched sides. As party-
hopping is not permitted by law, they were forced to give up their seats,
which necessitated a by-election. Twelve of them were victorious, only
this time as BJP candidates. The ideological fluidity that allows such
craven opportunism is striking. It has few parallels in other so-called
democracies, and it is bound up with a number of factors, including the
long-standing lack of distinguishable ideology in electoral politics, the
hollowing out of political parties, and the tightening grip of dark money.

Figure 27. DKS (in all-white, fifth from the left) keeps a close watch on his flock in a resort near Bangalore

For all the political parties India has—about 2,300 at last count—there's very little to tell most apart. Even the BJP has traditionally campaigned mainly on bread-and-butter issues, in much the same way as other parties (Modi's development-centric campaign in 2014 is a case in point). And the communists, supposedly at the other end of the ideological spectrum, lost power in Bengal after thirty-four years when voters turned on them for rushing to grant cultivable land to the country's biggest capitalists at the cost of farmers. With the exception of the BJP, which subsequently pushed its Hindu-first policy with vigour, most major political parties—seven 'recognized' national and fifty-nine state parties—could all be roughly called centrist, with no major distinct differences.

Apart from their leaders, that is. Indian parties are by and large oligarchic, run top-down and woven around a public personality. The party leadership, which the Indian media often calls the 'high command', is typically a group of people close to the main leader, who in turn is referred to as the 'supremo'. The 'high command' takes all major decisions. The concentration of power is symptomatic of the fact that Indian parties don't practise internal democracy. While they operate as the vote-harvesting machines of the world's biggest elections, they don't themselves hold elections to choose their leaders, an anomaly in the democratic world. Indira Gandhi suspended party elections in 1972, setting a precedent that other parties were only too happy to follow. As a result, with the exception of Left parties, dynasticism is rife across party lines. The Gandhis of the Congress—from Jawaharlal Nehru and his daughter Indira Gandhi to her son Rajiv, followed by his wife Sonia and children Rahul and Priyanka at present—are only the best known dynasts. There are many others. Almost all regional parties are cultish and dynastic. In 2014, as we've seen already, a fifth of the directly elected parliamentarians sitting in the Lok Sabha, or the directly elected Lower House, were from political families. That increased to nearly a third in the 2019 elections. The BJP, which likes to ridicule the Congress's dynasticism, is itself not much better. While 31 per cent of the Congress candidates in the 2019 national elections belonged to political families, 22 per cent of BJP candidates were dynasts.[2] Some 24 per cent of Modi's cabinet in his first term were dynasts, compared to 36 per cent in his predecessor Manmohan Singh's Congress-led coalition ministry.

In recent decades, as parties have become ever more functionally dependent on the wealthy, dynasts have been joined by criminal leaders, who raise funds to help meet the constantly rising costs of elections and tap into state-party patronage to boost their personal wealth. DKS is an example. He rose from a humble farming family to become one of the richest ministers in the country, with declared assets of 8.4 trillion rupees ($115 million), profiting handsomely from real estate. His rise to prosperity coincided with Bangalore's transformation into a heaving global metropolis from a laidback Indian town in the early 1980s. Holding key ministries, such as urban development, gave him a ringside view of policymaking and powered his rise as a poligarch. Many of Karnataka's top politicians have similarly made billions, mainly from land, education, or mining, with their money and political careers mutually reinforcing each other, often at the intersection of state policy and private business. As the quest for public office has turned into an exercise of profit maximization, party loyalties have become secondary, even inconsequential.

Little wonder that 'party-hopping' is rampant. It is not entirely a new phenomenon. As the Congress began to weaken during the 1960s and new parties appeared, floor crossings became commonplace, destabilizing several elected state governments and two federal governments. One legendary turncoat, Gaya Lal in Haryana, who switched parties thrice in a fortnight in 1967, even inspired the Hindi epithet of '*Aya Ram, Gaya Ram*' (Ram has come, Ram has gone). Things got so out of hand that in 1985, the then prime minister, Rajiv Gandhi, introduced an anti-defection law stipulating disqualification for lawmakers who didn't vote in line with party directives and whips. Under this law, members are disqualified and lose their seat in the House if they defy the party whip, unless two-thirds of party lawmakers defect or rebel against the whip. The law did bring stability, but it has had an adverse effect on the quality of representation, with far-reaching consequences for executive–legislature relations. Parties now issue whips on every single vote in state legislatures and Parliament, in the process denying elected representatives their own voice, and the right to dissent from the party line. The result: lawmakers cannot question their own parties even if a party decision goes against the interest of their constituencies.

Temples of Democracy

Let that sink in: the Parliament, the highest embodiment of people's will, the living link between citizens and their government, disallows people's representatives to exercise their will freely. The lack of representative democracy in the hallowed halls of what Modi describes as the 'temple of democracy' is telling. Society's priorities are secondary to those of the parties, which are controlled by a handful of individuals, who are in turn beholden to anonymous financiers. As three-time Congress MP Shashi Tharoor puts it, the anti-defection law has reduced 'each MP to a cipher during every vote, a number to be totted up by his party whip rather than an individual of ability, conviction and conscience'. It is a travesty of the parliamentary process, believes Tharoor, reducing Parliament to a place to 'ratify decisions made elsewhere in party cabals or cabinet meetings'.[3]

In the classical literature on democracy, political parties have been described as oligarchies run by a handful of generals who monopolize strategy, raise funds, and issue commands to their foot soldiers on the battlefield of elections.[4] The description of the trend towards oligarchy has come to apply with a vengeance to India, even to a traditionally 'cadre-based party' such as the BJP. It is now essentially run by two men—Modi, and his confidante and powerful home minister, Amit Shah. In the cabinet structure of collective decision-making that India borrowed from the British parliamentary system, the prime minister is technically first among equals, with rights equal to other ministers. But in reality, every minister today owes his or her position in the government personally to Modi, and all their initiatives are either Modi's own, or cleared by him. Nobody in the cabinet would dare talk back to Modi, or voice an opinion he would not like to hear. Collective responsibility has morphed into 'collective resonating'.[5] All leadership positions in the party, down to the state level, are filled by people who have the blessings of Modi and Shah. China's all-powerful President Xi Jinping might still have rivals in his party—Modi has none in his.

Modi is part of an old pattern. Past prime ministers with absolute majorities in the House, such as Nehru, Indira and Rajiv Gandhi, enjoyed an equally unfettered grip on both government and party and, by extension, the Parliament. Numerical majority allowed them legislative dominance. The upshot is that the principle of the separation of governing powers is destroyed. If the party and the legislature are meant to be a check on the powers of the executive, then things don't work in this way. There's nothing to inhibit an electorally successful leader with a mass appeal, be it a Modi or powerful state leaders of regional parties, from seizing absolute domination over their executive, their party, and the legislature. The result: elective despotism.

The limited number of sitting days of legislatures offers a glimpse of their subordination. The legislature, which is expected to hold government to account, doesn't even decide its own dates of sitting. Since it is in the interest of the governing executive to allow less time for scrutiny of its legislation, the number of sitting days has sharply dropped over the decades. In Uttar Pradesh, for example, the Assembly met for an average of eighty-three days a year in the 1950s. That is now down to twenty-four days. Other state legislatures don't do much better, averaging about twenty-six days. Some are particularly bad, like Haryana, which averages just twelve days. And even when the House convenes, much of the time is wasted in disruptions and protests, which attract more media coverage than the boring work of lawmaking, and are hence preferred by politicians. Behind this charade of democratic dissent and protest, the legislatures in effect rubber-stamp executive decisions. They become rump parliaments. Bills are passed with little or no scrutiny. Most of them are introduced on the last day of the session, saving the members the trouble of studying and debating them. In 2014, the Haryana Assembly introduced and passed 129 bills on the same day.[6]

The national Parliament, too, sits a lot less these days. Till 1974, the number of sittings never dropped below a hundred days a year. Since 1989, it has never passed a hundred, averaging sixty to seventy. Even on the days the House sits, the level of participation and deliberation is alarmingly low. Unless the subject of legislation is contentious, with the possibility of grandstanding and telegenic disruptions, most of the business is conducted in virtually empty chambers with a scattering of disinterested MPs. Legislation and budget allocations are hardly examined, or debated. India's elective despotism makes a mockery of the principle that democracy is about preventing elite capture of the allocation of public resources, with elected representatives monitoring and determining who gets how much, when, and how. In most years, less than 10 per cent of the budgetary provisions are discussed. A global index of budget transparency gives India a score of 48 out of 100, right behind Afghanistan and Ecuador, which scored 49.[7]

European scholars rue that democracies are often snail-paced in their handling of large and small political matters, but in India it's exactly the opposite.[8] On just one day in 2018 (13 March), the Lok Sabha passed funding demands from ninety-nine ministries and government departments, along with two bills containing 218 amendments—all in thirty minutes and without any debate. The entire annual budgetary plan for a country of 1.3 billion people passed in half an hour. The House Speaker used a special parliamentary procedure called the 'guillotine', which enables the Speaker, backed by the brute majority of the ruling party, to railroad financial grants and proposals worth Rs 26 lakh crore ($375 billion). Most budgetary provisions that people think are examined and debated in the House are actually passed every year using the 'guillotine' method. Some years, *all* funding bills are passed in this way without debate, along with important non-financial regulations (Figure 28). The two government bills that were passed that day included the crucial 'Finance

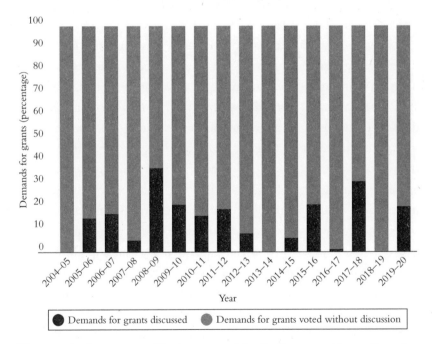

Figure 28. Percentage of budgets passed by Parliament without discussion, 2004–20

Bill' with the 218 taxation law amendments. Tucked away on page 90 of the 92-page Bill was an amendment allowing political parties to escape scrutiny on foreign funding.

On the last day of 2008, eight bills were passed in the Lok Sabha in seventeen minutes, without any discussion. That year, the Parliament had met for just forty-six days, the lowest ever. After a similar spate of bills in 2019, an exasperated opposition MP from Bengal, Derek O'Brien, tweeted: 'Are we delivering pizzas or passing legislation?' A valid question, but it's doubtful that more time would necessarily lead to greater scrutiny. MPs show increasingly less ability or inclination to engage with the business of the House. O'Brien's own party colleague from the TMC, Deepak Adhikari, popularly known as Dev, a Bengali film star, spoke all of 190 seconds in the five years of the sixteenth Lok Sabha (2014–19). It didn't matter. He was re-elected in 2019.

House Never Wins

In the Westminster model of parliamentary government favoured by the founding leaders, non-partisan cabinet subcommittees and parliamentary committees were afforded an important role in scrutinizing legislation to promote good government. These mechanisms are seldom used in state legislatures, and they've been losing their importance in Parliament in recent years. On paper, these committees allow member MPs from all parties the scope to study bills more closely, so enabling better-crafted legislation. But the declining quality of MPs means there's little appetite for this important process of parliamentary oversight. Nearly 40 per cent of MPs didn't bother attending even a single meeting of the two dozen parliamentary standing committees constituted to study the allocations made in the 2020 federal budget.

The parliamentary committees also lack teeth. Their recommendations are neither discussed in the House nor are they binding on the government. Their reports can be of great value, if the government doesn't block them. But they often do, if the findings cut too close to the bone. Using its majority in the standing committee on finance, the BJP government put on hold an adverse committee report on Modi's shock move to withdraw high-denomination banknotes from circulation in 2016, a decision that badly damaged the economy. The previous Congress-led government had similarly thwarted a critical report on the allocation of telecom licences that a committee headed by a BJP leader had been preparing. Intelligence agencies are also beyond the purview of parliamentary oversight. Restrictions on these kinds of key oversight mechanisms make democracy failures—unwise decisions, serious policy mistakes, corruption caused by accountability deficits—much more probable.[9] Matters are worsened by the fact that it's usually up to the government to decide which bills it will allow the committees to look into. In Modi's first term (2014–19), only 25 per cent of the bills were referred to parliamentary committees, down from 71 per cent in the Congress-led alliance government before it. In the first parliamentary session after his resounding 2019 re-election, the Modi government introduced and passed twenty-eight bills in thirty-seven days, without referring even one to a parliamentary committee. The government and a section of the media projected this as a 'productive' session. The legislature's loss was the executive's gain.

House rules and conventions provide various other means of strengthening elective despotism by allowing the government to sneak through legislation without deliberation. One popular channel is the use of 'money bills', which can be enacted into law through a majority in the directly elected Lower House, without any need for approval by the Upper House comprising members elected by state legislatures. A government that has a majority in the directly elected Lower House and is desperate to push through a certain piece of legislation, even if it has very little to do with taxation or borrowings or other matters financial, can simply frame it as a money bill. It can thus eliminate any vetting role for the Upper House altogether, defeating the whole purpose of having a second chamber as a check on the legislative power of the Lower House. And who decides if it ought to be a money bill or not? The Speaker, who hails from the ruling party.

Even in ordinary bills, the executive has ample room to subvert parliamentary scrutiny through a channel known as 'subordinate legislation'—a process by which the complex task of framing the detailed provisions of a law is delegated to the government. These provisions, which are the nuts and bolts of a law, are rarely ever discussed in the House. The government can also choose to bypass the route of bills altogether and simply push through a measure in the form of an ordinance. Other House rules similarly feed elective despotism. Any government, for example, can sign or ratify international treaties without approval from Parliament, unless it requires a new law to be enacted. Technically, any MP can introduce a bill, but seldom do bills introduced by 'private members', or members who are not ministers in the federal cabinet, ever become laws.

Given the raft of established House rules that so heavily tilt the balance in favour of the executive, it shouldn't come as a surprise that a government with sufficient numbers in both Houses, or at least the Lower House, treats itself as beyond democratic scrutiny. Modi's government, for example, blocked any examination by a parliamentary panel of either the handling of the coronavirus crisis or a freshly constituted prime ministerial relief fund, named 'PM CARES', which raised more than $1 billion through corporate and public donations to tackle the pestilence. PM CARES was thus shrouded in mystery, as the government refused to divulge any information on the donors, or how the money was being spent.

When the Parliament met for its 'Monsoon Session' in September 2020, under the shadow of the pestilence, the government decided to do away with the 'Question Hour', which allows members to demand answers from the government. Neither the lockdown-induced economic crash nor the ongoing border tussle with China, the two most important issues at the time, were debated. A controversial piece of legislation on the sale, pricing, and storage of agricultural products was railroaded. In the Upper House, where the ruling BJP did not have a majority, the government refused to put the three major agricultural bills to vote. Instead, it was passed by a dubious 'voice vote', sparking protests by the opposition in the House—the rumblings of discontent that triggered an unprecedented farmers' movement. The government hit back by suspending eight opposition MPs for unruly behaviour. When the opposition boycotted the House in protest, the government made full use of the empty House to pass unchallenged fifteen bills in just two days.

The next sitting of the House, the winter session, was inexplicably cancelled by the government altogether citing the pestilence even though daily life had returned to normal by then. Having thus shut down the Parliament, Modi held a gala ground-breaking ceremony for a new Parliament building—without a debate or the consent of other parties, who found the project wasteful, unnecessary and secretive. India's House didn't even get to deliberate on whether it needs a new building.

The Steel Frame

The growing stranglehold of the executive branch of government over the legislature in India is a particularly virulent version of what's happening in many other so-called democracies.[10] In essence, law-making in India is now the monopoly of the top executive. It is blessed with unreviewable powers. Responsibility to the electorate is secondary. Governments cease to be answerable to Parliament. Governments suppress information or inquiries that are to their disadvantage. They block threatening inquiries. They disapprove of independent committee hearings on their bills. They have no taste for legislative scrutiny that might result in better policy solutions. Conciliation ceases to be a word in their vocabulary; the readiness to compromise, the willingness to concede something to opponents who hold opposite views, is anathema. Under conditions of elective despotism, government patronage flourishes, on a scale that would have made monarchs of yesteryear blush. Parliaments lose their powers to scrutinize and assert proper control over government's military and foreign policy initiatives.

Treaties can be signed and ratified without consultation with Parliament. The upshot is that the legislature no longer publicly monitors the executive and the laws it makes. A strongly willed government gets away with many things, no matter what individual members of Parliament think, or want, or say.

The trend towards elective despotism is strengthened by executive control of investigative and regulatory agencies. Weaponizing taxmen against political rivals has been an old ploy. The use of bodies such as the Enforcement Directorate (ED), which specializes in tracking down economic crimes, is a relatively new addition to the government's arsenal. DKS himself was among its most recent victims. His attempts to stall a BJP government were avenged in a couple of months when he was thrown behind bars for nearly two months on charges of tax evasion and money laundering. Where the needle went the thread followed. For the federal government—of any party—there is the Central Bureau of Investigation, the country's apex investigative agency, and traditionally the weapon of choice for dealing with pesky opponents. As the rising cost of politicking entrenches dodgy deals and other forms of corruption, the ED's domain knowledge on the shadowy webs of national and international finance through which dark money travels in a globalized world makes the CBI far more potent than before. The duo is used to great effect in taming the government's enemies.

In the past few years, several regional and national opposition leaders have been picked up by the CBI, sometimes spending months, even years, in confinement, without any proven charges. So obviously partisan have the raids become that some opposition-ruled states have withdrawn the automatic permission granted to the CBI in conducting investigations in their jurisdiction, making it mandatory for the agency to first obtain the state government's permission. These raids and incarcerations by federal agencies are meant to punish, intimidate, and coerce. For the party in power in Delhi, it is important leverage in fending off foes, or even turning them into friends. In Maharashtra, Raj Thackeray, a far-right populist leader who once led violent campaigns against immigrants coming to Mumbai from poorer states like Bihar and Uttar Pradesh, made waves when he started weaving PowerPoint presentations and videos into his campaign speeches against the BJP in the run-up to the parliamentary election in 2019. A few months later, when it was time for state elections, the ED paid him a visit. They interrogated him for more than nine hours. Thackeray fell uncharacteristically quiet thereafter, fielded a handful of candidates, and hardly campaigned. Then, a few months later, he suddenly re-emerged in a new avatar—this time as a supporter of the BJP's contentious citizen verification project.

The raids and shakedowns by federal agencies such as the CBI and ED are widely reported. By contrast, the activities of organizations such as the Crime Investigation Department (CID) and Economic Offences Wing (EOW) that states have at their disposal are quietly weaponized by state governments. Relics of a colonial state that endowed government with unlimited powers to suppress dissent, organizations like the CID continue to be crucial tools of executive control. Maintenance of 'public order' and keeping an eye on 'subversive elements' are considered legitimate functions of the police and the CID. A power-hungry state government with little regard for democratic norms can easily tailor these definitions to its convenience, against opponents. The CID even provides informal election forecasts to state governments.

The political subservience of organizations like the CBI and the ED, or the CID and the EOW, are symptoms of a much larger structural vulnerability of India's bureaucracies and their potential to arm the executive with unlimited powers. Since the 'executive' can really mean just a small cabal, or even just one leader, the systemic risks of elective despotism are fairly high when parties and legislatures are tamed. The complicity of bureaucracies in the drift towards elective despotism holds for both the federal and state governments. It's worth noting that in India, as elsewhere, the bureaucracy, an unelected arm of government comprising civil servants, was designed as an institution that would be immune to the exigencies of the elected executive.

According to European scholars such as Max Weber, unelected government officials ought to be placed under the supervision of elected representatives. Bureaucratic experts were meant to be on tap, not on top. Ministerial responsibility was the phrase often used to describe this relationship of mutual interdependence and subordination of bureaucrats to elected executives. India's founding leaders differed: they accorded bureaucracy a much higher status that supposed it should be almost a parallel source of power. In the shape of the Indian Administrative Service (IAS), the top-level bureaucracy was meant to be an independent and apolitical 'steel frame', in the words of Vallabhbhai Patel, the first deputy prime minister.

The unelected bureaucracy was to be the protector of elected government. The idea was to have state machinery that ensured administrative memory and continuity amidst the flux of political executives, an intelligent bureaucracy that would be a bastion of the best and the brightest talent, capable of keeping elected governments in check and ensuring they governed wisely. The fresh wounds and mayhem of Partition and a young and extremely diverse nation being woven together were seen to necessitate a unified civil service drawn from an enlightened, young cadre free from sectarian baggage and schooled in the task of nation-building. In this conception, the executive was broadly responsible for framing policies while the bureaucracy's job was to provide advice and to implement those policies, assisted by some of the country's sharpest brains. The principled vision had practical effects: district magistrates and police superintendents came to wield enormous power. Further up the chain of command, ministerial secretaries can be at least as powerful as the ministers themselves, especially when governments are led by politically powerful executives, with strong leaders like Modi, or figures like Banerjee at the state level. Since policies are framed at the top, these leaders find it easier to deal directly with the bureaucrat, rather than the minister, who often has little or no domain knowledge. India's corridors of power buzz with stories of powerful bureaucrats patronized by their leaders.

With the quality of elected representatives in precipitous decline, a meritocratic and professional civil service can seem to be the best guarantor of administrative efficiency, especially in a country where public trust in politicians is so low. But ever since Independence, concerns have been mounting about the dangers of elitism and lack of accountability lurking within the theory and practice of a powerful centralized bureaucracy in which local representatives can have little say over bureaucrats. As the Congress began to lose its way and fall apart, and new political forces came on the scene, political partisanship began to creep into the civil services as well. Public service bureaucracies in India, as in many other so-called constitutional democracies, found themselves subject to intense pressures to become unaccountably partisan in the permanent campaigns waged by governments of the day.[11] Indira Gandhi even floated the concept of a 'committed bureaucracy' to institutionalize partisan loyalty. En masse transfers of bureaucrats with every change of government in Delhi and states are routine, so undermining the stated purpose of a permanent executive of neutral civil servants. Take H.D. Revanna, a minister and brother of the Karnataka Chief Minister H.D. Kumaraswamy, whose government DKS was trying to save. He earned the moniker of 'super CM' for engineering transfers of 700 civil service officials in twenty-four hours after his brother became the chief minister.[12]

As the elected executive has grown less and less bound to democratic values and institutional obligations, the unelected executive too has split more and more along partisan lines. Bureaucrats find it profitable to align with politicians who reward them for their loyalty. Given the say ministers have in confidential reports that determine a bureaucrat's career path, it pays to stay on the right side of power. The price of perceived animosity, or even unbending professionalism, can lead to unimportant postings, or punishment transfers. Take Ashok Khemka, a Haryana bureaucrat who (in November 2019) was transferred for the fifty-third time in his career. 'Transferred again. Back to square one . . . Reward of honesty is humiliation', he tweeted soon after.

Khemka shot to the limelight in 2012, when he cancelled a land deal that involved the firm of Congress president Sonia Gandhi's son-in-law. Naturally, he faced the ire of the Congress, which at the time was in power in both Delhi and the state. But Khemka was treated no better when the BJP came to power next. He was transferred from the science and technology department to the archaeology department in Haryana, a low-profile and low-impact posting. Still, Khemka is only the second-most transferred bureaucrat in Haryana. Pardeep Kasni, who was transferred seventy-one times in his thirty-five years of service, holds the unenviable record of most transfers. At the time of Kasni's retirement in 2018, he was posted to a department, Haryana State Land Use Board, that had actually ceased to exist in 2008. Parked in a non-existent job, he was essentially being paid not to get in the way. That's what elected despots do to sticklers for expertise and rules.

Private Militia

Ancient Hindu texts prescribe four *upaya* (techniques) for conflict resolution in politics, society, and interpersonal and international relations. These are *saama* (conciliation), *dana* (placating with gifts and bribes), *danda* (punishment using force to crush the enemy), and *bheda* (dividing and sowing dissension among the opposition). They are to be used individually or in a combination of measured doses, depending on the exigencies of a particular situation. For the state, *danda* is particularly effective in dealing with powerful foes and recalcitrant citizens who may not respond to the first two, or respond better if there's an implicit possibility of the fourth. The police, which wields the stick (whose Hindi word also happens to be *danda*) of state power internally, is hence a particularly effective tool of control. Unsurprisingly, among the arms of government, the police are the most prone to executive control.

As crime and high politics have come to be intertwined, the careers of hired muscle rise and fall with parties and politicians. The knot has tightened as ever more criminals enter politics directly and parties become increasingly dependent on their illicit money. Police are key not only to keeping allies and party men in play and ensuring money flows into politics. They are also vital for keeping the opposition in check, especially because police also control investigative agencies like the CID. So important is the police force for top leaders that most chief ministers prefer to handle the home ministry (under which police falls) themselves, rather than delegate it to others. It's the next best thing to having a private militia. India's policing laws, after all, stem from the nineteenth-century needs of the British gendarmerie to subjugate rather than to serve the population. Top police postings are accordingly highly coveted. They open the doors to extraordinary power and riches, not to mention direct access to elected despots.

Within months of a new BJP government taking over after DKS's failed bid and the collapse of his coalition government in Karnataka, leaked audio tapes surfaced in which a senior police officer was heard lobbying a political fixer for the top police job in the state. As soon as the BJP took charge, it transferred the incumbent police commissioner, Alok Kumar, then just forty-seven days into the job. Kumar's own appointment as police commissioner by the previous government had triggered loud complaints about his inexperience (he was the most junior-ranked candidate), his method of appointment (in a midnight shuffle), and questionable integrity (he had been facing suspension after being named in a dodgy lottery sale case).

The material rewards for police commissioners contrast with the poor salaries and working conditions of rank-and-file police. India has 151 police personnel per 100,000 people, a quarter of the number of private security employees and two-thirds of the United Nations' recommendation of 222. It's even worse in some states, like Bihar (seventy-five per 100,000) and Uttar Pradesh (ninety). Yet more than a fifth of the positions nationwide are unfilled. Uttar Pradesh alone had about 130,000 unfilled police positions as of 2019, 30 per cent short of its sanctioned strength. Bihar was short by 40 per cent and West Bengal, 35 per cent. Working conditions are usually horrendous. Nearly half the police officers in a recent study were found to be working more than twelve-hour days. Only one state, Maharashtra, gave all personnel at least one weekly day off. A fifth of the police stations didn't have toilets. According to a separate government study, more than 70 per cent of police personnel don't get government housing, while 75 per cent of those who do are dissatisfied by the tiny, dismal, and dilapidated police quarters.[13]

Understaffed, underpaid, and under-equipped, cops make easy pickings for political manipulation, not just at the top but throughout the chain of command, all the way to the bottom. Corruption is built into the system to keep cops in line. Bribery and protection rackets come with the territory, with the money collected at the lowest levels travelling all the way up the chain. 'Auctions' for lucrative postings in areas with greater scope for bribes are not uncommon. Apart from material benefits in a poorly paid job, political patronage offers physical security (from the far better equipped goons backed by politicians), rigged appointments, favouritism, and professional advancement. Not falling in line can mean hazardous transfers and other forms of departmental punishments. That's why police transfers jump markedly in election years. A quarter of the transfers take place well under two years, the supposedly fixed tenure period recommended to minimize political interference. In 2006, the Supreme Court ordered states to implement seven reform measures to eliminate political interference with the police, including a minimum tenure for heads of police. To date, no state has fully implemented the directives.[14]

Monopoly control of a system of sanctioned violence is too much to give up for elected despots. They presume that, ultimately, political power grows from the barrels of guns.

Justice Defiled

'No proof, no witness. How could anyone believe such a thing? They had to kill somebody. So they killed somebody.'

Jayamma's face steeled as she defended her dead son. At a tiny hut in a desolate corner of Gudigandla village, about 180 kilometres from Hyderabad, this mother was fighting a lonely battle against state narratives and popular anger. Her 20-year-old son, Chintakunta Chennakeshavulu was among the four who were arrested and killed by police in the closing months of 2019. The four men had allegedly raped and murdered a 27-year-old veterinarian. The sensational case rocked the country.

The entire village deserted the family. Chennakesavulu brought shame to the community, they said. But Jayamma held her ground, protesting against the vigilante justice meted out to her son. 'See here, he was a kidney patient and was on medication', she said, rifling through a thick file of her son's medical records that she had just taken out of the cupboard. 'He didn't even touch alcohol and they say they drank all day in their lorry before committing the crime.'

Jayamma only had Renuka, Chennakesavulu's pregnant wife, by her side. All television channels, said Renuka, reported the police account as the absolute truth. 'They showed it all day, how can anybody *not* believe it?' He was a kind man, she insisted. He could not have committed the crime he was accused of. 'His only crime was that he was poor and had no political backing. It was easy to frame him.'

The two women fought a losing battle. The custodial killing of Chennakesavulu and his three friends was greeted by mass celebrations.

To Jayamma and Renuka, their killing was an offence. For everybody else, their life was. People distributed sweets and garlanded cops. The killings, they said, brought closure. Rape had to stop and rapists needed to be afraid. As cops became saviours, suspects became convicts, without so much as a trial. Thoughtful editorials on the dangers of summary justice notwithstanding, social media reactions and scenes of jubilance suggested most Indians were convinced that justice had been delivered (Figure 29).

A semblance of justice, however questionable, has come to be preferred to its utter absence. Inordinately slow, poorly organized, and popularly perceived to be the playground of the rich and the powerful, the criminal justice system is seen to be so broken that even the dysfunctional and corrupt police force is reckoned to have a better shot at ensuring justice than the courts. Former Supreme Court judge Madan B. Lokur, who admits the criminal justice system 'has collapsed or is definitely near collapse', believes there's 'a big question mark on the faith and public trust in the functioning and independence of the judiciary'.[1] Going by the celebrations in Hyderabad, India may be well past the 'question mark' stage. Like its democracy, public trust in the judiciary is demonstrably dying.

Figure 29. Jayamma (right) and Renuka suffered vigilante justice

Chronicle of a Death Foretold

Disha, as the media called the young vet (Indian laws forbid using rape victims' real names), had left her bike that fateful evening in November 2019 at an expressway toll booth near her home, to take a cab to her clinic. The four men, said to be lorry workers, deflated a tyre of her bike while she was away. When she returned that night to collect the bike and go home, they offered to help her. Disha called her sister to say that she was stranded and a group of strangers had offered to fix her bike, but that the men looked scary.

Her phone then went dead. When her family tried to find her but couldn't, they rushed to the nearest police station. The officers refused to file a complaint and told her mother that Disha must have eloped with her lover. They kept asking her if Disha had a boyfriend. Finally, they directed her to go to another police station, as the toll booth, they said, was not in their jurisdiction. Disha's charred body was found the next day. It had been wrapped in a blanket and doused with kerosene before it was set on fire.

The police detained the four based on CCTV footage. Protests broke out as a shocked nation digested the details of yet another gang rape. #HangRapists trended on social media. Politicians bayed for their blood in primetime news. The four accused had to be moved to a secure jail after protesters stormed a police station where they were being held. It was the 2012 Delhi bus rape all over again. During that incident, Delhi was paralysed for days as hundreds of thousands took to the streets to demand justice. The law was subsequently made stricter to protect women, but sexual assaults have since continued unabated. There is a rape every sixteen minutes in India. The actual figure is a lot higher. Government data show 99.1 per cent of sexual violence cases aren't reported.[2]

Lack of public trust in police, low conviction rates, and the fear of social stigma are among the reasons that prevent women from reporting sexual assaults. Filing the FIR (first information report, the document that determines what happens next) at an Indian police station can be challenging. As registering more cases adds to the case load and bumps up the crime rate, police are inclined to record as few cases as possible. The practice of 'burking'—which in nineteenth-century Scotland meant artfully murdering a person to make money and today means not registering a police case—is fairly common.

For complaints of sexual assaults, a male-heavy police force is an additional deterrence. Women comprise just 7 per cent of India's police personnel, and less than 1 per cent of supervisory positions.[3] For women, police premises thus feel like forbidding fortresses of male domination and gender discrimination. That's how it felt to Disha's mother and her sister that night. When they broke down at the police station, pleading the cops to help, one duty officer barked at them, telling them not to 'create a scene', and to 'go outside and cry'. None of this made for good copy when the media came down on the government after Disha's body was discovered. It didn't help that a senior minister told reporters that Disha should have called the police hotline instead of her sister. The anger on the street was palpable. *Something* had to be done to bring matters under control. 'Something more than arrest' was needed to 'calm public anger', Hyderabad's *Deccan Chronicle* offered a dark hint, reporting that 'various options and scenarios were being discussed.'[4]

It so happened that the police officer in charge of the Disha rape and murder case was also in charge of the team that in 2008 arrested and gunned down three men who had attacked women engineering students with acid in the city of Warangal, about 200 kilometres from Hyderabad. That acid attack had similarly shocked the country, and the young police officer became an instant hero when the culprits were killed after arrest, without a trial. And so, lo and behold! Within a week of the arrest of Disha's alleged murderers, police announced that the four had been killed in a dawn 'encounter'. To recreate the crime, they said, they had taken the suspects to the scene of the crime, where the four suddenly attacked them with stones and sticks. They even 'snatched' two weapons from the cops and started firing at them, 'forcing' the police team to shoot them dead. Four more names had thus been added to India's ever-lengthening list of victims of 'encounter'—an Indianism for extrajudicial killings often glorified in movies featuring honest cops fighting the 'system'. It would be a matter of shame in any functional democracy, but apart from Jayamma and Renuka and the sundry few media commentators still attached to the faintly quaint idea of 'rule of law', everybody else seemed mighty pleased.

Court Decay

Given the speed at which rape cases—or all cases, for that matter—crawl through a clogged and corrupted legal system, the chances of swift justice were non-existent. There were 127,800 rape cases pending as of the end of 2017, growing every day. Overall, nearly 38 million cases are pending in Indian courts, 3.7 million of them for more than a decade, according to the National Judicial Data Grid. A High Court judge once estimated that it would take 320 years to clear the backlog of cases.[5] If justice delayed is justice denied, that's a whole lot of injustice right there. More than 200,000 cases are more than twenty-five years old, 1,000 of which haven't been processed even after fifty years. In 2 million of the 9 million pending civil cases, even summons haven't been served.

In 2016, India's then chief justice, Tirath Singh Thakur, broke down at a public function while appealing to Modi to reform the judiciary. 'In the name of development and progress, I beseech you to rise to the occasion and realize that it's not enough to criticise [the judiciary]', he said, addressing Modi. He was cracking under pressure. Judges are so overworked that higher courts stay closed for about five months a year, so adding to the unending pipeline of cases. Many of the judges' posts remain unfilled. Judges in the busiest courts in India spend an average of 2.5 minutes to hear a case and about five minutes to decide one.[6] Between 2018 and February 2020 alone, the number of pending cases in High Courts increased 29 per cent. But it is in the lower courts that most cases are marooned. Nearly 88 per cent of the 38 million pending cases are stuck in the district and subordinate courts.

A three-year study of district courts near Bangalore shed insights into the workings of the subordinate court, the first court of appeal for most litigants. Cases in general were found to remain pending for an average of 3.5 years.[7] Antiquated processes stall cases at elementary stages, such as issuing warrants or summons. Almost 60 per cent of staff positions lie vacant. The infrastructure is poor, with not enough light, ventilation, clean water, or restroom facilities.[8]

The decaying and sluggish court system ensures that India has one of the world's highest rates of 'undertrials', or people awaiting trial and sentencing in prison. Nearly 70 per cent of Indian prisoners are undertrials, more than twice the number of convicted prisoners. This compares with 20 per cent in the United States, which has the world's highest incarceration rate. The provision of detention without trial is used wantonly, pulping the principle of presumed innocence until proven guilty. Only 45 per cent of Indian prisoners are ever convicted of their crimes. The rest spend years, even decades, in jail without conviction. There is no restitution for those wrongly detained, however long (Figure 30).

Deepak Joshi, 75, lodged in a jail in Kolkata, has been awaiting trial and conviction since his arrest in 1980 in connection with a murder case. In April 2019, Nirmalakka from Telangana was released after twelve years in jail. Police failed to prove the 157 cases it had filed against her after she was arrested in the eastern state of Chhattisgarh on the suspicion of being a Maoist rebel. In July that year, three Kashmiri citizens, Mohammad Ali, Latif Ahmed Waja, and Mirza Nisar, were released from jail after twenty-three years of wrongful imprisonment. They had been arrested for a bomb blast they had nothing to do with. Numerous other victims rot away, even die, in custody. Many of them miss hearings—and their cases drag on—often because there are not enough policemen to escort them to court.[9] In

Figure 30. Seven out of ten Indian prisoners have not been convicted

Uttar Pradesh, one correctional staff member handles nearly 100,000 prisoners.[10]

By meting out instant justice, the Hyderabad police might in fact have spared Chennakesavulu and his friends prolonged misery. Once detained on suspicion, there was no telling when they would have been convicted, if at all. And while in prison, they would have been subject to the customary custodial torture endemic in the system. In the northern state of Haryana, for example, half of the prisoners were reported to have been brutally tortured. Electric shocks, bricks hung from private parts, and sexual assaults are among the common methods.[11] India records a custodial death every six hours. In October 2020, 31-year-old convicted prisoner Asghar Ali Mansoori hanged himself at Nashik Central Prison in Maharashtra after fourteen years as an inmate. Before he killed himself, the unlettered Mansoori dictated a two-page suicide note to a cell mate detailing the torture meted out to him by five prison officials, wrapped it in plastic, and swallowed it to ensure it would be discovered during autopsy. It was, just as he had planned. But no action was ever taken against any of the prison staff he named even though other prisoners corroborated Mansoori's account of custodial torture.

The states share the blame with the federal government for the incompetence, corruption, and injustice of the law enforcement mechanisms of the police and the courts. India overall spends just 0.08 per cent of GDP on its judiciary; some states spend far less. Legal aid is a glaring lapse. Nearly 80 per cent of India's 1.3 billion people qualify for legal aid designed to bring social justice by helping the disadvantaged. But lawyers and paralegal volunteers are hard to find, and the quality of legal aid, when available, is often rotten. Other innovations to facilitate justice have had similarly limited success. The alternative preventive and remedial service of Lok Adalats that promote mutually agreed settlements at the pre-litigation stage has been around since the 1980s, but it isn't very effective.

Rule of Law

A clogged and corrupted court system hastens the breakdown of the social foundations of Indian democracy. The pain of rape victims and their families, burking, inadequate policing, custodial deaths, undertrials: these and other injustices generated by the judiciary compound the social injustices suffered by millions of citizens. It's as if the two separate spheres are working secretly in tandem, conspiring to worsen India's social emergency and bring down its democracy, to prepare it for the kill. The infirmities of the Indian judiciary violate the spirit and substance of the rule of law, the principle that legal institutions and written laws should have the practical effect of curbing and balancing the ambitions of the powerful, and those seeking power over others. According to that principle, rule of law is the cure for despotism. The system of laws imposes meaningful restraints on crooks and thugs and schemers hungry for power. No person is above the law, or escapes the hand of published and publicly available laws. The laws are clearly stated and consistent. They rule supreme and apply equally to all without exception. That's the theory. For many in India, the principles of rule of law and the practical avenue of seeking legal remedies are instead a blind alley. Impaired by poor resources, delays, and corruption, the justice system works best for the well-resourced. They are the ones who can withstand—and game—its debilitating inefficiencies and sluggishness.

For anybody with even a passing familiarity with a typical Indian court compound, the decay is self-evident. Bogus witnesses, fixers, hapless victims from the hinterlands, and rotting case files and typewriters barely hide the corruption and anachronism that bedrock the judicial system. But insiders prefer not to speak about it too much. The price for breaking the *omerta* can be steep. A High Court judge was recently stripped of his powers and later demoted after he alleged large-scale corruption in Bihar's courts. The chief minister of the northeastern state of Arunachal Pradesh, Kalikho Pul, who hanged himself in 2016, left behind a sixty-page suicide note in which he made shocking allegations of bribery against top judges, including the then chief justice of the Supreme Court and his successor. The case was neither investigated nor followed up by mainstream media. It was eventually closed unceremoniously.

Monuments to systemic exploitation, bureaucratic sloth, antiquated procedures, and corruption, India's courts are where power comes to be validated and the powerless shown their place. 'No wonder... that citizens do not feel empowered enough to insist on their rights being respected by the state. It is as if the rights we hold are no more than concessions granted by the state, rather than something that inhere in the citizens. This outcome undermines the faith people have in the rule of law', writes lawyer and writer Harish Narasappa.[12] When people in a democracy cheer Taliban-style summary killings, it is because the justice system has been undermined enough for them to have given up on it.

Narasappa is among those legal observers who argue that given the central role of the state and the enormous power and discretion state institutions enjoy in the everyday life of Indians, it is imperative that they function according to rule of law principles. The oligarchic nature of the legislature unfortunately means that new laws and policies are foisted on people in an opaque manner. They are seldom debated by people's representatives; and, on the rare occasion they are, the exchanges take the form of theatrical performances rather than reasoned debates. The legislature is supposed to enact laws, the executive implement them, and the judiciary test their constitutionality, to examine and decide whether they violate constitutional rights. With the legislature's role rapidly becoming ornamental, it's the executive, in effect, that both enacts and arranges the enforcement of laws. This puts India firmly on the road to a new kind of despotism. Citizens are stripped of their powers as voters and citizens. As subjects, they elect lawmakers but are divorced from lawmaking. The injustices of the legal system only increase this distance between people and the law.

With the legislature the playground of corrupt politicians and most of the society excluded, the burden to examine laws falls squarely on the judiciary. This sets the stage for judicial meddling with the affairs of the executive—and the backlash of the executive against the judiciary. Tensions between the judiciary and the executive have run high from the very first days of Independence, when the first Indian cabinet under Nehru pushed through the First Amendment, without waiting for scrutiny by the first elected Parliament. The First Amendment—in contrast to its American counterpart—curbed free speech and expression, put limits on the right to property and equality, and allowed exemptions to the fundamental rights prohibiting discrimination on the basis of religion, race, and caste. The reason for the hasty railroading of the amendment was the government's concern that the courts would sabotage its programme of affirmative action for lower castes and land reform initiatives, such as the seizure and redistribution of big landholders' property, that directly conflicted with some of the basic guarantees provided by the Constitution.[13]

Checks and Balances

Tensions between the executive and judiciary are to be expected and welcomed in a democracy where those who exercise power, as the famous eighteenth-century French writer Montesquieu said, can be expected to abuse it, so power must always be used to restrain and temper power.[14] The relationship between the executive and the judiciary has since those initial years of the republic, till recently, been one of an uneasy compact, in which the two kept each other at arm's length, but without giving each other too much room. That's what is stipulated by the democratic principle that nobody is above the law, that authorities must constantly be scrutinized and tested, so that in the age of monitory democracy, when democracy has come to mean much more than free and fair elections, the public monitoring and restraint of arbitrary exercises of power by bodies such as independent courts is vital for the freedom, equality, and well-being of citizens. In 1973, along these lines, in the famous Kesavananda Bharati case, also known as the Fundamental Rights Case, the Supreme Court asserted the right of the courts to strike down constitutional amendments that violated what it called the 'Basic Structure', or the fundamental architecture of the Constitution. In subsequent years, it delivered significant rulings on matters that it held pivotal to this 'Basic Structure', such as secularism and the judiciary's independence in appointing judges. The executive hit back periodically by blocking the career path of judges who issued inconvenient rulings. The intended separation and mutual contestation of powers preserving the architecture of India's brand of monitory democracy was well served and honoured. Except for times when the judiciary opted to fall tamely in line, rather than push back. These were the dark and foreboding moments that spelled long-term danger for Indian democracy.

The bleakest of them all was the famous 'ADM Jabalpur' case in 1976, when a five-member Supreme Court bench ruled that personal liberties could be suspended during the Emergency that Indira Gandhi had imposed. In a majority ruling of four to one, the judges upheld the executive's prerogative to detain people and ruled that the right to life and the remedy of moving a habeas corpus ('to produce the body') petition for release against illegal detention didn't hold during a period of emergency rule. A habeas corpus petition, a vital instrument against state coercion, allows judges to order the authorities to bring the accused before their courts to verify if they had been detained in accordance with the law. During the twenty-one-month Emergency, the ruling that liberty was not an absolute freedom, that even the right to life could be suspended in extraordinary circumstances, enabled indiscriminate arrests of Indira Gandhi's political opponents. The lone Supreme Court judge on the five-member bench who dissented against the four-to-one majority ruling was denied elevation to the position of chief justice. Sixteen judges from nine High Courts who had earlier upheld personal liberties were also sidelined.

Soon after Indira Gandhi lost the election in 1977, the opposition alliance that rose to office passed the 44th constitutional amendment. It reversed the despotism of the previous *habeas corpus* ruling by upholding that the right to life could not be suspended, not even during an Emergency. But the ghost of ADM Jabalpur was to live on, until late 2017, when a nine-judge Constitution bench finally overturned the 'seriously flawed' ruling. ADM Jabalpur, it said, was an 'aberration' that needed to be 'buried ten fathom deep with no chance of resurrection'.

Within two years, however, the old ghosts of the Emergency rule returned. *Habeas corpus* stirred back to life from 'ten fathom deep', in historian and constitutional lawyer A.G. Noorani's words, as 'habeas carcass'.[15] In August 2019, with the stroke of a pen, Modi's government revoked the autonomous status of the restive state of Jammu and Kashmir. The federal government stripped it of its statehood and split it into two federally administered units, without the consent of its elected representatives. It imposed an information blockade by shutting down telephony and the Internet, and put thousands of Kashmiris, including all its political leaders, in detention. The draconian Public Safety Act of 1978 allowing preventive detention—modelled after the colonial-era Rowlatt Act that once galvanized protests led by Mahatma

Gandhi—was back with a vengeance in independent India, used indiscriminately to imprison even young boys. Under determined government pressure, the Supreme Court simply chose to look away. In a political system already showing clear signs of a slide towards despotism, the court's inaction allowed the government to get away with a move already made by despots in Hungary, Poland, Turkey, Russia, and elsewhere: to tame the judiciary to the point where executive power guts constitutional precepts and rulings to ensure that the courts are the playthings of the reigning political powers.[16]

To the multiple habeas corpus petitions challenging preventive detentions, the Supreme Court issued 'permission' to petitioners to travel to Kashmir and meet the detainees in question, even though there have never been any legal restrictions on internal travel in India. The court even placed conditions on petitioners, instructing them to avoid any political activity while in Kashmir. The Supreme Court thus not only abdicated its duty to protect fundamental rights by asking the executive for justification of its actions in Kashmir. By seeking to enforce some of the clampdown regulations, it became an arm of the executive (Figure 31).

Figure 31. Kashmir, a testing ground for judiciary and executive collaboration

Road to Despotism

If institutional checks and balances are intended to keep the executive and the judiciary on their toes, and to prevent arbitrary exercises of power, tensions between the two should serve a democracy in good stead. With Modi's rise to power in 2014, tension turned into open war between the two wings. Within four years, the Supreme Court found itself in uncharted territory, when four of its most senior judges called a press conference and alleged government meddling with judgments. The chief justice, they felt, was not working independently and was using his privilege as the 'master of the roster' to assign important cases to specific, 'reliable' judges in a way that predetermined their outcome to the satisfaction of the government. 'The four of us are convinced that unless this institution is preserved and it maintains its equanimity, democracy will not survive in this country', Justice Jasti Chelameswar, the second-most senior judge after the chief justice, told reporters.[17] Two months later, he shocked the legal community with a letter to the chief justice, asking him to convene a full court to take up the issue of executive interference in the judiciary, warning 'bonhomie between the judiciary and the government in any State sounds the death knell to democracy.' The chief justice was a member of a team of four senior judges who comprise the all-powerful collegium that takes the most important decisions related to India's higher courts, such as promotion, appointment, and the transfer of judges. The federal government is required to act on the recommendation of the collegium.

The unusual protest by the country's most senior judges marked the apogee of a simmering turf war with the government, which had been trying to end the collegium's monopoly in judge-related matters by instituting a panel called the National Judicial Appointments Commission (NJAC) designed to give the executive a say in judges' transfers and appointments. The NJAC Act was the first piece of legislation that Modi's government steered through the Parliament after he took office in 2014. But the Supreme Court upheld the collegium system and struck down the NJAC Act, keeping the power of promotions and appointments with the judges, and maintaining the separation of powers between the judiciary and the executive.

One of Modi's senior ministers called the verdict 'the tyranny of the unelected', and the government retaliated by sitting on collegium recommendations on judges even as vacancies piled up, using its veto power, not unlike some of its predecessors in similar battles of nerves with the high priests of justice. A chief justice breaking down in public was a sign that their lordships weren't winning. By the end of his tenure in 2016, the number of vacant posts for High Court judges had risen to nearly 500, with the government declining most of the recommendations by the collegium. His successors might well have concluded that for the sake of peace and quiet it would make more sense to abide by the government's wishes.

Courts are dependent on governments both for the implementation of their orders and the resources needed for their sustenance. Especially when the courts are losing legitimacy in the eyes of citizens, governments can bring the judiciary into line using blackmail, withdrawals of favours, and threats of funding cuts. Balancing legal principles with the government's sensitivities as a way of judicial self-preservation is thus built into the system. Nobody probably understood this better than Ranjan Gogoi, one of the four protesting judges at the peak of the 2018 tussle between the executive and the judiciary. Gogoi was soon to take over as the next chief justice. By the time he finished his stint at the top of India's judicial pyramid two years later, the collegium had become far more collegial towards the government's preferences for judges in its recommendations for transfer and appointments. The executive–judiciary status quo was radically transformed. It went from one of guarded cordiality interspersed with periodic friction into a relationship of active collaboration—to the point that the two sets of institutions sometimes looked like conjoined twins, as in the established despotisms of governments led by Viktor Orbán and Vladimir Putin.

Citizenship Matters

Kashmir proved to be a testing ground for this convergence of the judiciary and the executive under the new chief justice. Gogoi himself headed the benches listening to the most high-profile habeas corpus cases, as if he was the executive. His greatest executive cameo, however, was reserved for a citizenship verification project called the National Register of Citizens (NRC) in the north-eastern state of Assam. Its purpose was to separate Indian citizens from undocumented Bengali-speaking migrants who once came from what is now Bangladesh, itself once part of Pakistan and, before that, undivided British India. All modern states lay down rules of citizenship, but the NRC used a verification process similar to Nazi Germany's Nuremberg Race Laws on citizenship that provided the legal framework for the systematic persecution of Jews leading to the Holocaust. The 'family tree' recorded in the so-called 'ancestor pass' (Ahnenpass) issued to those determined to be of 'Aryan blood' has a strong resemblance to the family tree of lineage that the people of Assam have had to prove to pass the test of Indian citizenship.

The Assam NRC was an important test case for Modi's government. It later went on to announce a nationwide NRC. To protect Hindus from the risk of failing the citizenship test, the government introduced a new law disallowing Muslim refugees from applying for citizenship. The all-India NRC plan and the citizenship law triggered an outpouring of public protests that roiled India for much of 2019.[18]

Gogoi, who is an ethnic Assamese, adopted the Assam NRC project as if it were his baby. He co-managed the verification process directly with the NRC 'state coordinator', a federally appointed bureaucrat. The final NRC list in 2019 eventually disenfranchised 1.9 million people, most of whom have never known any other place but Assam as their home. Rule of law was swept aside. The verification drive was poorly implemented, and it resulted in arbitrary detentions, suicides, and penury. It destroyed lives and families, especially among the poor, who lacked the privilege of 'documents' to establish their ancestry and the financial resources for legal recourse. But the apex court's executive control over the whole exercise meant there was no place left for the aggrieved to appeal against rights violations. They were left with no rights to rights. The Supreme Court's takeover of the NRC process 'amounted to taking a knife and slashing right through this constitutional fabric', according to constitutional scholar Gautam Bhatia, who saw in it the rise of what he calls the 'Executive Court', in which the 'Court has departed so far from the fundamental principles that it is unrecognisable as a "Court" under the classical model'.[19]

Not only were NRC orders coming from the court itself, the basis of the orders was enveloped in secrecy as well. The Supreme Court often asked for reports in 'sealed cover' from the state coordinator. The practice was not exceptional. The NRC is one of the many instances in recent years when the delivery of verdicts based on evidence in 'sealed cover'—evidence that only judges can see—has become commonplace. In the process, citizens and their representatives are robbed of the right to seek justice through the democratic scrutiny of judicial action. The use of sealed cover reinforces the trend towards arbitrary power oiled by secrecy. It is yet another way the judiciary, like the executive and the legislature, becomes an aloof, inaccessible institution wielding state power without the participation of citizens or the public accountability exercised by independent watchdog institutions.

'Sealed covers' have been effectively used to put the lid on several inconvenient cases for the government, from public interest litigations (PILs) on a controversial deal to buy French fighter jets to those challenging the government's disputed electoral bond scheme that helps flood politics with dark money. 'Sealed cover' also featured in Gogoi's best departing gift to Modi's populist government: the resolution of a decades-long dispute over a plot of land between Hindus and Muslims. The Supreme Court received in sealed cover the reports from parties to the dispute, as well as a settlement plan from the court-appointed mediation panel. The plot, in Ayodhya, Uttar Pradesh, which Hindu

activists claim to be the birthplace of the Hindu god Ram, has been a
political flashpoint for decades. The BJP supports the local Hindu
view that a sixteenth-century mosque that stood on the site was built
by the Mughals after demolishing an ancient Ram temple. The party's
rise to national prominence began with the launch of a movement to
build a temple in place of the mosque and reclaim 'lost' Hindu pride.
In 1992, a frenzied Hindu mob destroyed the mosque, triggering
nationwide riots. Gogoi worked tirelessly in his final days to resolve
the matter. In his last week in office, a bench headed by him handed
over the entire site to a Hindu trust to build a Ram temple. The ruling, in November 2019, brought down the curtains on one of the
most divisive political issues in India, but it raised serious doubts
about the independence of the court. As several former judges and
legal luminaries pointed out, the ruling curiously placed the belief
of Hindus that a temple once existed at the site above the material
proof of a mosque's actual existence for 460 years.

The judiciary's full-throated support for the temple was part of the
more general drift towards a neutered and compliant court within a
state structured by the rules of elective despotism. The five-member
Constitution bench that heard the Ayodhya case began its proceedings
(6 August 2019) just a day after the Modi government abrogated
Kashmir's special status. The Supreme Court bench heard the mosque/
temple case on a daily basis but showed no urgency to deal with the
pressing issues of fundamental rights arising out of the lockdowns and
detentions in Kashmir. The bench headed by Gogoi even told Kashmir
petitioners, including those pressing PILs seeking restoration of
Internet facilities for hospitals and release of children in detention,
that it had no time for them because it was 'too busy' hearing the
Ayodhya case. To the daughter of an imprisoned Kashmiri leader
seeking permission to meet her mother, Gogoi said: 'Why do you
want to move around? It is very cold in Srinagar.' Gogoi's cavalier
approach was more of a piece with a populist demagogue than the
chief justice of a constitutional, power-sharing monitory democracy.
When an academic applied for bail following his arrest by police in

the eastern state of Odisha, Gogoi remarked, 'If you are facing threats, there is no safer place than jail.' When a bench led by him was approached to hear a matter related to cases of lynching of Muslims by Hindu mobs, Gogoi said the issue 'does not merit urgent hearing'. This was a court, and a chief justice, as Bhatia puts it, that had 'liberated itself from that annoying little thing called the Constitution'.[20]

The haughty disdain of the chief justice for justice was on full display when handling a sexual harassment complaint directed at him. When a former junior court assistant brought charges of sexual misdemeanour against him, Gogoi convened an urgent sitting by three judges on a Saturday while the court was on vacation 'to deal with a matter of great public importance touching upon the independence of the judiciary'. He presided over the hearing, proclaimed his innocence before the judges, including himself, and claimed the accusations were part of a larger conspiracy to destabilize the judiciary. The complainant wasn't given a chance to speak before this special court. An in-house panel comprising three of his colleagues cleared him of all charges, saying it found 'no substance' to the allegations. The probe report was delivered in sealed cover, inaccessible even to the complainant.

Personal conduct aside, Gogoi's reign at the top helped normalize the replacement of rule of law by what can be called the phantom rule of law: government decision-making whose power to shape things comes wrapped in the trimmings and trappings of law but is in reality 'rule through law'. Law is weaponized as an instrument of power and control by the state, which makes itself exempt from rule-of-law rigours. Tongues wagged when one of the five senior-most judges of the Supreme Court described Modi as an 'internationally acclaimed visionary' and a 'versatile genius who thinks globally and acts locally'—at an open forum with Modi on the dais. It's difficult to recall a moment of greater obsequity by a member of the higher judiciary in the history of independent India. A newly appointed chief justice of the Patna High Court described Modi as a 'model and hero'. That many members of the judiciary decided that Modi's massive

electoral victory required a downgrading of the rule of law isn't only a
sign of the frail courage of individual judges. It is equally a symptom
of the structural weakness óf the judiciary that Supreme Court judges
in recent years increasingly refuse to cross swords with the executive.
In cases where a judgment may put them at odds with the executive's
stated position, they either delay through indefinite adjournments, or
direct petitioners back to the government, or simply accept the government's explanation as the gospel truth and then close the case.
Gogoi grasped these altering power dynamics early and well. So well
that by the time he retired in November 2019, he had grown convinced that the only way to shore up the judiciary was to have it collaborate with the executive. Within four months of retirement, he
accepted the federal government nomination to sit in the Upper
House.

Gogoi is not a freakish aberration. He's a symptom of the compliance of the judiciary with the institutional power of the executive to
get judges to fall in line. The bulk of the litigation that reaches the
Supreme Court is initiated by the government. It also happens to be
the biggest employer of retired Supreme Court judges. Little wonder
that, prior to retirement, senior judges are tempted to think about
taking up lucrative appointments in publicly influential regulatory
bodies in such areas as environment, telecoms, and human rights. For
that to happen, Supreme Court judges mustn't blot their copybooks
with the incumbent government. The data shows that even just one
ruling handed down in favour of the government significantly boosts
the chances of a lucrative post-retirement government job.[21] Other
judges have become just as excessively deferential to executive power.
When the executive fills up the prisons with dissenters on unproven
and often ridiculous charges, as the Modi government has done in
recent years, they are happy to look away. Even when the prisoners
include 80-year-old activists with serious health conditions. But when
it comes to the regime's favourites, their lordships are a picture of
concern. When Arnab Goswami, chief of a rabidly pro-BJP television
channel, was arrested in November 2020 in an opposition-ruled state

on charges of abetting a suicide, almost every minister in Modi's cabinet tweeted support for him, and the top judiciary swung into action.
A disgusted president of the bar association wrote to the secretary-
general of the Supreme Court, saying, 'it is, to say the least, deeply
disturbing as to how and why every time Mr Goswami approaches
the Supreme Court, his matter gets listed instantly.' Goswami was
bailed right away. But when Father Stan Swamy, an 83-year-old Jesuit
priest and a defender of tribal rights, arrested as an alleged Maoist terrorist, appealed for a straw and sipper as he has Parkinson's disease and
cannot steadily hold a cup, a lower court asked him to wait twenty
days for a hearing.

As head of the highest constitutional court, Gogoi's indifference to
the fundamental rights issues in Kashmir was unexceptional. His successor has shown similarly little urgency in cases involving pressing
constitutional questions such as the validity of electoral bonds or a
new law that links citizenship to religion, which goes against the grain
of India's secular Constitution. It is almost as if the top constitutional
court tries extra hard to avoid constitutional issues. The increasing
trend of admission of civil cases (through its discretionary appellate
jurisdiction) over the years has in fact 'cannibalized' the Supreme
Court's role as an effective constitutional court.[22] More than 11 per
cent of the Supreme Court's cases are disputes over such matters as
salary and transfer, while about 5 per cent are related to constitutional
matters. The Supreme Court in fact hears more cases relating to
admissions and tuition fees at private engineering and medical colleges (0.8 per cent of cases) than to constitutional cases such as habeas
corpus (0.2 per cent). And when it does hear cases of preventive
detention, it does it so slowly and allows government so much leeway
that its intervention is essentially stillborn. In the handful of habeas
corpus petitions where the Supreme Court bothered to stir and act in
the last two decades, it took on average more than two and a half years
to dispose of the case—the subject of trial remaining in detention
during the time.[23] Such judicial compromises with the executive,
accelerating in the Modi years, have a telling effect on the international

standing of India's Supreme Court. Studying judgments delivered by the apex courts of forty-three countries whose legal systems are similar to India's (in that they are influenced by the common law system and thus more likely to cite the Indian Supreme Court), lawyer Mitali Gupta finds that international citations of Indian rulings have drastically fallen since 2014 (Figure 32).

As one Indian public intellectual puts it, the Supreme Court was never perfect, but there are signs that it is slipping into a 'judicial barbarism' that sustains India's new 'democratic barbarism'. With 'creeping hues of a Weimar judiciary', the highest court has become complicit in the despotic executive's brutal imprisonment of dissenters and strangling of fundamental rights. In the process, some of the traits of the elected despots have rubbed off on the top judiciary. The courts, too, have become intolerant of criticism and mocking, 'excessively concerned with the judiciary's own version of lese majeste like a "scared monarch"'.[24] Be it a top lawyer or a comedian or a cartoonist, even a tweet with the slightest hint of reproach of their lordships is met swiftly with dire criminal contempt proceedings. There couldn't be a sign more manifest of India's passage to despotism—not to mention the trenchant irony—than the highest constitutional court of the 'world's biggest democracy' using intimidation to silence criticism.

Within days of initiation of a contempt of court proceedings against stand-up comedian Kunal Kamra for his tweets against Supreme Court

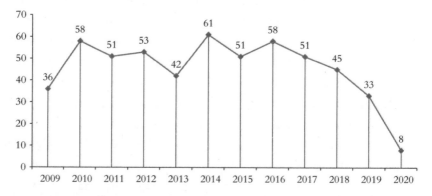

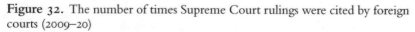

Figure 32. The number of times Supreme Court rulings were cited by foreign courts (2009–20)

judges for fast-tracking a bail hearing for pro-BJP television anchor Goswami, a parliamentary panel headed by a BJP Member of Parliament summoned Twitter's India policy head and demanded to know why the 'obscene tweet' had not been removed. The judges and the elected despots have each other's backs. The nomination of a former chief justice to the Parliament immediately after retirement is symptomatic of this despotic alliance. Gogoi's appointment understandably set off alarm bells about his past performance, but he said he was driven by 'a strong conviction' that the legislature and the judiciary must 'work together for nation-building'.[25] Gogoi the jurist was rejecting the democratic principle of an independent judiciary. Instead of defending the separation of powers, he was justifying the despotic concentration of power.

An independent judiciary wasn't the only component of monitory democracy that had come to heel. A curious 'order' that came out of the unusual weekend court hearing of sexual harassment allegations against Gogoi, by a bench presided over by Gogoi, issued a gentle warning—for the media. The judges let it be known that they expected the media to behave, 'to show restraint, act responsibly as is expected from them and accordingly decide what should or should not be published as wild and scandalous allegations undermine and irreparably damage reputation and negate independence of judiciary'. They also urged the media to 'take off such material which is undesirable'.

The most curious case of Ranjan Gogoi turned curiouser. The judiciary was now threatening the freedom of the press. Many editors got the message. Few media houses dared to follow up the case of the woman who lost her job for complaining that the chief justice had 'touched me all over' and was charged with conspiring to destroy India's judicial independence, then a few months later quietly reinstated. Like the judiciary, India's mainstream media had by now also come to make peace with the dictates of elective despotism.

Bad News

Media Conspiracies

On the mid-April day the great 2020 lockdown was scheduled to end, just before the government announced its extension by several weeks, hundreds of migrant workers desperate to return home suddenly gathered near Mumbai's Bandra station. Social media was flooded with videos of police baton-charging the milling crowds in a losing battle to enforce physical distancing. Unable to stem the swell of migrant workers, police used the loudspeaker of the nearby mosque to appeal to the crowds to return to their slum shelters. But the crowd grew bigger as more and more migrant workers joined in, hoping the government would try to find a way for them to get home if it saw a sizeable gathering. It was a desperate bid by distressed migrants, stripped of their livelihoods and cooped up in their wretched city shelters, to make a last-ditch attempt to return to their village homes and families.

But that is not how India's pro-government media reported that afternoon's news. Portraying the crowd at Bandra as an impromptu gathering of distraught workers would have been an admission of the stress caused to millions by a poorly planned nationwide lockdown announced at a notice of just four hours. It would have reflected badly on Modi. It wasn't interesting either—bedraggled men from the hinterlands never are. And it didn't fit the script—of an alarmist Islamophobic angle, the stock-in-trade of most national-level news channels ever since the BJP's rise to power.

All past pestilences witnessed scapegoating. Thousands of Jews were murdered after being accused by municipal governments, bishops, and the Holy Roman Emperor of spreading the bubonic plague in mid-fourteenth-century Europe. Jews were again targeted in the first recorded speech of Hitler, delivered in 1919 in Munich's Hofbräukeller, where they were accused of 'lust for money and domination' and spreading 'racial tuberculosis among nations'.[1] In India 2020, Muslims became the new Jews. That evening, many television channels began to spin bizarre interpretations laced with leading questions. Who instigated the crowds? Who orchestrated the protest? What was their motive? Why was it that the crowd had assembled in front of a mosque? (Because the mosque is next to the train station.) Why was the mosque public address system being used to whip up the protest? (Because the police wanted to use it and asked the imam and other community leaders to join in the appeal to workers to return to their barracks.) Arnab Goswami, the 'nationalist' anchor who HBO show host John Oliver calls 'Tucker Carlson of India', and whose periodical wrinkles with the law are unfailingly ironed out by the Supreme Court's lightning interventions, fulminated on what he called the 'Lockdown Villains'. The massing migrants, he pronounced, were in fact paid actors faking a protest as part of a larger 'conspiracy'. The top band of the news screen on another channel read: 'Conspiracy of "Corona Blast" at Bandra Station?'

The anti-Muslim rants were part of a sustained media campaign, the twin takeaways from which were unambiguous. One, Modi's handling of the coronavirus crisis was perfect. A timely, decisive lockdown was working fine, till the Muslims spoiled it all and endangered the lives of all decent Indians. Two, this was not just an unfortunate mistake. It was a concerted plot by Muslims to spread disease and disorder in India. This line of reportage had been shaped by the discovery of Covid-19 cases in a Delhi gathering of an Islamic missionary organization by the name of Tablighi Jamaat. Most of the coronavirus news in India in those early days of the pestilence became disproportionately focused on the Tablighi. More so because the government itself was interested in talking about little else, even as health journalists complained bitterly of the lack of more substantive information on the spread of the disease, preparations, testing data, and the migrant crisis.

A large chunk of mainstream media began to portray the Tablighi, a non-political organization with no history of terrorism, as a radical group plotting an attack on India. Tablighi had clearly become the country's single-biggest cluster for the disease at that point, just like the Shincheonji Church of Jesus in South Korea. Except that the mistakes of the secretive Korean church during the early phase of the pestilence didn't become an excuse for attacking Korean Christians. In India, the attribution of intended mischief to this one Muslim organization was in no time extended to the entire Muslim community. Tablighi, Taliban, and Muslim became interchangeable words in media narratives. Bizarre 'news' posts flooded social media, with some making their way to news channels. These were often based on video mash-ups featuring Muslim vendors spitting on fruits; Muslim restaurant chefs spitting in food; Muslims licking utensils; or Muslims sneezing in unison or spitting at police. These were subsequently all proven to be concocted. But by the time a gutsy band of fact-checking media outfits like Alt News and Boom could get around to debunking the stories, the lies had spread far and wide.

The virus was transformed into a 'communal virus', a Radio Rwanda–style weapon to attack Muslims, the country's biggest minority. As a result of the misinformation campaign, Muslims were killed, assaulted, hounded, and ostracized by calls to boycott Muslim vendors in particular and the community in general. Some neighbourhoods and apartment blocks decided to bar Muslims from entering. Hospitals denied treatment to Muslim patients, some began to segregate Muslim patients from the rest. One cancer hospital took out an advertisement declaring it would admit Muslims only if they weren't carriers of the coronavirus.

Media Frames

Ever since the BJP's rise to power, media framing of Muslims as the 'enemy' has become routine. A sizeable section of the media, especially television channels, has worked tirelessly to peddle the image of Muslims as the dangerous 'Other'. Barely two weeks before the 2020 lockdown was announced, one of the top anchors and the editor-in-chief of a popular news channel ran an entire show explaining all the different types of jihad being waged in India—complete with a flow chart—that included 'population jihad', 'love jihad', 'land jihad', 'economic jihad', 'history jihad', 'media jihad', 'education jihad', 'film and music jihad', 'secularism jihad', and even 'victim jihad'.

Communications scholars have long argued that media sets the agenda for public opinion, first by drawing the attention of citizens to a particular issue, and then by defining it by means of comprehensible media 'frames' that act as cognitive shortcuts to understand issues. 'Frames' are distinct narrative structures that ascribe set meanings to events, which help readers grasp the news but often strip it of nuance and ambiguity. Although media frames don't always tell audiences what exactly to think, they suggest to them what to think about and how to think about it. India's most successful news segments—and framing vehicles—are soft news shows that are a cacophony of hectoring and self-righteous anchors and squabbling talking heads. The shouting matches they generate make for great television. They effectively compete with teledramas, keep up ratings and, most importantly, help cut outdoors reporting costs by keeping the shows entirely studio-centric. Anti-Muslim messaging, generally subtle, has been the default media frame for this set ever since the BJP came to power in 2014. With the pestilence, as the ratings race became more vicious, chasing whatever little advertisements remained in a crashing economy, it was time to set the dog whistle aside and bring out the bugle (Figure 33).

Figure 33. Many Indian TV channels now megaphone the ruling party's views

As in other so-called democracies, journalists working within India's mainstream media are engaged 24/7 in framing narratives, making them indispensable for any government. Especially so for one that's as headline-obsessed as Modi's. His coming to Delhi coincided with a recasting of newsrooms through the sidelining of top editors with proven 'liberal' values. Liberalism has become an embarrassing liability in the new order, a dirty word, in fact. Once prized as a virtue, inclusive tendencies exhibited by 'sickulars' are the antithesis of the Hindu-first worldview of Modi's party. 'Secularism' is systematically disparaged by his cyberwarriors, who condemn it as a sign of opportunism and national untrustworthiness. There has been a coordinated campaign to discredit the high priests of mainstream media. These 'presstitutes' of power and privilege are said to be relics of an earlier, corrupt regime in which they traded their watchdog responsibilities for patronage. The 'New India' that Modi intends to build has no place for such leeches.

Modi presumed that government must make every effort to beguile and bewitch its subjects. Just as early modern Russian despots bathed in the splendour of glorious entries, coronations, weddings, name days, funerals, and sumptuous ceremonies, so his government uses television, radio, print, and digital platforms as the media of seductive political performances. Power is meant to flow only in one direction: from top to bottom. Senior editors no longer accompany the prime minister on foreign trips. There are no press conferences by the prime minister. Interviews are granted to handpicked journalists, with both the questions and the answers tightly scripted. The new crop of editors, especially in television, are granted access to power on the condition of their deference to power. Modi, after all, doesn't need journalists to reach his people. Not with 67 million followers on Twitter. Like Vučić, Trump, and other budding despots, getting a message across simply means sending a tweet. The press takes it from there. Modi even has his own app, NaMo, that provides real-time updates about him. It passed 10 million downloads in February 2019. He has his own radio programme called 'Mann Ki Baat' (Heart to Heart), as well as his own television channel, NaMo TV, which goes to air during elections.

Flooding the Zone

Modi's rise to power in 2014 coincided with the coming of communicative abundance, the profusion of new communication networks and technologies, and rapidly changing media consumption habits.[2] Aided by throwaway data prices and cheap Chinese products flooding the market, smartphone users in India passed 500 million in 2019 from just 156 million in 2014. With more than 400 million Indians on WhatsApp and nearly 250 million on Facebook, India has become the biggest market for both social media platforms, which are powerful weapons in the hands of the BJP's formidable IT cell, the party's most efficient and effective outreach medium. Ahead of the 2019 elections, described by the BJP's social media chief as the first 'WhatsApp election', the party drew up plans to have three

WhatsApp groups for each of the nearly 1 million polling booths. In Uttar Pradesh alone, the party said it was setting up a 'cyber sena' (cyber army) of up to 200,000 social media workers, with the goal of having in place at least one dedicated 'cyber yodhaa' (cyber warrior) for every polling booth.

The IT cell and myriad faceless organizations backed by the ruling party make sure these extensive, informal, networked channels of information are kept constantly watered. Secretive organizations frame sophisticated misinformation campaigns to spread fake news and false claims through social media. They ensure BJP campaigns go viral, with the help of proxy Facebook pages, engineered WhatsApp forwards, trending tweets, and through other online platforms.[3] Social media allows inexpensive micro-messaging for specific target groups, however toxic. Micro influencers not officially connected to the party but inspired by Hindu supremacism help spread these messages, allowing the party to maintain distance and plausible deniability even as these supposed 'fringe' elements help charge its core base with inciteful lies and prejudices. In this parallel universe of 'news' and 'information', protests against the gruesome rape and murder of a Dalit girl are turned into an international Islamist conspiracy; a film star's suicide becomes a sinister conspiracy hatched by a cartel of Bollywood insiders, drug mafia, and opposition figures; random acts of criminality with no Muslim participation become concerted acts of an organized 'jihad'. Following the playbook of powerful despotisms like Putin's Russia, the strategy is to feed endless nonsense into public life, to create fogs of disinformation in order to disorient and 'gaslight' audiences. In this new-age propaganda, described by former Donald Trump aide Steve Bannon as 'flooding the zone with shit', the overload of misinformation disrupts established patterns of media framing and makes it difficult for gatekeeping legacy media to sift fact from fiction, issues from trivia, information from distraction. The line between facts and claims is blurred. Citizens are denied the accurate information they need to make enlightened political choices. Democracy is hacked.

To dominate public narratives requires more than slick social media strategies. It helps if legacy media is on message as well, so that the 'news' environment is turned into a constant echo chamber of pro-government messaging. It helps if the legacy media amplifies, and legitimizes, the most improbable of social media propaganda by picking up fiction from WhatsApp forwards and repurposing them as 'news'. In the age of Modi, partisan support is willingly given by a new crop of top editors, especially in the field of television. As a result, a once-proud media landscape is now littered with shells of news outlets eager to please the executive. Few prominent newspapers or television channels dare criticize Modi or his regime. Journalists who don't toe the government line are forced out.

In such a media environment marked by features common to despotisms like Vietnam, Iran, and Russia, where independent journalism is all but dead, self-censorship and toad-eating are rife. News reports that might show the government in a bad light are underplayed, or quashed. Sometimes, when they appear, they are taken offline without explanation. If any breakout media platform stumbles upon a critical story, others pretend it's not happening. Bad news is best avoided. Newspapers are extra-cautious with headlines and content so as not to offend the rulers. Television anchors eager to please the executive prefer to demand answers from government's critics and opposition figures rather than ministers or the ruling party. This contributes to a culture of 'anticipatory obedience' and 'creeping quiet'.[4] When *Time* magazine put Modi on the list of '100 most influential people' in 2020 for wrecking India's multicultural democracy, stifling dissent, and attacking Muslims, most mainstream Indian media outlets reported it like it was a cause for celebration, conveniently omitting the acid critique or even the mention of why he was on that list. Foreign media companies active in India are also alive to the need for self-censorship, and active cooperation, to prosper in this lucrative market. Facebook has been found to systematically amplify Hindu right-wing voices. Its India head of policy was outed as an ardent BJP follower.[5] Twitter has blocked accounts of some

prominent anti–Modi voices. When HBO's John Oliver aired an episode critical of Modi, Hotstar simply removed the episode from its
platform even before the government asked it to do so. It was bracing
for what was coming. The government later issued new rules to
regulate all digital content and assumed the right to crack down on
content endangering 'national security' and the 'sovereignty and
integrity of India'. The central government can now order social
media platforms to break encryption and disclose the 'first originator'
of 'mischievous' posts. 'Cyber crime volunteers' are urged to flag up
'anti-national' digital content. In early 2021, makers of an Amazon
Prime series had to agree to make changes in the script and apologize for 'hurting Hindu sentiments'. In print media, the Press Council
of India has been ominously warning newspapers to 'publish foreign
extracts with due verification' or 'be responsible for the contents
irrespective of the source'.[6]

Media monitors have spotted this drift. India has been falling steadily on the World Press Freedom Index compiled by Reporters Without
Borders. From 80th in 2002, it ranked 142nd out of 180 territories in
2020, behind South Sudan, Myanmar, Afghanistan, and junta-ruled
Thailand. From Modi's disastrous currency ban to a covert military
strike on terror pads across the border in Pakistan, 'nationalistic
anchors', newspaper headlines, and social media buzz relentlessly con-
vey the competence and triumphs of the government. The reportage
is at odds with how international media covers the same subjects. The
dissonance was most strikingly evident when Modi abrogated
Kashmir's autonomous status and pumped in extra troops. Domestically
reported as yet another 'masterstroke' by Modi designed to improve
the lot of Kashmiris, almost all Indian mainstream media outlets followed the government narrative of peace and calm in the restive
region, despite its change of status. #KashmirWithModi trended on
Twitter even as the Internet there was switched off as part of the
information blockade. It was only foreign media organizations like
the BBC and Reuters that reported the rage bubbling up in Kashmir,

the impromptu protests and police firings to quell protesters. The government dismissed the reports as 'fabricated', much in the manner of any despotic state warding off prying foreign media.

The legislature and the judiciary weren't the only institutions that decided to look the other way when the ruling executive suspended fundamental rights in Kashmir. It had the enthusiastic support of the country's media watchdog statutorily tasked with ensuring freedom of the press. When a Kashmiri editor approached the Supreme Court to seek a relaxation of restrictions on free reporting, the Press Council of India opined that journalists' right to free and fair reporting should be balanced with concern for the 'national interest of integrity and sovereignty' of the country. When a country's statutory media body supports a media clampdown, democracy and irony die a thousand deaths. The Press Council didn't stop there. As if it had consulted a handbook on how to build a despotism, it reminded the court of the need to curb the rights of journalists, and even urged journalists to exercise self-regulation.

Behemoths

Until 1991, India had only a single state-owned television channel. Daily life has since been colonized by a plethora of news channels, talk shows, web platforms, news aggregators, and citizen journalism that trades in on-the-spot video clips, opinions, and news reports. India is now one of the biggest media markets in the world with nearly 120,000 publications, 550 FM radio stations, and 880 satellite TV channels. But this vast market is capitalized and controlled by a handful of people.

Big business ownership of media enterprises is something of a tradition in India. The concentration of business media power has accelerated in recent years, along with a discernible shift towards such products and practices as sexed-up 'breaking' news, paid content 'advertorials', private treaties (granting advertising space to companies in exchange for equity shares), and editorial coverage targeted at the 'three Cs' for which (middle class) Indians supposedly have a passion: crime, cricket, and cinema. A study of fifty-eight leading media outlets with the largest audience shares in India found the print media market to be highly concentrated. Just four outlets, for example, control three-quarters of the national Hindi-language market.[7] It is the same with all vernacular markets in the country. These media behemoths, in turn, are often owned by large conglomerates entangled in a whole range of other businesses, which make them dependent on the government. Media fields provide rich pickings for poligarchs. India's democrats stress the vital importance of media as a counterweight to centralized power and protector of citizens' interests. The trouble is that media laws relating to the concentration of ownership are poorly laid out and ineffectual. There's no regulatory framework to prevent monopolization and cross-industrial holdings and, even if there were, they would be difficult to implement given the maze of legally approved cross-holdings and complex ownership structures.

A study of filings with the registrar of companies in 2016 showed Mukesh Ambani, the richest Indian and owner of the country's largest conglomerate Reliance Industries, and two other closely connected tycoons, together controlled between 20 and 70 per cent of five big media houses, either through equity holdings or loans or other modes of investment that can be converted into equity. The takeover of Network18, one of these media houses that Reliance bought just as Modi took power, combined with Reliance's telecom business, made it the biggest media house in India.[8] It was on course to grow bigger. In April 2020, in the midst of the great pestilence, Facebook bought 9.99 per cent of Reliance's digital and Internet businesses in a $5.7 billion deal. Three months later, Saudi Arabia's sovereign fund and Google invested billions more.

Reliance's stellar performance has helped Ambani race up the global billionaire rankings since Modi's re-election in 2019. The opposition calls him a Modi crony, but the cosy connections between Indian media, big business, and governments have deep roots. Many media owners and editors have for a long time openly allied with one party or the other, and been rewarded as poligarchs with parliamentary seats, political sinecures, or favourable deals. At the state level, such associations can be even more overt, with powerful political families openly owning influential media houses. The fortunes of media barons and editors have fallen and risen with parties and leaders many times before Modi happened. Like the wider trend towards elective despotism, Modi's arrival in Delhi only intensified the media pathologies that have long been on display.

Purse Strings

Some of these pathologies are a function of the business model that underpins Indian media companies. Indian media essentially runs on advertising rather than subscription. This has allowed a wider spread of information and democratized news as newspapers and channels can be accessed at throwaway prices. But the over-reliance on advertisements also has distortionary effects on the spirit and substance of democracy. It makes media funding overly dependent on corporate and government advertisement budgets and, by extension, their framing and content preferences.

The poor coverage of rural news in response to the corporate advertising model biased towards the more resourceful urban consumer in a country where 70 per cent of people live in villages, is a case in point. The trend has been apparent for several decades but has been intensifying since market liberalization began in the 1990s. The average national daily in India gives 0.67 per cent of its front page to rural India. In non-election years, even less.[9] India has seen more than 350,000 farmers' suicides since 1995. In 2019, according to the National Crime Records Bureau, 10,281 farmers and 32,559 farm workers committed suicide. In Punjab alone, the first state where industrial farming was introduced, farmer suicides have increased more than twelve

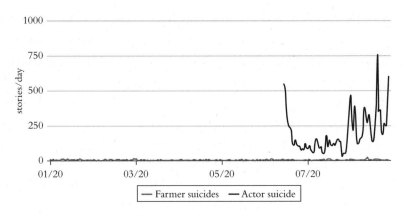

Figure 34. Media coverage of farmers' suicides compared with actor Sushant Singh Rajput's suicide

times in five years. But mainstream media hardly covers this social emergency, unless farmers march to metro cities in protest. During the first six months of 2020, more than 1,000 farmers committed suicide in Maharashtra, but barely received any media attention. Indian news channels were instead seized with the suicide of a Bollywood star, Sushant Singh Rajput (Figure 34). The suicide triggered conversations about nepotism, corruption, and mental health that then morphed into a shadow political war between the BJP government in Delhi and the opposition-ruled Maharashtra state (Mumbai is its capital). An ugly primetime witch-hunt of his girlfriend ensued, followed by an even more bizarre media trial of Bollywood's supposed drug connections (Rajput was said to be a drug user), with arrests and questioning of some of the top stars by federal agencies. The Maharashtra state government hit back by slapping charges on Goswami, the pro-BJP 'nationalist' anchor, which eventually led to a giant ratings scam. The resultant non-stop coverage related to the celebrity suicide and the chain reaction triggered by it blanked out other significant news stories, such as the deaths and social injuries caused by the pestilence, mounting worries about an unprecedented economic collapse, and intensifying border skirmishes with China.[10]

The media obsession with celebrity, political news, and the urban rather than the rural is endemic. A study of six news channels revealed that on any given day, rural news doesn't receive more than seven minutes of prime time.[11] As a result, the implosion of India's social foundations—the effects of which are most acutely felt in rural and semi-urban areas—are hardly covered in the media. The market censorship helps explain why there's so little public outrage and so much complacency about famine and hunger, environmental despoliation (except when air pollution reaches critical levels in Delhi), poor health care and sanitation, low levels of education, transport dangers, and the new slavery of labour markets. Unlike political dramas, matters of defence, and sports or celebrity news, these things seem not to matter. Advertisers battling to tap the purchasing power of the upper and middle classes would rather put their money on the content those segments prefer. The logic is summarized by India's most famous media baron, Vineet Jain (who controls Bennett, Coleman & Co, which produces *The Times of India* and owns the *Times Now* channel, among others): 'We are not in the newspaper business', he says, 'we are in the advertising business.'[12]

The corporate media bias towards advertising shapes its content in other ways. Investigative reportage on corporate groups is a strict no-no for newsrooms. As advertising from the government is no less important, similar self-censorship when covering the land's most powerful political leaders is not uncommon either. Before the Congress was pushed from power, the Gandhi family enjoyed a degree of media deference.[13] The kowtowing to Modi is an escalation of this pre-existing condition. The senior BJP leader and Modi's mentor Lal Krishna Advani, who stood up to Indira Gandhi's draconian gagging laws, once famously chided journalists for their sycophancy during the Emergency days, saying: 'You were asked only to bend, but you crawled.' Having said this long before Modi's rise to power, Advani must now marvel at the subservience his protégé has extracted from the media. It's not just that the new leaders of newsrooms recast in the wake of Modi's rise kowtow to him. A whole new crop of media ventures has emerged that owe fealty to him and the ruling party. In particular, several channels evangelizing Hindu-first populism have emerged. One of them, Sudarshan TV, openly rejects job applications from Muslims, regularly spreads communally charged fake news with morphed videos, and runs provocative shows targeting Muslims. Since channels like these also receive generous government advertisements, their rabid sectarian agenda, ironically, gets funded by taxpayers of a republic that claims to be secular on paper. Muslim taxpayers are basically funding mass-media calls for their own annihilation as citizens.

Government advertisements are among the most powerful weapons of media control, both in Delhi and in the states. Consolidated numbers of state and federal government ad spending are difficult to obtain, but they are sizeable enough to have become vital to the bottom line of many newspapers and television channels. Delhi's ruling Aam Aadmi Party, a tiny city party with national pretensions, is given to splurging taxpayers' money on countrywide media ads glorifying its founder-leader. In November 2020, the Andhra Pradesh government forged an 80 million rupee deal with Bennett, Coleman & Co (Times Group) to improve the 'image of the state and its leaders on the national stage'. In its first four years, Modi's government alone spent more than Rs 4,300 crore ($590 million) in advertisements and publicity. In the 2019–20 financial year (April 1 to March 31 of the following year), it spent nearly 20 million rupees ($270,000) on average *every day* on advertisements, not including the ad spend on foreign media. The smaller the media outlets, the more dependent they are on government handouts and, hence, more vulnerable to political control.[14] Governments should logically use circulation figures or ratings to determine which media outlet should get what percentage of the government advertising budget. More ads should go to bigger outlets because they reach more people. In practice, however, decisions are taken much more arbitrarily. There's nothing stopping governments from freely punishing big media houses for adversarial reportage and rewarding tiny publications, with limited reach, with advertising bounty for doing their bidding. Soon after Modi returned to office in 2019, it came to light that his government had frozen advertisements to three major newspaper groups—Bennett,

Coleman & Co, the ABP Group (which owns *The Telegraph*, *Anandabazar Patrika*, and several news channels), and the Hindu group, whose eponymous newspaper *The Hindu* had run a series of tough investigative reports on a controversial defence deal in the run-up to the 2019 election.

The same dynamic works at the state level. Editors of local editions of national newspapers in non-BJP states often complain that much of their energy is spent scrubbing off the pro-BJP tilt sent through by Delhi editors and 'maintaining balance', lest it offends local ruling parties hostile to the BJP. These mandatory balancing acts are crippled by a contradiction: while even-handedness keeps alive the democratic spirit of pluralism among media platforms and journalists in their employ, the obligation to please two masters at once tempts journalists and their bosses into becoming conformists who, for the sake of keeping their jobs and reputations, keep well away from the electric fences operated by executive power.

It's not just the government that holds the media bottom line. Political parties themselves—especially when in power—are major sources of advertisement revenue, primarily during elections. Full-length front-page ads of a smiling Modi or a regional leader in the local press or in television spots are common during election season. India has an acute problem of 'paid news', the practice of media houses trading favourable coverage for political ads. After his re-election, in a moment of honesty, Haryana's Congress chief minister Bhupinder Singh Hooda told the magazine *Outlook*: 'When I noticed the leading paper of my state printing baseless reports on its front page day after day, I called them up and offered money to print the right picture. The paper apologised.'[15] The Press Council of India detailed the news-for-cash phenomenon in national and especially the regional press. A parliamentary standing committee corroborated these findings by documenting the widespread use of 'paid news'. In just one state, Gujarat, it found 126 cases of paid news, with sixty-one candidates saying they had bought positive coverage in the state election.

Much of this kind of media advertising is also routed through business backers of candidates. When in power, governments use their corporate allies to pressure or reward media houses with advertisements. Given the interdependence of government and big business, ruling parties, in addition to government advertisements, have at their disposal the extra weapon of their corporate friends' advertising budgets to keep media platforms in line. The hand of elective despotism is strengthened through the state–corporate–media compact among poligarchs.

Mightier Than the Pen

In the early days of the 2020 Covid lockdown, Siddharth Varadarajan had some surprise visitors at his Delhi home. A group of about eight policemen from the adjoining state of Uttar Pradesh came to serve the founding editor of the online magazine, *The Wire*, a notice to appear in the temple town of Ayodhya, in connection with a police report for making an 'objectionable comment' about chief minister Adityanath. The police had driven all the way from Ayodhya, about 600 kilometres away, despite the lockdown. The immediate provocation was an article in *The Wire* that had misquoted Adityanath as saying Lord Ram would protect his devotees from the coronavirus. It was a flimsy excuse. The publication had already fixed the error the very next day and posted a clarification. The shakedown was payback for something else: the fact that it existed.

Pesky journalists like Varadarajan, and a new crop of similarly doughty media platforms that provide space for views that don't echo the established narrative, are a thorn in the side of despotic power. Their journalists well understand that in India, as elsewhere, the unfinished digital communications revolution of our time can be used by despots to circulate materials, such as deepfake mash-ups, lies, and bigoted messaging, designed to stir up public confusion, hatred, and subjugation. But they refuse talk of the inevitability of such decadence. They resist the anti-democratic rot. They offer critical reportage and perspectives that aren't often found in mainstream media. By contributing to a diversity of views, they threaten the echo chamber that despotic power builds to fortify itself. The price they pay is intimidation, and worse. Knocks on the door by personnel from the UP Police—with its formidable track record of 124 deaths from nearly 6,500 'encounters' in three and a half years (at the time) under Adityanath—can be daunting.

Varadarajan was one of the many journalists targeted by a vindictive executive looking to settle scores in the middle of the pestilence. As many as fifty-five journalists were targeted by the police across India within two months of the lockdown for daring to report on the poor handling of the pestilence.[16] Journalists, public intellectuals, and activists critical of government action found themselves thrown into jail at a time when other countries were decongesting prisons to reduce contagion risks. Many of them were booked under the draconian Unlawful Activities (Prevention) Act, or UAPA, a law from the 1960s that restricts some of the fundamental rights of individuals if deemed a threat to the sovereignty and integrity of India. With new amendments, the federal government can now label an individual—rather than an organization—as terrorist if it merely believes so, with no need for proof. The burden of proof lies entirely on the accused. It is among the several extraordinary laws that limit dissent, including by journalists, on the ground of national security. There are others, such as the National Security Act and the Public Safety Act, both of which allow for detention without charge or trial on vague grounds. Then there are colonial-era sedition laws that continue to be used with impunity by both state and federal governments. Journalists in states often end up in jails for Facebook posts and retweets critical of the local despot that determines these as 'inflammatory' and a threat to 'law and order'. Social media posts against the government are now treated as cybercrime in Bihar and a ground for the withdrawal of a passport in Uttarakhand. In brief, despite India's much-celebrated media freedom, the state has sufficient legal tools at its disposal to discipline an adversarial media. Journalists across India are subject to imprisonment and legal harassment for the most routine of media activities, from covering protests to train derailments. If a despotic executive enjoying a free hand from the legislature and the courts considers any journalist or reportage as prejudicial to its cause, there's little legal room to push back. If it's not charges of sedition, there are always defamation suits that governments and political parties can use to intimidate and break upright journalism.

And, there's violence: virtual and physical, real and potential. India's marauding troll armies—whose murder threats and graphic rape messages coincide with the BJP's rise to dominance and the social media explosion—are by global trolling standards a particularly ugly lot. They give turpitude a bad name. Trolls go to war every day, making and unmaking Twitter trends, scaring and scarring their victims. Hunting in packs, they pounce on anybody with a point of view that dares to diverge from their own. These trolling campaigns are often potent. Facing a boycott call on social media, Snapdeal had to sack Aamir Khan as its brand ambassador after the Bollywood star spoke out against growing intolerance in India. Tanishq, a top jewellery chain, was forced by online outrage to withdraw an ad featuring an interfaith couple. Some of the vilest trolls are followed by Modi himself and other senior government leaders. One of India's most respected anchors, Ravish Kumar, who received the 2019 Ramon Magsaysay Award for standing out with his sober and objective presentation in a media space crowded by pro-government screamers, wrote an open letter to the prime minister asking if his life was in danger. He noted he was being repeatedly threatened and abused over WhatsApp by people followed by Modi himself on Twitter. The fear is real. More than a few of these threats don't just stay online.

India ranks as one of the most dangerous countries for journalists. In 2015, it was judged the third most dangerous, after Iraq and Syria, in terms of the number of media workers killed that year in their line of work. A 2018 list compiled by Reporters Without Borders found no journalist had been killed in Iraq that year but six were killed in India, the most after Afghanistan, Syria, Mexico, and Yemen. 'Violence against journalists including police violence, attacks by Maoist fighters and reprisals by criminal groups or corrupt politicians is one of the most striking characteristics of the current state of press freedom in India', the report noted. The shooting of Gauri Lankesh, editor of a Kannada-language weekly tabloid in Bangalore, by right-wing extremists in 2017, trained the global spotlight on the dangers faced by Indian journalists.

But most of the killings and silencing in fact take place in villages and small towns. Away from the media glare in big metropolitan cities, they go relatively unnoticed. Local-level corruption is the most common reason. As media houses tend to underspend on non-metro reportage, they make do with freelance journalists out in the field with no institutional protection. Their salaries are often tied to the volume of copy generated. The challenges they face are made much worse by a relatively less talked about aspect of Indian journalism: the journalist as an advertisement agent. Freelance journalists in small urban centres are often tasked by their employers as procurers of advertisements, for a commission. As the advertisements come from the same people whose work the journalists are supposed to monitor, they are victimized and co-opted by local power networks whose corruption they are expected to reveal. In one of the greatest perversions of the spirit of democracy, journalists are forced to plug themselves into local patronage networks both for their livelihood and safety. Those who still persist with journalistic integrity, defying the intertwined power interests of local business, politics, and government, pay with their careers, or lives. In November 2020, television journalist Isravel Moses in Tamil Nadu's Kancheepuram district was hacked to death. Fellow journalists said Moses had received death threats from local drug dealers after he reported on their activities. That same month, a journalist in Uttar Pradesh was burnt alive at his home in a village not far from the state capital. The attackers doused him and his friend in alcohol-based sanitizer before setting them on fire. In a 2.5-minute video recorded before his death at the local hospital,

Rakesh Singh 'Nirbhik' (the self-given last name meaning 'fearless'), said he was paying the price for exposing the corrupt deals of the village head.

Moses and 'Nirbhik' are among the eighty or so journalists who have been killed in India since 1992, according to a compilation by the Committee to Protect Journalists (CPJ). Many, like them, were investigating and exposing corruption. Forty have been killed in the five years between 2014 and 2019 alone.[17] The Press Council of India says 96 per cent of the cases of murder remain unsolved, either because they drag on in the courts or because the investigations hit a dead end.[18] In its Global Impunity Index, the CPJ consistently ranks India as one of the countries with the worst records of bringing to book the killers of journalists.

The killing and muzzling of journalists in a tightening entanglement of media with shadowy webs of tough party bosses, business behemoths, criminal politicians, and bridled judges, marks a major milestone in the forward march of elected despots. By choking the free flows of information that are foundational for democratic accountability, the poligarchs who kill democracy go scot-free.

Towards Despotism

Remaking the People

So what fate awaits a political system called a democracy when its social foundations inflict indignity on millions of citizens and its basic governing institutions begin to lose their bearings and fall apart? And fall prey to power-greedy governments intent on reshaping those institutions with the help of big business friends, compliant courts, police violence, and election victories dominated by dark money, media manipulation, and muscle power?

Historians remind us that democratic institutions can be so twisted and stretched to snapping point by cunning and conflict that the resulting chaos is ultimately resolved only by a military *coup d'état*. There are other possibilities. When things fall apart, social resistance by disaffected citizens and calls for a revolutionary overthrow of the rotting political system can happen. Social disorder and street violence and even civil war may result, followed perhaps by martial law or foreign military intervention. These are the fates that disaffected and dysfunctional democracies have commonly suffered in past times. But times have changed. Things are now different. Nowadays another type of outcome is possible, and more likely. Let's call it the killing of democracy in the name of democracy by despots and despotic politics.

In broad-brush outline, here's how despotism is born of a corrupted democracy. A cunning and tightly disciplined political party, behaving as if it has a hotline to 'the people', begins to win elections. Millions of dissatisfied people find its message attractive. Victory grants the party and its leaders capture and control of the decaying institutions of government. Electoral success convinces them that governing necessitates more than strengthening their loyal base of willing followers. Winning office tempts them to begin kidnapping the legislature, the courts, and other key state institutions, to exploit their weaknesses and profit from their remaining strengths, and to outflank and politically crush their listless opponents. The governing party machine, in the hands of a big boss leader who daily sounds and looks ever more like a media-trained demagogue, stirs up talk of 'democracy' and 'the people'. It operates a spoils system to reward 'friends' and punish 'enemies'. There are stern warnings about subversion and the collapse of law and order. With the backing of men in uniform and investigative agencies, and a few whiffs of tear gas, the government of 'the people' begins to swoop like a hawk on its opponents. Bans on public assembly and Internet crackdowns are enforced. Arrests, detentions without trial, and unsolved murders happen. There are sensational media accounts of opposition party scandals and impending threats to public order. The ruling party, helped by cunning media tactics, finally outmanoeuvres and wins control of the legislature. It neuters the courts and other power-monitoring institutions and turns them into empty shells, phantoms of their former selves. State power turns steel tough. Demagogic talk of 'democracy' and the need for firm rule backed by 'the people' grows louder, and more militant.

With power-sharing democracy on its knees, blindfolded, elections prove useful to its killers. Elective despotism prevails. Elections become rowdy plebiscites. Politics morphs into spectacles, permanent campaigning and vote harvesting by the dominant party led by a demagogue messiah. The redeemer makes promises of betterment and offers rewards. Using state-of-the-art tools ranging from media message bombing and legal trickery to calculated silence and brute force, the forces of despotism effect a metamorphosis. They liquidate democracy by restyling government as strong-armed rule led by a despot who centre stage plays the role of guide and guardian of 'the people'. Elections are by now more than elections. They are elections without democracy, public rituals, carnivals of political seduction, a celebration of the mighty power of the government, endorsed by the votes of millions of people. But during the transition from democracy to despotism, something more significant happens. In the hands of the ruling party and its despot leader, the razzamatazz, promises of justice, vote buying and election harvests have a more drastic effect: they aim to redefine who 'the people' are. Desperate to tighten their grip on state power, the governing party offers bread and roses to its followers. But it also plays filthy and stops at nothing. It cheats and lies with impunity. The government gaslights. Rumours, exaggerations, and bullshit are spread by its loyal media organs. The signature tactic is stirring up trouble about who counts as 'the people'.[1] Peddling doubts and fears, the governing despots move to ostracize people deemed not to belong. They repeat, and repeat again, that they are the government of those who truly belong to the polity. So elections become an exercise in electing an alternative people, a 'true' and 'pure' people rid of misfits and miscreants. Winning elections thus means creating a new 'sovereign' people—a pasteurized people who (it's said) are the true bedrock of a more authentic and strong state democracy ruled by an exceptional leader whose strength and legitimacy are grounded in the true 'people'. Elections are turned upside down. The government votes in the people.

Demagogues

Experience teaches us that well-organized despots, unless stopped in their tracks by citizen resistance, robust watchdog institutions, unforeseen outcomes and plain bad luck, can quickly remould sickly democratic institutions into a different political order we call despotism. Despotism isn't old-fashioned tyranny or military dictatorship, or describable as a single-ruler horror show the ancients called autocracy. It mustn't be confused with 20th-century fascism or totalitarianism.[2] Despotism is rather a new type of strong state led by a demagogue and run by state and corporate poligarchs with the help of pliant journalists and docile judges, a top-down form of government that has the backing of not just the law-enforcement agencies but also the backing of millions of loyal subjects who are willing to lend their support to leaders who offer them tangible benefits and daringly rule in the name of 'democracy' and 'the sovereign people'. Hungary, Kazakhstan and Turkey—to name just several recent cases—show that a transition from democracy to despotism can happen rapidly, in not much more than a decade. India may be next on the list. The local details of these transitions usually differ, but the end result is generally the same: in the name of democracy, democracy is metamorphosed into a different political system. The butterfly of democracy becomes the caterpillar of despotism. A weird new kind of phantom democracy is born.

The lethal dynamics gripping the upper levels of Indian politics indicate what's at stake. India is showing how despotism happens, or might happen, if the supporters of what remains of its democracy allow it to happen. Despotism is the auto-immune disease of a sick democracy. It sucks life from what remains of its spirit and institutions. Despotism feeds upon periodic elections and voter support. Despots take full advantage of rights of assembly and association, and they make use of media freedoms to spread their message. Despotism also taps into the democratic sense that power relations aren't set in stone, and that things can be different. It nurtures hopes of redemption. It raises expectations that the 'sovereign people' are entitled to expect improvements in their daily lives. It promises solutions to the headaches and heartbreaks of famine, joblessness, putrid air and water, mountains of rubbish, dysfunctional transport systems and poor healthcare. Despots do all they can to win loyal followers by offering them material gifts: cash-for-votes, new homes and toilets. But when viewed in terms of democratic values and institutions, despotic politics actually makes things worse. By inflaming and damaging the cells, tissues and organs of what remains of the democratic body politic, despotism has killing consequences. It hastens the demise and death of democracy.

When a democracy allows its social foundations to be torn apart, it encourages leaders to play the role of messiahs, and to experiment with the dark arts of despotic politics. Weak governing institutions that are fundamentally malleable and tilted in their favour only feed such despotic trends. The current anxieties about India's democratic decline are stoked by the flagrant violation in the Modi era of the freedoms guaranteed by India's Constitution, and by the manifest capitulation of state institutions. But the social decay that allows despotism to take root has been at play much longer, predating Modi by decades. If, as we have shown earlier in this book, the destruction of social life is a form of democratic decline, the story of India's journey to despotism becomes much more complex. The qualifications are important to note. Under India's federal arrangement, it's the state governments that are mainly responsible for such areas as health, education, nutrition, mobility and environment, all of which have witnessed democracy failure. Modi's supporters tend to lionize him as the saviour from Congress's 55 years of these failures. It is a specious argument. Even as it managed to retain power in Delhi for much of India's existence as an independent nation, the country's Grand Old Party hasn't ruled many states in ages. In Gujarat, for example, which has witnessed steady economic growth but rising child malnutrition, the BJP has been in power since 1995. Two of the poorest and the worst governed states, Uttar Pradesh and Bihar, haven't had a Congress government for 30 years. In Tamil Nadu, the Congress has been absent since 1967. In West Bengal, since 1977. Many parties—national and local, left, right and centrist—have ruled in states and in Delhi, by themselves or in coalitions, and cannot escape responsibility for the social decay and the resultant dynamics of despotism.

On the other hand, the suggestion that Indian democracy was doing just fine till Modi showed up, is equally fallacious. Many of the institutional pathologies outlined in this book have intensified under Modi, but neither the many curbs on fundamental rights and the dissolution of the checks and balances of power, nor the spate of unlawful arrests of the regime's discontents are an entirely new phenomenon restricted to the machinations of one party or leader. One of Bollywood's most celebrated lyricists, Majrooh Sultanpuri, found himself in jail for criticizing Nehru in 1949. It was under Nehru again when one of the most flagrant exercises of mass detentions in India took place—during the 1962 war with China, when about 3,000 Indian-Chinese were rounded up from Assam and West Bengal and taken to an internment camp in the deserts of Rajasthan. All because the Nehru government deemed them a security risk simply because of their ethnicity. Their property was seized and auctioned, and many of them were deported to China, even though they were Indian citizens who had lived in India for generations. India's colonial-era sedition laws and the draconian security and anti-terror laws designed in subsequent years have consistently allowed rulers to attack their real and imagined enemies with impunity. To what extent the rulers use these provisions is subject to their inclination and legislative might. Only now, it seems to be part of the natural order of things, a functional requirement of governing. Unlike the US Bill of Rights, India's fundamental rights are not inviolable.[3] Rights such as free speech and expression, assembly and movement can be—and regularly are—tempered by 'reasonable restrictions' on the grounds of protecting the inviolable but conveniently inexact notions of preserving 'law and order' and the 'sovereignty, unity and integrity' of India. Modi is not the first or the only politician to define these conditions to his advantage. But the current concentration of power by a demagogue at the head of a legislatively unchallenged party with a fork-tongued strategy pushing a majoritarian ideology that is in open conflict with the country's constitutional norms of secular democracy heighten the real dangers of a passage to despotism.

The Biggest Boss

Killing a democracy and building despotism always requires big-mouthed demagogues, political bosses who play the role of earthly avatars of 'the people'. Here again, it may be thought that demagogy is a recent phenomenon, all Narendra Modi's fault, but the brute fact is the cupboards of Indian politics have long been stocked with determined and power-greedy figures like him. At local levels, despots abound. Mamata Banerjee, fondly known among her supporters as '*Didi*', or 'elder sister', is a middle-class woman who plays the role of champion of the poor. She's a poet and painter dressed in simple sarees. A leader included by *Time* magazine (in 2012) in its '100 most influential people'. A woman of the people who has a taste for sound-bite sayings, such as 'Our policy is very clear: whatever policy will suit the people', Banerjee delivers rousing speeches and municipal tax breaks for painting homes after her party colours, harbours few qualms about letting loose a vigilante cadre on her political opponents, and brooks no dissent within her party, or without. Indian democracy also features big boss men who play the role of political messiahs. Figures like Kalvakuntla Chandrashekhar Rao, better known as KCR, the first chief minister of the new southern state of Telangana (carved out of Andhra Pradesh in 2014). Dressed in white and pink (the colours of his TRS party), he's a supremo lion and fox who ruthlessly uses the state machinery to gag the opposition and distribute patronage to the 'true natives' of his state. KCR built himself a splendid palace, sprawled across a nine-acre compound in the heart of Hyderabad, complete with bulletproof windows. He peddles the principles of astrology and numerology, and convenes days-long Hindu festivals of *yajna* (offerings to sacred fire) performed by thousands of priests, and attended by millions. During the 2020 pestilence lockdown, he vowed personally to order curfew violators 'to be shot on sight'. To those who complain about his despotic habits, he proudly replies that 'KCR is definitely Hitler for dealing with thieves and the corrupt' and boasts that if necessary he can be 'Hitler's grandfather' who does what it takes to stop 'injustice'.[4]

Demagogues of this kind are neither incidental nor accidental features of despotic politics. Since 'the people' is a fiction of the political imagination, an abstraction incapable of speaking and acting together, in harmony, with one voice, what's needed in practice is a Leader who's capable of simplifying things by performing the role of the equivalent of 'the people', to cheer them up and confirm who they are: The People. The aim is to make the Leader and the People mirror images of each other. Despotic politics is ventriloquism. It's demolatry. 'When I see you, when you see me', the Venezuelan despot Hugo Chávez liked to say during election campaigning, 'I sense it, something says to me, "Chávez, you are no longer Chávez, you are a people."'[5]

Narendra Modi, arguably the biggest big boss in Indian politics since Independence, takes things further. The Big Leader sometimes claims he enjoys a mandate from the heavens, 'chosen by God' to undertake the 'difficult tasks' for the country.[6] *Vox princeps, vox populi, vox dei*. His demagogy is a strangely anti-democratic throwback, a twenty-first-century version of 'the ruler has two bodies' principle of early European monarchies that supposed that the body of the crowned ruler was the visible sign of heavenly power and the visceral manifestation of the unified body of loyal subjects.[7] He plays the role of tea seller and servant (*dass*) of 'the people', charming them with his tunes and grand public performances. After election campaigns, instead of putting his feet up, he carries on campaigning by heading out to meditate in holy caves, photographers in tow. Having cemented his grip on power with a thumping re-election, he has grown his beard longer in the manner of a Hindu ascetic king. He concentrates on lofty matters of nation building, political philosophy, and principles of high governance in his speeches, advises students how to beat exam stress, celebrates Diwali with soldiers guarding the border, waxes eloquent on self-reliance, lays foundation stones and flags off major projects—and leaves policy details and politicking to his underlings. With the opposition parties in disarray and no rival national-level leader of his stature in sight, he appears as the goliath of Indian politics (Figure 35). The BJP's own grassroots cadres and social media, an obliging mainstream media (derisively termed 'Modia' by the regime's critics) that megaphones the government, a submissive judiciary, and a captured bureaucracy help insulate the new guru

Figure 35. Narendra Modi takes a ride on a tank while spending Diwali with soldiers

from the rigours of democratic accountability. His popularity seems immune to the most egregious failures of his government—be it a whimsical and painful currency ban, or a poorly thought-out lockdown, a crashing economy, heart-wrenching epic migration by distressed workers, or even loss of territory and soldiers to China. It's almost like he has transcended to a celestial plane of power far removed from the usual rules of politics.

His journey to political divinity has been eventful. Born the son of a humble railway station chaiwallah into a low-ranking Ganchi caste family in the small town of Vadnagar in Gujarat, he became a preacher for the Rashtriya Swayamsevak Sangh (RSS), the massive Hindu supremacist volunteer organization whose political wing is the BJP. The True Man of the People began his political career as a little-known BJP bureaucrat loaned to the party by the RSS. As chief minister of the state of Gujarat, he presided over the 2002 pogroms that resulted in the deaths of hundreds of Muslim citizens and the displacement and homelessness of many thousands of others. More than a few observers denounced him as a provincial Pol Pot, a dangerous threat to Indian secularism. He drew the ire of overseas commentators, including the government of the United States, which banned him from crossing its borders. But his unapologetic stance on the riots also earned him the loyalty of a hardcore Hindu base. Modi bounced back. His fortunes rose as the public mood turned against a corruption-ridden, Congress-led coalition government that ruled India from 2004 to 2014. The business elite rallied behind the man they credited for dynamic pro-business policies in Gujarat. The self-declared '56-inch-chested' leader blended in his persona the muscular appeal of Hindutva, or Hindu nationalism, and the aspiration of national and personal economic power. Once considered a pariah by the national media elite, he underwent an elaborate image makeover—with the help of the same, corporate, media. He went from being a parochial provincial to a messiah of the disesteemed who would right wrongs and give direction to a rudderless India. Millions of rich, urban, upper-class voters—over 60 per cent of them, according to National Election Study surveys—were also attracted by his promises of enrichment, political stability, order, and clean government. Western governments set aside their old aversions and began to court him as he looked increasingly likely to win the national election in 2014. And so Narendra Modi seized the moment, to climb the ladders of power. He became a media celebrity. His Twitter fans multiplied (nowadays he has about 67 million followers). The bellicosity, contrived histrionics, and strong-arm tactics practised in Gujarat became his stock-in-trade campaign and governing tactics at the national level.[8]

Institutional Vandalism

It happened a few times, for instance in the United States, that demagogues, against their worst intentions, surprised posterity by unleashing positive pressures for democratic reform.[9] Might demagogues have similar effects in India? By definition, we don't know the future effects of self-glorifying leaders. Only certain is that demagogy generally feeds centralized state power. A decade before becoming the first prime minister of India, in a pseudonymous attack upon his own public fame, Jawaharlal Nehru claimed to be worried about the dangers posed to democracy by the hubris of elected leaders, or what he called 'Caesarism'. 'His conceit is already formidable', Nehru wrote on Nehru in a monthly journal. 'He must be checked. We want no Caesars!' A more explicit warning about the dangers of demagogy surfaced in B.R. Ambedkar's final speech (in 1949) to the constituent assembly drafting the Constitution, when he quoted the nineteenth-century liberal philosopher John Stuart Mill, to urge Indians never to 'lay their liberties at the feet of even a great man, or to trust him with power which enables him to subvert their institutions'. Hero worship, he warned, 'is a sure road to degradation and to eventual dictatorship'.[10]

Ambedkar's worst fears may be coming true. Supported by Caesars large and small sprinkled throughout the political system, demagogy is spreading black-and-white thinking about how society should be organized and government should operate. Fuelled by hopes of betterment, seething anger at social injustices and upper class fears of disorder, demagogy is stirring up friend-versus-enemy politics and peddling impatience and disrespect for institutional pluralism. State capture and top-down rule, a kind of slow-motion coup d'état, are its thing.

The spreading hostility to institutional pluralism—putting an end, for instance, to the watchdog roles of legislatures, media platforms, and the courts—isn't accidental, for in order to define anew and retain the loyalty of 'the people', big boss leaders and their party machines must engage in institutional vandalism. Despots have no taste for the give-and-take compromises of institutional politics. They're driven to do everything they can to weaken or destroy outright any institutions that block their advance, or loosen their grip on high office. Centralized power is their aphrodisiac. Unchecked ambition is their guru.

In Alberto Fujimori's Peru, *democracia plena* (as the despot called it) meant hostility to the idle talk (*palabrería*) of the political class and its established media. Buoyed by election promises to bring an end to oligarchy, state secrecy, and silence, the Fujimori government, in the name of 'the people', browbeat and bribed legislators, judges, journalists, bureaucrats, and corporate executives into submission. Fujimori not only contradicted his promises. He failed: he became the first elected head of state to be extradited to his home country, tried, and convicted of human rights violations. Other despots have succeeded, so far. In Hungary, the government of Viktor Orbán managed to collar mainstream media, the judiciary, and the police and breathed fire down the necks of the universities and other civil society organizations. Donald J. Trump's presidency (2016–20) similarly witnessed attempts to attack and tame flanking institutions such as Congress, the Supreme Court, mainstream media platforms, federal bureaucracies, and the Federal Reserve. Amidst a widening gap between rich and poor, Trump's despotic methods exacerbated political divisions, spread fear, incited violence and aggravated social conflicts. Elective despotism in India pushes in the same direction.

A psychological sense of a lack of personal control, typically fuelled by social degradation, increases the demand for messiah leaders who are seen to be able to serve the interest of group members, at the expense of non-group members, to restore 'order'. Politics becomes more polarized as 'in-group' favouritism and 'out-group' derogation by such despotic figures becomes desirable.[11] Menacing language as political communication becomes attractive as existential anxiety leads to fanaticism. Suspicion of insiders and authority increase, and levels of trust in society and democratic institutions and practices shrink. Survey findings are notoriously fickle, but telling is that a 2017 study by the Centre for the Study of Developing Societies (CSDS) found the percentage of Indians who supported democracy dropped from 70 per cent to 63 per cent between 2005 and 2017. The proportion of people 'satisfied with democracy' plunged from 79 per cent to 55 per cent. Less than half (47 per cent) of 'graduates and above' expressed satisfaction with democracy. More than half of all respondents said they would back 'a governing system in which a strong leader can make decisions without interference from parliament or the courts'. Two-thirds said technocrats, not elected officials, should make policy decisions. Research by the World Values Survey indicates similar trends. In 1999–2004, some 43 per cent of Indians supported rule by a strong leader. By 2010–14, that figure had risen to 56 per cent. Recent Pew surveys separately find Indians to be the most ardent supporters of 'autocratic rule'. Together with Vietnam, South Africa, and Indonesia, it is one of only four countries in the world where a majority of citizens (53 per cent) say they would be prepared to support military rule.[12]

Despots gain from this preference for centralized power in a strong and decisive leader trusted to take good decisions in a weak and faltering state.[13] The decline of political parties as mass organizations and their degeneration into oligarchic clubs reinforce the dependence on political personalities. Despotic politics has everything to do with promises of redemption. As it feeds upon the indignities of social life, it is energized by people's compensatory yearnings for tough but uncorrupted leaders who get things done. Modi's rise was powered by widespread anger about poor welfare provisions and disaffection with the corrupt poligarchs. He is seen as a charismatic redeemer backed by a well-funded and well-oiled party machinery. Someone who has proven that his government can build roads, homes, and toilets, and supply electricity and cooking gas, expanding his social base. Someone who is trying to make a difference. His popularity has also been fuelled by his reputation as a provincial outsider untainted by Delhi's old oligarchic clubs of patronage. An incorruptible anomaly who neither comes from a dynasty nor is building one. A leader whose take-no-prisoners brand of Hindutva signals political honesty.

The closest allies of Modi regard him as a Leader who never loses; defeat is not a word in their dictionary. Since he fancies himself as the saviour and redeemer of India, Modi himself demands unconditional personal loyalty from his confidantes, advisers, and party functionaries. In his influential mid-twentieth century reassessment of democracy, the Austrian political economist Joseph Schumpeter was sure that rule by manipulative political party machines would mark its future. 'The psycho-technics of party management and party advertising, slogans and marching tunes', he wrote, 'are not accessories. They are the essence of politics. So is the political boss.'[14] He would have been astonished by the operative psycho-technics of the Modi government, and its concomitant subjugation of every governing institution. It has downsized the number and role of cabinet ministers and fast-tracked the centralization of decision-making. States, long used to being independent nodes of power in India's federal structure as a result of coalition governments before Modi, have again begun to feel the tightening clasp of a domineering Delhi. Independent experts, bureaucrats, and opposition politicians are regarded with deep suspicion. Editors who cast doubts on the government, judges who refused to play ball, and vice chancellors who publicly defended the autonomy of the universities and students' right to protest are placed on hit lists. One-way communication, government by soliloquy, is the norm. Modi doesn't do press conferences. Like despots everywhere, the Prime Minister's Office harnesses calculated silence, such as when hate crimes are committed by Hindutva bigots. Striking is the rainbow quality of his government's multi-media, public pronouncements. Bent on maximizing the number of loyal people who count as the true people, its Hindu nationalism comes tinged with a khichri of different political symbols, loaded keywords and weasel phrases like 'jobs', 'God', 'growth', 'good days ahoy', 'friends', 'self-reliance', '$5 trillion economy', 'the people', and of course, 'democracy'.

New Licence Raj

The centralization and concentration of state power breeds other deadly pathologies. Since politics is turned into battles to crush enemies and win friends on the slippery road to capturing state power, with the help of followers persuaded they are the promised people, secret deals and alliances with chums in high places is mandatory. Ancient Greek democrats used a (now obsolete) verb *demokrateo* to describe how demagogues bent on ruling the people typically team up with rich and powerful aristocrats to snuff out the spirit and substance of democracy. There are strong parallels with what's been happening for some time in India, where, for all the talk of 'democracy' and 'the people', despots practise 'in-grouping' with rich and powerful buddies whose loyalty requires that they be treated well, showered with deals, gifts, and favours.

In-grouping between business tycoons and government is an old practice in Indian politics. It's traceable back to the Licence Raj period of Nehru, but ever since the beginning of economic reforms three decades ago, poligarchs—bigwig politicians and fat-cat businesspeople—have been actively weakening the spirit and substance of democracy as never before. The New Licence Raj of the despots is bolstered by a half-baked neoliberalism that still allows the state considerable policy discretion over business. The rapid economic growth post-liberalization, on the other hand, has endowed the seekers of favourable policy with far greater resources to offer party and government bosses in return for state discretion. The ability of despots at state and national levels to 'raise funds' has risen exponentially, allowing them more power over other party leaders and centralize authority. Ever since Modi started a biennial 'Vibrant Gujarat' in his home state in 2003 as chief minister, similar business 'summits' have become a fixture at the state level where corporate and political bosses hobnob in pageantries of poligarchy. Local despots use these glitzy events

to burnish their 'business-friendly' credentials by parading local and
foreign investors, who, in turn, pledge millions of rupees in fresh
investments. The promise of new jobs and prosperity bolsters the despot's credentials.

The investigative and revenue agencies at their disposal, along with
the tools of control of general economic policy and regulations, give
despots at the federal level added leverage over corporate players, forcing them to fall in line and forge new state–business alliances.
Proximity to the despot in Delhi can smooth the path to a lax reading
of the tax returns, friendlier policy, and debt-fuelled growth. Banks
wrote off more than Rs 2 trillion of bad loans in 2018–19 alone, taking
the total to Rs 5.7 trillion since Modi came to power in 2014–15.
More than 90 per cent of these loans were taken from public sector
banks, long used by India's rogue industrialists for private enrichment.[15] 'Modi toadies', understandably, shower him with petals of
flowery praise.[16] The toadying and adoration extend far beyond India's
borders, to include foreign admirers such as Rupert Murdoch (who
shortly after meeting the prime minister tweeted that he was 'the best
leader with best policies since independence'), successive American
presidents, and crowded stadiums of overseas diaspora citizens voicing
their support with loud chants of 'Modi! Modi! Modi!' The hard work
of the corporate toadies is rewarded with favourable policies in areas
where the state plays a major role in determining winners, such as
telecommunications and transport infrastructure.[17] The big winners
include Mukesh Ambani, whose Reliance Industries achieved a
near-monopoly of private hydrocarbon assets under the previous
Congress-led government and now dominates telecommunications
and retail, among many other industries; and the billionaire indus-
trialist Gautam Adani, who the *Financial Times* calls 'Modi's
Rockefeller'. When the Modi government decided (in 2018) to
privatize some smaller airports, all six of them went to Adani, in a
feat an opposition leader called an 'act of brazen cronyism'.[18] As an
already struggling economy crumbled under the weight of the

pestilence and the world's most stringent lockdown, and the shadow of job losses and poverty grew longer, Adani's personal wealth in 2020 increased $20 billion. Ambani's rose $17 billion, making him the fourth richest in the world, from fortieth on the Forbes list when Modi took over in 2014.[19] Following the Covid lockdown in March, India drew $36 billion of record foreign investments from April to August. More than half of it went to Ambani alone.

Backed by friends like these in high places, the new despotism harnesses the popular ambivalence about democratic accountability to the cause of tough and uncompromising government that delivers. Soon after Modi's re-election (in 2019), Rao Inderjit Singh, one of his ministers, told a public meeting that India is 'a democracy, sometimes it's a boon, sometimes it's a curse. China has developed so much faster than us because it is not a democracy...We are handicapped.'[20] The next year, Amitabh Kant, one of Modi's most trusted advisers, declared that 'too much' democracy in India keeps it from effecting meaningful reforms. Singh and Kant were probably dog whistling 'the people' against democracy—trying to persuade more Indians that if democracy is what people want, and most people want strong leadership that gets things done, and don't give a damn about freedom of speech or independent judiciary and media, then despotism is actually very democratic. Whatever 'the people' want.

Enemies of the People

Satyajit Ray's famous film *Ganashatru* (1990) tells the story of an honest doctor whose efforts to alert a community to the typhoid contamination of holy water of a famous temple are rebuffed by crooked local politicians and sycophant journalists and gullible citizens filled with wrath. He becomes an enemy of the people. The film was clairvoyant in spotting the way corrupt despots strengthen their grip on power by picking political fights with deviants and dissenters defined as not belonging to 'the people'. Despotism does more than 'in-grouping'. It practises 'out-grouping'. Its talk of 'We the People' actually means 'Others Don't Belong'. Despotism thrives on friend–enemy alliances and has deeply exclusionary effects, but its targets are flexible. Just as despots like Rodrigo Duterte in the Philippines and Jair Bolsonaro in Brazil variously spit at 'liberals' and 'foreigners', unpatriotic people who hail from nowhere, socialists, 'terrorists', environmental activists, same-sex, transgender, and religious minorities, so in India the outcast marginalia of The People who are deemed 'not even people' (Eric Trump)[21] are subject to ongoing redefinition. Heads high and sticks in hand, local despots and their followers hunt Western civil society organizations such as Amnesty and Greenpeace, or domestic NGOs receiving funds from foreign sources that do not bow to their wishes. They hound 'urban Naxals' (Left-leaning individuals), citizen activists, scientists, secular filmmakers and writers, intellectuals, 'Westernized' women, liberal journalists ('presstitutes'), and 'immoral' film stars. They hurl abuse at 'Hindu-baiters', spy patterns of 'Hindu-phobia' in voices dissenting against the government, and equate opposition to government with disloyalty to the nation. 'Go to Pakistan' is their message to anybody who dares to cross the despotic worldview of India's right-wing Hindus.

The struggle to elect a pasteurized people cleansed of those considered to be non-people helps explain why despots everywhere are morbidly attracted to violence, or urge or practise violence. Building despotism requires physical force: guns and sticks during election campaigns. It needs military-style street-level policing, the rough-tongued and violent treatment of targeted groups by private militia masquerading as social activists. Under the new dispensation of Hindutva despotism, the howling and hunting are mainly directed at the country's 200 million Muslim citizens. They are the prime targets of verbal insults, institutional discrimination, police inaction, political propaganda, and street-level thuggery, such as lynching and harassment. Muslims are also the intended victims of new citizenship laws audaciously designed to remake 'the people'.

For the first time in constitutionally secular India, the Modi government, emboldened by its re-election in 2019, linked citizenship to
religion, privileging non-Muslim immigrants from neighbouring
Islamic countries with fast-track citizenship. In tandem with a proposed national citizenship verification drive, known as the National
Register of Citizens (NRC), the elected despots redoubled their
efforts to define the 'true people' (Figure 36). The new citizenship law
helps Hindus and other non-Muslims retain citizenship if they can't
produce the necessary documentary evidence of citizenship. They can
claim to have roots in a neighbouring Muslim country where they
were persecuted, and so be considered refugees entitled to automatic
citizenship. Muslims without documents would have no such rights.
In an all-India citizenship verification, all 1.35 billion Indians would
be automatically considered outsiders, the onus being on individuals
to prove they are not. But with the new citizenship law, everybody
gets a free pass to remain—except Muslims, who are deemed no
longer part of 'the sovereign people'.

Figure 36. The citizen verification drive in Assam required establishing a
'family tree'

The prospect of a nationwide NRC and general anxiety about the future of citizenship triggered widespread protests across India. There were rallies, marches, and boycotts led by students, citizen activists, intellectuals, artists, film personalities, and voices from the middle class. Confronted by mass outpourings of popular rage for the first time, the new despots predictably stood firm. They showed that those who build despotism have tough minds and rough hands—and that they do all they can to win the backing of people who are attracted to a muscular, masculine vision of respect and reverence for the state. The peaceful protests were framed by BJP leaders as a 'deep-rooted con- spiracy' led by 'anti-national elements' of jihadis and Maoists (code for Muslims and Left liberals) bent on destroying the Indian state from within. In Uttar Pradesh, the local despot chief minister Adityanath, whose own rise to power was marked by violent rabble-rousing and sectarian violence, oversaw a nasty wave of state reprisal. There was terror, torture, and the imprisonment of hundreds of activists and protesters, even schoolchildren, on trumped-up charges. The priest- politician with a tendency to openly issue death threats to political dissenters and Muslims reminded citizens that 'there is no place for violence in a democracy', and simply banned public demonstrations. In a new low for state high-handedness, the government seized and auctioned the properties of activists who dared to raise their voice. Posters of protesters were put up in public places to name and shame them. Adityanath's actions were closely coordinated with his party bosses in Delhi as the establishment worked overtime to criminalize principled dissent.

Using well-crafted social media disinformation campaigns, normal- ized and amplified by regime-friendly legacy media, the government began to project the protests as yet another insidious plot to destroy India. The opposition, imploding and rudderless since Modi's victory in 2014, failed to counter the narrative or rally to the defence of the protesters. In no time, legitimate democratic pickets and roadblock protests became metaphors for Muslims obstructing Hindu India's triumphant march towards a brighter future under the Leader. 'Shoot the traitors' became a popular slogan for BJP party workers. Party goons were unleashed on campuses that showed the most resistance. Incendiary speeches by senior BJP leaders against protesters set the stage for riots in Delhi between Hindu and Muslim mobs, which turned into a pogrom against Muslims. Police remained passive observers, sometimes active collaborators. Hordes of armed Hindu vigilantes targeted Muslim homes and businesses in days-long orgies of violence. With the announcement of the pestilence lockdown, the crackdown intensified. In the following months, prominent rights organizations, academics, activists, politicians, and student leaders were charged and arrested by the police in an elaborate witch-hunt. Police submitted a 17,000-page chargesheet blaming anti-citizenship-law protesters for hatching the riots 'conspiracy'. A pan-India civil rights movement faithful to India's inclusive Constitution was thus neatly packaged as high treason. A hopeful moment of democratic resistance succumbed to the might of the despotic state.

Hopes

The use of iron hands to crush democratic dissent in the name of the 'people' has deepened fears over where India is heading. Intellectuals, journalists, politicians, and citizens are today engaged in robust conversations about what current trends mean, and how to define the steeling of state power. A public phrase struggle has begun. There's talk of the rise of fascism, the birth of an 'ethnic democracy', the 'revolt of the upper castes against democracy', and the 'retreat' and 'backsliding' of democracy towards 'crony capitalism', 'authoritarianism', and a 'majoritarian state'.

From Hungary and Poland to Turkey and Russia, despotism in the twenty-first century is a distinctively *global* problem for democracy. As the eighteenth-century French political writer Montesquieu first spotted ('democracy usually degenerates into the despotism of the People'), and as Tocqueville confirmed a century later when visiting

America ('democratic times should especially fear despotism'), despotism is a dangerously seductive by-product of an ailing democracy and therefore demands that thinking people track its current growth, and its possible future triumph.[22] India's metamorphosis into despotism, a centralized state that wields power over its loyal subjects in the name of a phantom 'people', hence calls on democrats everywhere to think with an urgent sense of caution about what the future may hold.

India's despotic drift has an added dimension, in the nearly century-old majoritarian ethno-nationalist Hindutva movement that backdrops the BJP's rise to hegemonic power. The political obliteration of Muslims, as evidenced from a drastic drop in Muslim representation through a concerted pan-Hindu voter mobilization, is only one facet of India's slide towards a new despotism. There are others, such as the systematic invisibilization of Muslims in rewritten official histories, renamed public spaces and all spheres of public life. There are state-orchestrated denigrations of India's founding leaders who stood for an inclusive secular democracy; new laws to prevent Muslim men from marrying Hindu women; renewed legislation to protect cows and a National Cow Commission dedicated to promoting the benefits of all things bovine, from cow dung to urine. Even Bollywood, the country's mightiest cultural force, is fair game in this elaborate project to remake India's cultural life in a Hindu-first mould. It is not for nothing that some Indian political thinkers are declaring the arrival of a 'second republic' as the first 'socialist, secular, democratic republic' transitions to a 'quasi-democratic, firmly majoritarian, and crony-capitalist republic', if not an outright theocratic Hindu state.[23]

Is Indian democracy nearing the end of its life then? Given the profound social decay and government corruption in today's India, it would be tempting to conclude that the democratic spirit of equality and institutions designed to prevent bossing and bullying of citizens and their everyday lives don't stand a chance. But India doesn't lend itself to simple, reductive conclusions. The counter-currents to despotic power are substantial. Despite widespread talk of Modi's complete domination of Indian politics, the fact is that the drift towards elective despotism remains vulnerable to voters' resistance. Even though the BJP won more than 50 per cent of directly elected seats in the Parliament in the last two elections, it had the support of a little less than a third (31 per cent) of the voters in 2014 and a little more than a third (37 per cent) in 2019. The victories were inflated by the first-past-the-post voting system, a strangely imperial hangover that can make even a low vote share look like a thumping majority because of the fragmentation of the vote. The sobering fact, too, is that the BJP hasn't seized full control of the states. Many regional parties remain powerful, and Indian voters often vote differently in national or state elections, where these local parties tango and tussle with the dominant national forces according to their own calculus, rather than the dictates of some or other big-boss Leader.

India's plurality of languages, ethnicities, caste and class divisions, and other identities also doesn't lend itself to political monotheism. Pluralism is intrinsic to India's being. It is more comfortable in its multiple avatars. From ending Jammu and Kashmir's autonomy to centralizing welfare schemes and markets, and pressing for simultaneous state and national elections, Modi likes to justify what he does as a binding quest for 'One India'. But the fact is that his government's efforts to define an 'Indian people' by dressing in a coat of many colours and speaking in tongues are contradicted by its monochromatic Hindu nationalism. It also breeds resistance. Recurrent social media campaigns like #StopHindiImposition and other forms of social protest show that the BJP's philosophy of 'Hindi, Hindu, Hindustan'—one language, one culture, one country—sits at odds with India's intrinsic diversity. There's no single idea of Hindu or Hindu-ness, just as there's no one Indian language, or homogeneous 'Indian culture'.

There are other indications that the spirit and substance of democracy are still very much alive in India. If the dignity of women is a key indicator of the vigour of any given democracy, then trends such as shrinking public toleration of domestic violence and rising school enrolment of girls and women tell a hopeful story. Women's collectives, self-help groups, micro-finance schemes, and expanding education, along with female participation in business and economic life, are quietly altering gender balances. Reservation of elected seats at the local level for women have demonstrably raised expectations. Adolescent girls in villages with female leaders are now more likely to want to marry after 18, less willing to be housewives bogged down in household chores or have their occupations determined by their in-laws, and more likely to want a job that requires an education.[24] The advent of communicative abundance is also raising the public visibility of women's condition and challenging old patriarchal ideas. The introduction of cable television in rural India in the early 2000s, for example, led women to speak up against domestic violence and old preferences for male offspring.[25] The spread of mobile telephony is accelerating these trends. After a gang of Hindu thugs attacked women in a pub in the southern city of Mangalore in 2008, an initiative known as the Consortium of Pub-Going, Loose and Forward Women attracted widespread public attention when they launched a 'Pink Chaddi' Facebook campaign to crowdsource pink underwear to send to the gang's leader. Four years later, social media mobilization after the gruesome Delhi bus rape brought the capital to a standstill as hundreds of thousands of protesters took to the streets. More recently, a concerted online campaign in 2018 forced the Modi government to withdraw taxes on sanitary napkins.

The same spirit of women's refusal of arbitrary power was evident in Delhi's Shaheen Bagh area, where Muslim women held a 101-day sit-in protest on a major roadway against the new citizenship law, unshaken by the bitterest cold in Delhi's history and the deadly riots, unbowed until the lockdown and the spreading fear of pestilence forced them to go home. Bilkis 'Dadi' (grandma), the 82-year-old Muslim woman who led the sit-in that inspired similar protests across the country, was featured in *Time* magazine's list of 100 most influential people of 2020 for her spirited resistance (Figure 37).

This satyagraha tradition of non-violent political mobilization remains vibrant. Democratic instincts sharpened over decades by

Figure 37. Protesters at Shaheen Bagh flying the flag of hope

innovations such as public interest litigations (PILs) encourage public-spirited individuals and organizations to file petitions against predatory power. Civil society campaigns have brought about landmark court judgments, such as the banning of child labour in the carpet industry, and pressed home the right of citizens to access information and audit government programmes in open public forums. A decades-long campaign led to the enactment of the right to information (RTI), which allows any Indian citizen to demand any information from the government on its structures and functioning that are not in the public domain. RTI activists are often subject to violence and intimidation, but the 4–6 million RTI applications still filed every year across the country help citizens tease out important information from the government, despite its reluctance to part with secrets. Helped along by digitally networked media platforms, local citizen initiatives abound, be they rescuing livelihoods, saving lakes, fixing roads, or opposing flyovers, nuclear power plants, or protesting against government policies deemed unfair, such as the massive farmers' protests near Delhi from the end of 2020 against new laws pushing agricultural reforms.

Farmers mainly from northern states, most at risk of losing guaranteed farm prices due to reforms aimed at encouraging corporate

participation in agriculture, congregated at the capital's border, enduring biting Delhi cold like the rebellious gang of Bilkis 'Dadi' the
previous winter. A government that had first introduced the policy by
force through an ordinance and then railroaded it through Parliament,
overriding the opposition's pleas, was forced to negotiate with farmer
bodies. When talks failed, it tried to use familiar tactics. Federal probe
agencies were sent after prominent supporters of the agitation. The
peaceful protests were criminalized by calling these the machinations
of Pakistan and China. A vicious social media campaign sought to
tarnish Sikh protesters as terrorists and 'anti-nationals' and
'Khalistanis'— by evoking the '80s separatist movement for a sovereign state in the Punjab region that led to Mrs Gandhi's assassination.
The newly branded 'non-people', at war with the government of 'the
people', held their ground. Farmers stood together across ethnic and
provincial lines, asserted their constitutional right to dissent, rejected
the government's compromises and launched its own newspaper, and
dug in for the long haul. The great refusal forced the people's government to fortify itself against the 'non-people'. The months-long farmers' protest attracted international attention and again raised doubts
about India's democratic standards. The government was finally forced
to offer to put the new laws on hold and appoint a special commission to review the laws. The farmers stuck to their demand for full
repeal of the laws and carried on with their protests.

All these refusals to accept things as they are and question despotic
power 'are a tremendous source of inspiration and hope', write two
seasoned observers of Indian politics. Public mobilizations such as
these 'are a living expression of the constitutional values of liberty,
equality and fraternity. They have forged new solidarities across old
divides and unleashed an unprecedented wave of creative thinking and
action around democratic ideals.'[26] Some activist public intellectuals
are pointing out that struggles to 'rescue Indian democracy' now
require battles to 'save the Indian model of a diverse nation' and to
redeem the 'promise of an inclusive welfare state'.[27] Still others have

emphasized democracy's 'unceasing capacity to surprise, exceed, and evade our expectations'.[28] The Constitution itself is an example of democratic anticipation in action. It wasn't designed by the founders as simply a lengthy set of tedious procedural rules for managing conflict and constraining the power of government. It aimed to bring democracy to a society that knew and felt little about democracy. It supposed that people could be remade, that colonial subjects could be transformed into thinking and acting citizens who regarded themselves as equals living together in dignity.

Among the most potent long-term gifts of the democracy founded in India last century is the way it has stirred up hopes for a dignified society of equal citizens. The founding democratic vision was built on hope. It remains the condition of possibility of hope. Think of how democracy stirs up a sense of possibility. When confronted by setbacks and sticky situations that tempt people to conclude, 'Well, that's the way things are', wise citizens think twice. They're encouraged to say: 'Actually, things can be different.' This sense of possibility could be defined as the capacity of people to see that the way things currently are has no privileged status, so that the way things are can be challenged by the way things might become. In this sense, democracy 'denatures' power relations. It gets people to see that things aren't fixed in stone, and that they can be changed, for the better.

Even when people are ground down by social indignities, a democracy encourages them to look beyond their present miserable horizons, to expect and to demand positive improvements. Democracy even stretches the scope of hope. Hope isn't just the anticipation of a future that's judged to be possible. Hope can also be the active remembering of a past that can be rescued and resuscitated, brought back to life in much-changed circumstances, with an eye to the future. Hope can be a way of remembering past wisdoms in support of struggles to bolster the dignity of those who are presently wronged, to help them move towards a better future. That's the operative principle within the fine work on the subject of equality by Aishwary Kumar and other scholars. They remind their Indian audiences, and the rest of the world, of the global importance of B.R. Ambedkar's and Periyar E.V. Ramasamy's understanding of democracy as a way of life that not only licenses citizens to rebel against social injustice and lawless power but also enables them to see that if despotism replaces democracy then this isn't because despotic power is somehow inevitable, but because citizens allow it to happen.[29]

That means, when the going gets really rough, democracy fosters hope against hope. It stirs up insurrections. It gives energy to the sense that it's possible to change things, to build a better future guided by precious precepts: no famine and slavery, more freedom with clean running water, better schooling and decent healthcare, greater social equality, less political bossing and bullying. In moments when democracy falls sick, this is perhaps its most important virtue: it inspires citizens to take full advantage of what they have, and what comes their way, to build a better future for everybody, not just for the rich and powerful few.

Notes

A DISTANT RAINBOW

1. Ramachandra Guha, 'Two Anniversaries', *The Telegraph Online*, 29 August 2020, available at: https://www.telegraphindia.com/opinion/73-years-of-indian-independence-how-the-india-story-ended/cid/1789162

2. Winston Churchill, *India. Speeches and an Introduction* (London 1931), pp. 30, 136, 77; Hira Lal Seth, *Churchill on India* (Sant Nagar, Lahore 1942), p. 16.

3. Ashsis Nandy, *Time Warps: The Insistent Politics of Silent and Evasive Pasts* (Delhi 2003), pp. 5–6 and *The Tao of Cricket: On Games of Destiny and the Destiny of Games* (New Delhi 2000).

4. Sandeep Shastri, Suhas Palshikar, and Sanjay Kumar (eds.), *State of Democracy in South Asia*. Report II (Jakkasandra 2017), p. 23; https://www.pewresearch.org/global/2017/11/15/the-state-of-indian-democracy/

5. The data is drawn from a Centre for the Study of Developing Societies (CSDS) survey, as reported in *India Today* (31 August 1996), pp. 30–9; see also Yogendra Yadav, 'Understanding the Second Democratic Upsurge: Trends of Bahujan participation in electoral politics in the 1990s', in Francine Frankel et al. (eds.), *Transforming India: Social and Political Dynamics of Democracy* (Delhi 2000), pp. 122–34. The disproportionately low turnout of poor people in US presidential elections is analysed in J. Harder and J. Krosnick, 'Why Do People Vote? A Psychological Analysis of the Causes of Voter Turnout'. *Journal of Social Issues*, 64, 3 (2008), pp. 525–49.

6. Peter Ronald de Souza, *In the Hall of Mirrors: Reflections on Indian Democracy* (Hyderabad 2018), pp. 155, 239, 122.

7. Sunil Khilnani, *The Idea of India* (London 2003), p. 60.

8. Henry Kissinger, *White House Years* (Boston and Toronto 1979), p. 849.

9. Compare Rajni Kothari, *Politics in India* (Delhi 1970) and the different emphases in his *The State Against Democracy: In Search of Humane Governance* (Delhi 1988).

10. Gyan Prakash, *Emergency Chronicles: Indira Gandhi and Democracy's Turning Point* (Princeton, NJ 2019).

11. John Keane, *The Life and Death of Democracy* (London and New York 2009), pp. 70–77, 89–101; and Eric W. Robinson, *The First Democracies: Early Popular Government Outside Athens* (Stuttgart 1997), pp. 114–18.

12. Steven Levitsky and Daniel Ziblatt, *How Democracies Die* (New York 2018), p. 3.

13. Bálint Magyar, *Post-Communist Mafia State: The Case of Hungary* (Budapest 2016); Bálint Magyar and Júlia Vásárhelyi (eds.), *Twenty-Five Sides of a Post-Communist Mafia State* (Budapest 2017); and Bálint Magyar (ed.), *Stubborn Structures: Reconceptualizing Postcommunist Regimes* (Budapest 2019).

14. See Ramachandra Guha, 'India's descent from a 50–50 to a 30–70 democracy', *Hindustan Times*, 21 March 2020, available at: https://www.hindustantimes.com/columns/india-s-descent-from-a-50-50-to-a-30-70-democracy/story-CBlmSCCeaxXpO8rPL7nycI.html; Pratap Bhanu Mehta, 'There is no Emergency', *The Indian Express*, 5 November 2016, available at: https://indianexpress.com/article/opinion/columns/emergency-period-india-ndtv-ban-media-freedom-3737771/; and Yogendra Yadav's comment when launching his *Making Sense of Indian Democracy: Theory as Practice* at Delhi's CSDS (3 September, 2020).

15. Pratap Bhanu Mehta, *The Burden of Democracy* (New Delhi 2003), pp. 52–3.

16. See Periyar E.V. Ramasamy, *Ivarthaam Periyar* [This is Periyar], edited M. Nannan (Chennai 2019); and Periyar E.V. Ramasamy, *Women Enslaved* (New Delhi 2009).

17. See Amartya Sen, *Commodities and Capabilities* (Amsterdam 1985); 'Well-being, Agency and Freedom: The Dewey Lectures 1984'. *Journal of Philosophy*, 82, 4 (1985), pp. 69–221; and 'Capability: Reach and Limit', in E. Chipper-Martinetti (ed.), *Debating Global Society: Reach and Limit of the Capability Approach* (Milan 2009), pp. 15–28.

18. Aishwary Kumar, *Radical Equality: Ambedkar, Gandhi, and the Risk of Democracy* (Stanford 2015), p. 336; Pratap Bhanu Mehta, *The Burden of Democracy*, p. 176.

19. C.B. Macpherson, *Democratic Theory: Essays in Retrieval* (Oxford 1973), essays 1 and 3.

HEALTH OF A DEMOCRACY

1. Mandeep Singh, 'Turned Away From Hospitals, My Father-In-Law's Death From COVID Shows Delhi Is A Mess', *Huffpost*, 4 June 2020.

2. Sohini Ghosh, 'Civil Hospital worse than dungeon, says Gujarat HC', *The Indian Express*, 24 May 2020.

3. Prabha Raghavan, Tabassum Barnagarwala, and Abantika Ghosh, 'Covid fight: Govt system in front, private hospitals do the distancing', *The Indian Express*, 30 April 2020.

4. Sohini Ghosh, 'Civil Hospital worse than dungeon, says Gujarat HC,' *The Indian Express*, 24 May 2020.

5. Lant Pritchett, 'Is India a Flailing State?: Detours on the Four Lane Highway to Modernization', *Scholarly Articles 4,449,106*, Harvard Kennedy School of Government (2009).

6. C. Sohini, 'In India, do not ever say "dengue"', *This Week in Asia*, 23 December 2017.

7. 'Measuring performance on the Healthcare Access and Quality Index for 195 countries and territories and selected subnational locations: A systematic analysis from the Global Burden of Disease Study 2016', *The Lancet*, 23 May 2018.

8. Manas Chakravarty, 'India's dismal record in healthcare', *Live Mint*, 25 May 2017.

9. Ali Kazemi Karyani, Enayatollah Homaie Rad, Abolghasem Pourreza, and Faramarz Shaahmadi, 'Democracy, political freedom and health expenditures: evidence from Eastern Mediterranean countries', *International Journal of Human Rights in Healthcare*, 21 September 2015.

10. 'Global study highlights role of democracy in improving adult health', *The Lancet*, 13 March 2019.

11. Timothy Besley and Masayuki Kudamatsu, 'Health and Democracy', *American Economic Review*, 96, 2 (2006).

12. 'Mortality due to low-quality health systems in the universal health coverage era: a systematic analysis of amenable deaths in 137 countries', *The Lancet*, 392, 10, p. 160, 17 November 2018.

13. 'The Global Burden of Disease Study', *The Lancet*, 396, 10258 pp. 1129–306, 17 October 2020.

14. World bank data.

15. Jean Drèze, Aashish Gupta, Sai Ankit Parashar, and Kanika Sharma, 'Pauses and reversals of infant mortality decline in India in 2017 and 2018', *SSRN*, 8 November 2020.

16. Jean Drèze and Amartya Sen, *An Uncertain Glory: India and its Contradictions* (Harmondsworth and New Delhi 2013).

17. JustActions, 'The Missing Piece: Why Continued Neglect of Pneumonia Threatens the Achievement of Health Goals', New York, 2018.

18. Michael J.A. Reid et al., 'Building a tuberculosis-free world: The Lancet Commission on tuberculosis', *The Lancet*, 20 March 2019.

19. T.S. Ravikumar and Georgi Abraham, 'We need a leap in healthcare spending', *The Hindu*, 7 February 2019.

20. Sakthivel Selvaraj, Habib Hasan Farooqui, and Anup Karan, 'Quantifying the financial burden of households' out-of-pocket payments on medicines in India: a repeated cross-sectional analysis of National Sample Survey data, 1994–2014', *BMJ Open*, 31 May 2018.

21. Pramit Bhattacharya and Udayan Rathore, 'The staggering costs of India's failing health systems', *Live Mint*, 24 September 2018.

22. 'The Global Burden of Disease Study', pp. 1129–306.

23. Samar Halarnkar, 'The Tamil Nadu or Uttar Pradesh model: What lies ahead for India in 2019?', *Scroll*, 7 February 2019.

24. 'Democracies contain epidemics most effectively', *The Economist*, 6 June 2020.

25. John Keane, 'Democracy and the Great Pestilence', *Eurozine*, 17 April 2020.

26. Center for Disease Dynamics, Economics & Policy (CDDEP) in the United States.

A MILLION FAMINES

1. Thomas Robert Malthus, *An Essay on the Principle of Population; or A View of Its Past and Present Effects on Human Happiness* (London 1798).

2. Focused on the Bengal famine, Bhabani Bhattacharya's masterpiece is *So Many Hungers!* (New Delhi 1947).

3. Jasper Becker, *Hungry Ghosts: Mao's Secret Famine* (New York 1998).

4. Amartya Sen, *Development as Freedom*; compare his *The Argumentative Indian: Writings on Indian History, Culture and Identity* (London 2005), p. 51; and 'Democracy as a universal value', *Journal of Democracy* 10, 3 (1999), p. 12.

5. Quoted in Michael Massing, 'Does Democracy Avert Famine?', *The New York Times*, 1 March 2003,

6. John Keane, 'Hypocrisy and Democracy: The gap between ideals and perceived reality is widening', *WZB-Mitteilungen*, 120 (June 2008), pp. 30–32.

7. 'Identity Verification Standards in Welfare Programs: Experimental Evidence From India', *NBER Working Paper* 26744, February 2020.

8. 'Subnational mapping of under-5 and neonatal mortality trends in India: The Global Burden of Disease Study 2000–17', *The Lancet* 2020.

9. October 2019, The State of the World's Children 2019 Statistical Tables. Available at https://data.unicef.org/resources/dataset/sowc-2019-statistical-tables/

10. Ashwini Deshpande and Rajesh Ramachandran, 'Stunting in India: Role of Education, Behaviour and Social Identity', SSRN, 20 March 2019.

11. Nkechi G. Onyeneho, Benjamin C. Ozumba, and S. V. Subramanian, 'Determinants of Childhood Anemia in India', *Nature*, 12 November 2019.

12. Neha Saigal and Saumya Shrivastava, 'India's Disadvantaged Lack Nutrition, Except We Don't Know How Much', *IndiaSpend*, 30 November 2020.

13. Emanuela Galasso and Adam Wagstaff, 'The Aggregate Income Losses from Childhood Stunting and the Returns to a Nutrition Intervention Aimed at Reducing Stunting', *World Bank Group*, August 2018.

14. 'Gujarat has over 3.8L malnourished children', *Ahmedabad Mirror*, 28 February 2020.

15. Parth Shastri, Malnutrition contributing to child deaths in Gujarat', TNN, 6 January 2020. https://timesofindia.indiatimes.com/city/ahmedabad/malnutrition-contributing-to-child-deaths-in-state/articleshow/73113834.cms

16. Jean Dreze and Reetika Khera, 'Understanding Leakages in the Public Distribution System', *Economic and Political Weekly*, February 2015, 50(7).

17. 'Labouring Lives: Hunger, Precarity and Despair amid Lockdown', Centre for Equity Studies, Delhi Research Group & Karwan-E-Mohabbat, Rosa Luxemburg Stiftung, June 2020.

18. Survey by Gaon Connection and Centre for Study of Developing Societies (Lokniti-CSDS).

19. Rohan Venkataramakrishnan, 'Hunger hangs large over India. There is one thing Centre can do immediately to address the problem', *Scroll*, 17 April 2020.

20. Sarah Khan, 'Three-fourth poor households without ration card didn't receive government ration in lockdown', *Gaon Connection*, 2 November 2020; 'Over 1,500 Tonnes of Food Grains Wasted at FCI Godowns During Lockdown: Govt Data', *The Wire*, 5 October 2020.

21. MN Parth, 'Battling starvation during COVID-19: Struggle for survival intensifies for tribal families in Maharashtra's Palghar', *Firstpost*, 28 August 2020.

22. Jagriti Chandra, 'Three top panels on nutrition, but zero meetings in pandemic year,' *The Hindu*, 7 January 2021.

GROUND REALITIES

1. Justice M. B. Shah, *Commission of Enquiry, First Report on Illegal Mining of Iron and Manganese Ores in the State of Odisha*, June 2013.

2. Ministry of Rural Development, Government of India, 'Draft Report of the Committee on State Agrarian Relations and Unfinished Task of Land Reforms', 2009.

3. Robin Jeffrey, 'Whatever Happened To "Land Reform"? One Big Question and Four Naive Little Answers', *ISAS Working Paper* No. 149–8, June 2012.

4. 2013 draft National Land Reform Policy.

5. 'Draft report by the Committee on State Agrarian Relations'.

6. Mayank Aggarwal, 'The evolving story of India's forests', *Mongabay*, 27 February 2020.

7. John Keane, *Power and Humility: The Future of Monitory Democracy* (Cambridge and New York 2018).

8. Moin Qazi, 'India's Thirsty Crops Are Draining the Country Dry', *The Diplomat*, 6 April 2017; Mark Giordano, 'Global Groundwater? Issues and Solutions', *Reviews in Advance*, 28 July 2009.

9. Deepa Joshi, 'Caste, Gender and the Rhetoric of Reform in India's Drinking Water Sector', *Economic and Political Weekly*, 30 April 2011.

10. Cited in Jaideep Hardikar, 'A wish list on water from parched India', *LiveMint*, 11 June 2019.

11. E. Shajia et al., 'Arsenic contamination of groundwater: A global synopsis with focus on the Indian Peninsula', *Geoscience Frontiers*, 15 August 2020.

12. 'Aqualculture: An Investigation on Trends and Practices in India', Federation of Indian Animal Protection Organisations (FIAPO) and All Creatures Great and Small, 2020.

13. M. Rajshekhar, 'Cancer has exploded in Bihar as lakhs of people drink water poisoned with arsenic', *Scroll*, 24 April 2017; Sewa Singh and Harwinder Singh, 'Impact and extent of ground water pollution: A case study of rural area in Punjab State (India)', *International Journal of Environment and Health* 5, 4, pp. 277–292, December 2011.

14. Findings by New Delhi–based public-interest research group Centre for Science and Environment.

15. Bhasker Tripathi, 'Air Pollution Killed A Newborn Every 5 Minutes In 2019', 21 October 2020, citing 'State of Global Air 2020' report.

16. Venkata Krishna Munagala, Ramisetty M. Uma Mahesh, Jithendra Kandati and Munilakshmi Ponugoti, 'Clinical study of lower respiratory tract infections in children attending a tertiary care hospital', *International Journal of Contemporary Pediatrics*, 4, 5, 2017, p. 1733.

17. Survey by LocalCircles.

18. 'US Embassy purchased over 1,800 air purifiers before President Obama's India visit', *The Indian Express*, 2 February 2015; Aditya Kalra, 'Exclusive: Faced with Delhi's pollution, India's federal agencies bought air purifiers', *Reuters*, 20 March 2018.

19. Rahul Goela et al., 'On-road PM2.5 pollution exposure in multiple transport microenvironments in Delhi', *Atmospheric Environment*, 123, 2015.
20. Global report by researchers from the International Council on Clean Transportation (ICCT), George Washington University, and University of Colorado, Boulder.

MOTION SICKNESS

1. John Keane, *The Life and Death of Democracy* (London and New York 2009), pp. 3–126.
2. 'No Commuter Deaths On Mumbai's Local Train Network On June 26', *PTI*, 28 June 2019; 'Day after zero deaths celebrated, nine casualties reported on Mumbai trains', *Business Today*, 28 June 2019.
3. Pooja Dantewadia and Nikita Vashisth, 'Mumbai-Ahmedabad Bullet Train To Cost 70% More Than Highway Budget', *FactChecker*, 15 September 2017.
4. 'Promoting Low-carbon Transport in India: Low-Carbon Mobility in India and the Challenges of Social Inclusion: Bus Rapid Transit (BRT) Case Studies in India', Centre for Urban Equity, UNEP, 2013.
5. O.P. Agarwal, 'Compulsion to Choice: How Can Public Transport in India Be Transformed?' *EPW*, 29 January 2019; *Times of India*, 'For 1,000 people, just 1.2 buses in India', 25 September 2018.
6. Sriharsha Devulapalli, 'India's public transport challenge', *LiveMint*, 16 September 2019.
7. Dario Hidalgo et al., 'National Investment in Urban Transport in India: Towards people's cities through land use and transport integration', *World Resources Institute*, March 2013.
8. Athar Parvaiz, 'Road Accidents Killed 46% More People In J&K Than Armed Violence Over 13 Years', *IndiaSpend*, 8 August 2017.

WRITING ON THE WALL

1. Gary McCulloch, 'Empires and Education: The British Empire', in Robert Cowen and Andreas M. Kazamias (eds.), *International Handbook of Comparative Education* (Dordrecht, Heidelberg, London and New York 2009), pp. 169–79 [170]; see also J.A. Mangan, *The games ethic and imperialism: Aspects of the diffusion of an ideal* (London 1986); J.A. Mangan (ed.), *'Benefits bestowed'? Education and British Imperialism* (Manchester 1988); and 'Eton in India: The imperial diffusion of a Victorian educational ethic', *History of Education*, 7, 2 (1978), pp. 105–18.

2. L.E. Davis and R.A. Huttenback, *Mammon and the Pursuit of Empire: The Political Economy of British Imperialism, 1860–1912* (New York: Cambridge University Press 1986); see also Syed Mahmud, *A History of English Education in India 1781–1893* (1895).

3. The quotations are from John Dewey, *Democracy and Education: An Introduction to the Philosophy of Education* (New York 1916 [1925]), pp. 9–10, 95, 47, 387, 48, 53, 144–45, 86, 98, 101, 357, 115.

4. Latika Chaudhary, 'Colonial investments in education in India', *VoxDev*, 11 August 2017.

5. Jean Drèze and Amartya Sen, *An Uncertain Glory: India and Its Contradictions* (London and New York 2014), p. 25.

6. Vignesh Radhakrishnan, 'What is the dropout rate among schoolchildren in India?', *The Hindu*, 4 January 2019.

7. Drèze and Sen, *An Uncertain Glory*, p. 120.

8. 'Key Indicators of Household Social Consumption on Education in India', *NSS 75th Round*, National Statistical Office, Government of India, July 2017 to June 2018.

9. Oxfam, 'When schools continue to exclude, can education reduce caste discrimination in India?', 3 April 2015.

10. *Annual Status of Education Report* (ASER), 2018.

11. Lani Guinier, *The Tyranny of the Meritocracy: Democratizing Higher Education in America*, Beacon Press (13 January 2015).

12. Raj Chetty et al., 'Mobility Report Cards: The Role of Colleges in Intergenerational Mobility', *NBER Working Paper* No. 23618 (July 2017); Paul Tough, *The Years That Matter Most: How College Makes or Breaks Us* (New York 2019); and Louis Menand, 'Is Meritocracy Making Everyone Miserable?', *The New Yorker*, 23 September 2019.

13. 'Politics and Society Between Elections', Azim Premji University and CSDS-Lokniti, 2018.

14. According to global Multidimensional Poverty Index (MPI) 2018, by United Nations Development Programme and the Oxford Poverty and Human Development Initiative.

15. Nitin Kumar Bharti, 'Wealth Inequality, Class and Caste in India, 1961–2012', World Inequality Database, November 2018.

16. Ritika Chopra, '20 years on, where are the Board toppers? Over half are abroad, most in science and technology', *The Indian Express*, 29 December 2020.

17. Amit Thorat and Omkar Joshi, 'The Continuing Practice of Untouchability in India: Patterns and Mitigating Influences', *Economic & Political Weekly*, IV, 2, 11 January 2020.

18. National Sample Survey Organization (NSSO), 71st round, conducted during January to July 2014; Analysis of unit-level data from the 2017–18 National Statistical Office (NSO) survey on education by Roshan Kishore and Abhishek Jha, 'Mapping education inequalities', *Hindustan Times*, 1 August 2020.

19. Edward L. Glaeser, Giacomo Ponzetto, and Andrei Shleifer, 'Why Does Democracy Need Education?' *NBER Working Paper* No. 12128 (March 2006).

20. Anirudh Krishna, 'Examining the Structure of Opportunity and Social Mobility in India: Who Becomes an Engineer?' *Development and Change*, 45, 1 (2014).

21. 'Myths of Online Education', Azim Premji University, September 2020.

22. Nicholas Lemann, *The Big Test: The Secret History of the American Meritocracy* (New York 1999).

23. Yashica Dutt, *Coming Out as Dalit: A Memoir* (Aleph Book Company 2019).

24. Sukhadeo Thorat and Paul Attewell, 'The Legacy of Social Exclusion: A Correspondence Study of Job Discrimination in India', *Economic & Political Weekly* (13 October 2007); Surinder S. Jodhka, 'Caste and the Corporate Sector', *Indian Journal of Industrial Relations*, 44, 2 (October 2008), pp. 185–93.

A NEW SLAVERY

1. '21 Days and Counting: COVID-19 Lockdown, Migrant Workers, and the Inadequacy of Welfare Measures in India', *Stranded Workers Action Network*, 15 April 2020.

2. 'Technical Brief No 3: Young People Not in Employment, Education or Training', ILO, 2020.

3. Santosh Mehrotra and Jajati K. Parida, 'India's Employment Crisis: Rising Education Levels and Falling Non-agricultural Job Growth', Working Paper, Centre for Sustainable Employment, Azim Premji University, October 2019.

4. Oxfam estimates.

5. Karl Polanyi, *Origins of Our Time: The Great Transformation* (London 1945).

6. José Batlle y Ordóñez (writing anonymously), 'Instruccion Para Todos', *El Día* (4 December 1914); a fuller account is presented in John Keane, *The Life and Death of Democracy* (London and New York 2009).

7. 2003 NSSO report on landholding, cited in the 'Draft Report of the Committee on State Agrarian Relations and Unfinished Task of Land Reforms', *Ministry of Rural Development*, 2013.

8. Sandeep Kandikuppa, 'To What Extent Are India's Farmers Indebted?', *The Wire*, 30 November 2018; Sanjukta Nair, 'As Formal Farm Credit Grows, So Does Hold Of Moneylenders. Here's Why', *IndiaSpend*, 5 January 2018.

9. Sher Singh Verick, 'The Puzzles and Contradictions of the Indian Labour Market: What Will the Future of Work Look Like?' *IZA Institute of Labor Economics*, IZA DP No. 11376, February 2018.

10. Joseph E. Stiglitz, 'Some Lessons From The East Asian Miracle', *The World Bank Research Observer* 11, 2 (August 1996), pp. 151–77.

11. 'State of Working India 2019', Centre for Sustainable Employment, Azim Premji University.

12. Mehrotra and Parida, 'India's Employment Crisis'.

13. Prateek Goyal, 'A slaughterhouse for wombs: District Beed, Maharashtra', *News Laundry*, 31 July 2019: https://www.newslaundry.com/2019/07/31/a-slaughterhouse-for-wombs-district-beed-maharashtra; Patralekha Chatterjee, 'Hysterectomies in Beed district raise questions for India', *The Lancet*, 20 July 2019.

14. 'Karl Marx on India', *New International*, VIII, 6 (July 1942), p. 192.

15. Vijayta Lalwani, 'After 43 people die in factory blaze, fire official says: "Half of Delhi is like this" ', *Scroll*, 8 December 2019.

16. Paivi Hamalainen, Jukka Takala, and Kaija Leena Saarela, 'Global estimates of occupational accidents', *Safety Science* 44 (2006).

17. Dilip Kumar Arvindkumar Patel and Kumar Neeraj Jha, 'An Estimate of Fatal Accidents in Indian Construction', in P. W. Chan and C. J. Neilson (eds.) *Association of Researchers in Construction Management*, Vol 1, 32nd Annual ARCOM Conference, 5–7 September 2016, Manchester, UK.

18. Jagdish Patel, 'Difficulties of recording and notification of accidents and diseases in developing countries', ILO, 12 March 2019.

19. Guy Standing, *The Precariat: The New Dangerous Class* (London 2011).

20. Henry S. Farber, Daniel Herbst, Ilyana Kuziemko, and Suresh Naidu, 'Unions and Inequality Over the Twentieth Century: New Evidence from Survey Data', *NBER Working Paper* No. 24587 (May 2018).

21. 'India Wage Report: Wage policies for decent work and inclusive growth', ILO, 2018.

22. Soumya Kanti Ghosh, 'Profits And Wages In The Covid Era: Looking Under The Hood', *BloombergQuint*, 21 December 2020

23. Susmita Banerjee and Nabanita De, 'India's Informal Employment in the Era of Globalization: Trend and Challenges', *IOSR Journal of Business and Management*, 20, 4, Ver.III (April 2018).

24. Radhicka Kapoor, 'Understanding India's Jobs Challenge', *The India Forum*, 10 September 2019.

25. Aunindyo Chakravarty, 'Middle class takes a hit', *The Tribune*, 17 January 2021.

26. Santosh Mehrotra, 'India Does Have a Real Employment Crisis—And it's Worsening', *The Wire*, 6 February 2019.

27. Duha Tore Altindag and Naci H. Mocan, 'Joblessness and Perceptions about the Effectiveness of Democracy', *NBER Working Paper* No. 15994 (May 2010).

28. Anand Shrivastava, Rosa Abraham, and Amit Basole, 'State of Working India 2019', Azim Premji University.

VOTE, OR ELSE

1. Vineeth Krishna, 'Can you be a true democracy & let go of caste, Ambedkar asked Indians. We are yet to reply', *The Print*, 29 April 2018.

2. John Quincy Adams, 'Inaugural Address' (4 March 1825), in *The Addresses and Messages of the Presidents of the United States, Inaugural, Annual, and Special, from 1789 to 1846*, vol. 1, ed. Edwin Williams (New York 1846), p. 577.

3. John Keane, *The New Despotism* (Cambridge, MA 2020), pp. 98–109.

4. Partha Sarathi Banerjee, 'Party, Power and Political Violence in West Bengal', *Economic & Political Weekly*, XLVI, 6 (5 February 2011).

5. Amartya Lahiri and Kei-Mu Yi, 'A Tale of Two States: Maharashtra and West Bengal', UCLA, October 2004; Manish Basu, 'Study looks into why West Bengal's trade unions are now weaker', *LiveMint*, 22 October 2014.

6. Snigdhendu Bhattacharya, 'How one-teacher Ekal schools helped the spread of Hindutva in rural West Bengal', *The Caravan*, 10 October 2020.

7. Milan Vaishnav, *When Crime Pays: Money and Muscle in Indian Politics* (New York and London: Harper Collins, 2017).

8. The data are drawn from a study of twenty-two Assembly constituencies in eight states by Azim Premji University (APU) and Lokniti (Centre for the Study of Developing Societies (CSDS)), as reported by Shreehari Paliath, 'Indians Depend On Political Bodies, Social Networks To Access Govt Services', *IndiaSpend*, 6 August 2018.

9. Vaishnav, *When Crime Pays*.

CHREMACRACY

1. Frederick Charles Schaffer, *Elections for Sale: The Causes and Consequences of Vote Buying* (Boulder, CO 2007); Lisa Bjorkman and Jeffrey Witsoe, 'Money and Votes: Following Flows through Mumbai and Bihar', in Devesh Kapur and Milan Vaishnav (eds.), *Costs of Democracy: Political Finance in India* (Oxford 2019).

2. Shivam Shankar Singh, *How to Win An Indian Election* (India: Penguin Random House 2019).

3. Abheek Bhattacharya, 'India's $7 Billion Election', *Foreign Policy*, 23 April 2019.

4. Shemin Joy, 'Rs 60,000 crore spent during LS Polls 2019: Report', *Deccan Herald*, 3 June 2019.

5. Ingrid Van Biezen and Peter Kopecky, 'The State and the parties: Public funding, public regulation and rent-seeking in contemporary democracies', *Party Politics*, 13 (2007), pp. 235–54; see also the findings of the Money, Politics and Transparency Campaign Finance Indicators project at https://data.moneypoliticstransparency.org

6. Figures from the Association for Democratic Reforms (ADR) and National Election Watch, cited in T. Ramachandran, 'Most funds of national parties from "unknown" sources', *The Hindu*, 29 September 2013.

7. Nitin Sethi, 'Electoral Bonds Are Traceable: Documents Nail Govt Lie On Anonymity', *Huffington Post*, 21 November 2019.

8. Kunal Purohit, 'Inside Facebook's BJP bond: Key Tie-ups With Modi Govt, Its Special Interests', article 14, 26 August 2020; 'Analysis of Facebook ads prepared by the fact-checking website *Alt News*', 9 March 2019; and 'BJP is Leading Advertising Brand on Indian TV', *The Wire*, 23 November 2018.

9. Peter Mair, *Ruling the Void: The Hollowing of Western Democracy* (London and New York 2013); and Paul F. Witeley, 'Is the Party Over? The Decline of Party Activism and Membership across the Democratic World', *Party Politics*, 17, 1 (March 2009), pp. 21–44.

10. Mukulika Banerjee, *Why India Votes?* (Routledge 2014).

11. Larry M. Bartels, *Unequal Democracy: The Political Economy of the New Gilded Age* (Princeton, NJ 2008).

12. Neelanjan Sircar, 'Money in Elections: The Role of Personal Wealth in Election Outcomes', in Devesh Kapur and Milan Vaishnav (eds.), *Costs of Democracy: Political Finance in India* (New Delhi 2018).

13. Milan Vaishnav, *When Crime Pays: Money and Muscle in India Politics* (New Haven and London 2017).

ELECTIVE DESPOTISM

1. Thomas Jefferson, *Notes on the State of Virginia* (Philadelphia 1788), p. 126.

2. The figures are from data provided by the Trivedi Centre for Political Data (Ashoka University) and CERI (Sciences Po), as cited by Gilles Verniers and Christophe Jaffrelot, 'Explained: Why so many MPs are dynasts', *Indian Express*, 27 May 2019.

3. Shashi Tharoor, 'India's Crisis of Representation', *Open Magazine*, 17 August 2017.

4. Robert Michels, *Political Parties: A Sociological Study of the Oligarchical Tendencies of Modern Democracy* (New York and London [1911] 1962).

5. Gopalkrishna Gandhi, 'Silence is not golden', *The Telegraph*, 4 April 2015.

6. Abhijit Banare, 'Why Decline in Sittings of the Parliament & Assemblies Is Worrying', *The Quint*, 23 December 2018; Anil, 'Legislative Performance of State Assemblies', PRS Legislative Research, 27 May 2014.

7. PRS Legislative Research, 'Parliament and the Executive'; Open Budget Index 2017, compiled by non-profit International Budget Partnership.

8. David Runciman, *The Confidence Trap: A History of Democracy in Crisis from World War I to the Present* (London 2015).

9. Jean Drèze and Amartya Sen, *An Uncertain Glory: India and Its Contradictions* (London 2013), p. 80: 'Particular to India is the combination of insistence—for entirely plausible reasons—on having a large public sector, combined with a fairly comprehensive neglect of accountability in operating this large sector.'

10. Pierre Rosanvallon, *Good Government: Democracy Beyond Elections* (Cambridge, MA 2018).

11. Patrick Diamond, *The End of Whitehall? Government by Permanent Campaign* (London 2019).

12. 'Karnataka "super CM" transfers 700 officers in 24 hours', *The Print*, 5 October 2018.

13. Common Cause and the Centre for the Study of Developing Societies, *Status of Policing in India Report 2019*; Tata Trusts, *India Justice Report 2019* (October 2019); Shreya Raman, 'Leaky, Dingy, Tiny: Police Homes In India's Financial Capital', *IndiaSpend*, 7 October 2019.

14. 'Government Compliance with Supreme Court Directives on Police Reforms: An Assessment', Commonwealth Human Rights Initiative (September 2020).

JUSTICE DEFILED

1. Madan B. Lokur, 'India's Judiciary Is Facing An Increasing Lack Of Trust By Public', *Outlook*, 13 January 2020.

2. Pramit Bhattacharya and Tadit Kundu, '99% cases of sexual assaults go unreported, govt data shows', *LiveMint*, 24 April 2018.

3. Tata Trust, *State of Policing in India 2019*.

4. Vikram Sharma, 'Priyanka Reddy murder: Cops discuss "options other than arrest"', *Deccan Chronicle*, 30 November 2019.

5. 'Courts will take 320 years to clear backlog cases: Justice Rao', *PTI*, 6 March 2010.

6. Damayanti Datta, 'What made CJI TS Thakur cry in front of PM Modi', *India Today*, 27 April 2016.

7. 'How do Bengaluru's rural courts function?', *India Together*, 12 August 2019.

8. 'Building Better Courts: Surveying the Infrastructure of India's District Courts', Vidhi Centre for Legal Policy, Jaldi, Tata Trusts (August 2019).

9. Amnesty International, *Justice Under Trial: A Study of Pre-Trial Detention in India* (2017).

10. India Justice Report 2019, Tata Trusts.

11. Sabika Abbas and Madhurima Dhanuka, 'Inside Haryana Prisons', Commonwealth Human Rights Initiative (2019).

12. Harish Narasappa, 'The Dichtomy in India's Rule of Law', *India Together*, 24 July 2018; and *Rule of Law in India—A Quest for Reason* (Delhi 2018).

13. Tripurdaman Singh, *Sixteen Stormy Days: The Story of the First Amendment of the Constitution of India*. Penguin Random House (India, 2020).

14. Montesquieu, *The Spirit of the Laws* [1748], book XI.

15. A.G. Noorani, 'Habeas corpus is habeas carcass in Kashmir Valley', *The Asian Age*, 11 November 2019.

16. Keane, *The New Despotism*.

17. Debasish Roy Chowdhury, 'Modi, a dead judge, and ghosts from the past', *This Week in Asia*, 20 January 2018.

18. Debasish Roy Chowdhury, 'Modi's surgical strike on Muslims puts India at war with itself', *This Week in Asia*, 14 December 2019; and 'Abandoned in Assam: India creates its own Rohingya, and calls them "Bangladeshi"', *This Week in Asia*, 23 August 2019.

19. Gautam Bhatia, '"A little brief authority": Chief Justice Ranjan Gogoi and the Rise of the Executive Court', *Indian Constitutional Law and Philosophy* (17 November 2019).

20. Bhatia, '"A little brief authority"'.

21. Detailed study of the 1999–2014 period by M.S. Aney, S. Dam, and G. Ko, 'Jobs for Justice(s): Corruption in the Supreme Court of India', *Singapore Management University (SMU) Economics and Statistics Working Paper Series No. 06* (Singapore 2017).

22. Tarunabh Khaitan, 'The Indian Supreme Court's identity crisis: a constitutional court or a court of appeals?' *Indian Law Review*, 4, 1 (2020).

23. Shrutanjaya Bhardwaj, 'Preventive Detention, Habeas Corpus and Delay at the Apex Court: An Empirical Study', *NUJS Law Review*, 13, 1 (2020);

Aparna Chandra, William H. J. Hubbard, and Sital Kalantry, 'The Supreme Court of India: An Empirical Overview of the Institution', University of Chicago, Public Law Working Paper No. 660 (April 2018); Shreyas Narla and Shruti Rajagopalan, 'The Judicial Abrogation of Rights & Liberties in Kashmir', *article 14*, 25 September 2020.

24. Pratap Bhanu Mehta, 'PB Mehta writes: SC was never perfect, but the signs are that it is slipping into judicial barbarism', *The Indian Express*, 18 November 2020.

25. 'Legislature and Judiciary Must Work Together for Nation-Building: Ranjan Gogoi on RS Nomination', *The Wire*, 17 March 2020.

BAD NEWS

1. Ian Kershaw, *Hitler: 1889–1936: Hubris* (Harmondsworth 1998), p. 140.

2. John Keane, *Democracy and Media Decadence* (Cambridge and New York 2013).

3. Samarth Bansal, Gopal Sathe, Rachna Khaira, and Aman Sethi, 'How Modi, Shah Turned A Women's NGO Into A Secret Election Propaganda Machine', *Huffpost*, 4 April 2019.

4. Rasmus Kleis Nielsen, 'A creeping quiet in Indian journalism?' *Huffpost*, 15 November 2017.

5. Jeff Horwitz and Newley Purnell, 'Facebook Executive Supported India's Modi, Disparaged Opposition in Internal Messages', *The Wall Street Journal*, 30 August 2020; Billy Perrigo, 'Facebook's Ties to India's Ruling Party Complicate Its Fight Against Hate Speech', *Time*, 27 August 2020.

6. Rohini Mohan, 'Indian media perturbed by advisory on foreign content', *The Straits Times*, 3 December 2020.

7. Reporters Without Borders, *Media Ownership Monitor: Who owns the media in India?* (29 May 2019).

8. Krishn Kaushik, 'The Big Five: The Media Companies That the Modi Government Must Scrutinise To Fulfill its Promise of Ending Crony Capitalism', *Caravan Magazine*, 9 January 2016; Megha Bahree, 'Reliance Takes Over Network18: Is This The Death Of Media Independence?', *Forbes*, 30 May 2014.

9. Ruchika Goswamy, 'Media is a business, journalism a calling: P Sainath', *The Indian Express*, 24 November 2019.

10. Data pulled from 130 Indian news sources by MIT researcher Anushka Shah.

11. Anushka Shah and Zeenab Aneez, 'Cropped Out', *The Caravan*, 1 March 2018.

12. Ken Auletta, 'Citizens Jain', *The New Yorker*, 1 October 2012.

13. Swati Maheshwari and Colin Sparks, 'Political elites and journalistic practices in India: A case of institutionalized heteronomy', *Journalism and International Journal of Communication* (6 April 2018).

14. *Media Ownership Monitor India, A Delicate Handshake*, Reporters Without Borders.

15. Anuradha Raman, 'News You Can Abuse', *Outlook*, 21 December 2009.

16. Report by Indian think tank Rights and Risks Analysis Group.

17. Geeta Seshu and Urvashi Sarkar, 'Getting Away with Murder', Thakur Foundation (December 2019).

18. Chetan Chauhan, 'India "3rd most dangerous" nation for journalists after Iraq and Syria', *Hindustan Times* (4 November 2019).

REMAKING THE PEOPLE

1. The government tactic of bolstering its support by electing a new people is sketched in a sarcastic poem by Bertolt Brecht, '*Die Lösung ['The Solution 1953]'*, in *Poems. 1913–1956* (London 1981).

2. For further details of the changing history and present-day relevance of the term despotism and what it means in practice see John Keane, *The New Despotism* (London 2020); see also Nayanika Mathur's ethnography of Indian state structures, *Paper Tiger: Law, Bureaucracy and the Developmental State in Himalayan India* (Cambridge and Delhi 2015).

3. Sugata Bose, 'There will be no safe anchor until "We, the People" are able to decisively overturn current parliamentary majority', *The Indian Express*, 6 February 2020.

4. 'KCR can even be Hitler's grandfather to stop injustice: Telangana CM,' *FirstPost*, 18 August 2014.

5. Cited in Pierre Rosanvallon, *Good Government: Democracy beyond Elections* (Cambridge, Mass. 2018), p. 218.

6. 'I have been chosen by God: Modi,' *PTI/The Hindu*, 24 April 2014.

7. Ernst H. Kantorowicz, *The King's Two Bodies: a study in mediaeval political theology* (Princeton, NJ 1957); on the divinization of earthly rulers see also David Graeber and Marshall Sahlins, *On Kings* (Chicago 2017).

8. N. Kaul, 'Rise of the Political Right in India: Hindutva-Development Mix, Modi Myth, And Dualities', *Journal of Labor and Society*, 20, 4 (2017), pp. 523–48.

9. J.D. Dickey, *American Demagogue: The Great Awakening and the Rise and Fall of Populism* (New York 2019).

10. *Chanakya* (Jawaharlal Nehru), 'We Want No Caesars', *Modern Review* 62 (November 1937), pp. 546–7; B.R. Ambedkar, *Last Speech in the Constituent Assembly on the Adoption of the Constitution* (25 November 1949), available at: https://shodhganga.inflibnet.ac.in/bitstream/10603/38799/15/15_appendix.pdf

11. Hemant Kakkara and Niro Sivanathana, 'When the appeal of a dominant leader is greater than a prestige leader', *Proceedings of the National Academy of Sciences of the United States of America* (2 June 2017); M.A. Hogg and J. Adelman, 'Uncertainty–identity theory: Extreme groups, radical behavior, and authoritarian leadership', *Journal of Social Issues*, 69 (2013), pp. 436–54.

12. Bruce Stokes, Dorothy Manevich, and Hanyu Chwe, 'The state of Indian democracy', Pew Research Center, 15 November 2017, available at: https://www.pewresearch.org/global/2017/11/15/the-state-of-indian-democracy/; John Gramlich, 'How countries around the world view democracy, military rule and other political systems', *FactTank*, 20 October 2017, available at: https://www.pewresearch.org/fact-tank/2017/10/30/global-views-political-systems/; and Christophe Jaffrelot and Gilles Verniers, 'A New Party System Or A New Political System?', *Contemporary South Asia* (June 2020), pp. 9–10.

13. Neelanjan Sircar, 'Not vikas, Modi's 2019 election was built on politics of vishwas', *The Print*, 30 May 2020.

14. Joseph Schumpeter, *Capitalism, Socialism, and Democracy* (New York and London 1942), p. 283.

15. Sai Manish, 'India's banks wrote off Rs 2 trillion worth of bad loans in 2018–19', *Business Standard*, 29 November 2019.

16. Mihir S. Sharma, 'Modi, myths and man', *Business Standard*, 21 January 2013.

17. Andy Mukherjee, 'India's New Economy Can't Be a Monopoly Board', *Bloomberg*, 25 August 2020.

18. Stephanie Findlay and Hudson Lockett, ' "Modi's Rockefeller": Gautam Adani and the concentration of power in India', *The Financial Times*, 14 November 2020.

19. Rajesh Mascarenhas, 'Adani's wealth grows most on India rich list', *The Economic Times*, 20 November 2020.

20. Debasish Roy Chowdhury, 'Modi thinks he is Xi Jinping, but protests show India is not China', *This Week in Asia*, 4 January 2020.

21. Sophie Tatum, 'Eric Trump: Democrats in Washington are "not even people" ', *CNN*, 7 June 2017, available at: https://edition.cnn.com/2017/06/07/politics/eric-trump-hannity-democrats-obstruction/index.html

22. Montesquieu, *My Thoughts* (Indianapolis 2012), p. 566; Alexis de Tocqueville, *Democracy in America* (New York 1945), volume 2, book 4, chapter 6, pp. 334–9.

23. Yogendra Yadav, *Making Sense of Indian Democracy: Theory as Practice* (Hyderabad 2020), passim.

24. Lori Beaman, Esther Duflo, Rohini Pande, and Petia Topalova, 'Female Leadership Raises Aspirations and Educational Attainment for Girls: A Policy Experiment in India', *Science*, 335 (February 2012), pp. 582–6.

25. Robert Jensen and Emily Oster, 'The Power of TV: Cable Television and Women's Status in India', *NBER Working Paper* No. 13305 (August 2007).

26. Jean Drèze and Amartya Sen, 'India adrift, optimism hard to sustain', *Telegraph India*, 15 March 2020, available at: https://www.telegraphindia.com/opinion/india-adrift-optimism-hard-to-sustain/cid/1754027

27. See the conclusions of Yogendra Yadav, *Making Sense of Indian Democracy* (Ranikhet 2021), pp. 325 ff.

28. Sudipta Kaviraj, *The Enchantment of Democracy in India* (Ranikhet 2011), p. 23; other examples of this way of thinking about democracy include Pratap Bhanu Mehta, *The Burden of Democracy* (New Delhi 2003) and Sunil Khilnani, *The Idea of India* (London and New York 2003), pp. 15–60.

29. Aishwary Kumar, *Radical Equality: Ambedkar, Gandhi, and the Risk of Democracy* (Stanford 2015), p. 252 and ff.; the topic of remembering the past and restorative justice is examined in detail in John Keane, *Power and Humility: The Future of Monitory Democracy* (Cambridge and New York 2018), pp. 94–100.

Further Reading

Readers wishing to venture beyond the materials quoted in this book's footnotes may like to consult the following short selection of relevant books:

Ahmad, Irfan and Kanungo, Pralay. *The Algebra of Warfare-Welfare: A Long View of India's 2014 Election*. New Delhi, 2019.

Aiyar, Shankkar. *The Gated Republic: India's Public Policy Failures and Private Solutions*. Noida, 2020.

Beteille, André. *Democracy and its Institutions*. New Delhi, 2012.

Bhargava, Rajeev (ed.). *Secularism and its Critics*. New Delhi, 1988.

Bhatia, Gautam. *The Transformative Constitution: A Radical Biography in Nine Acts*. Noida, 2019.

Chand, Vikram (ed.). *Reinventing Public Service Delivery in India: Selected Case Studies*. New Delhi, 2006.

Chatterjee, Partha. *The Politics of the Governed: Reflections on Popular Politics in Most of the World*. New Delhi, 2004.

Curato, Nicole. *Democracy in a Time of Misery. From Spectacular Tragedies to Deliberative Action*. Oxford, 2019.

De, Rohit. *A People's Constitution: The Everyday Life of Law in the Indian Republic*. Princeton and Oxford, 2018.

Drèze, Jean. *Sense and Solidarity: Jholawala Economics for Everyone*. Ranikhet, 2017.

Feenstra, Rámon. *Kidnapped Democracy*. London and New York, 2020.

George, Cherian. *Hate Spin: The Manufacture of Religious Offense and Its Threat to Democracy*. Cambridge, Massachusetts; London, 2016.

Godbole, Madhav. *India's Parliamentary Democracy on Trial*. New Delhi, 2011.

Gudavarthy, Ajay. *India After Modi: Populism and the Right*. New Delhi, 2019.

Guha, Ramachandra. *India After Gandhi: The History of the World's Largest Democracy*. New Delhi, 2008.

Hansen, Thomas Blom. *The Saffron Wave: Democracy and Hindu Nationalism in Modern India*. Princeton, 1999.

Jaffrelot, Christophe. *The Hindu Nationalist Movement and Indian Politics: 1925 to the 1990s*. New Delhi, 1999.

Jaffrelot, Christophe, Chatterjee, Angana, Hansen, Thomas Blom (eds.). *Majoritarian State: How Hindu Nationalism is Changing India*. London, 2019.

Jaffrelot, Christophe and Anil, Pratinav. *India's First Dictatorship: The Emergency, 1975–1977*. London, 2021.

Jayal, Niraja Gopal (ed.). *Democracy in India*. Oxford, 2001.

Jha, Sanjay. *The Great Unravelling: India after 2014*. Chennai, 2020.

Jodhka, Surinder S. *Caste in Contemporary India*, New Delhi, 2015.

Kannabiran, K.G. *Wages of Impunity: Power, Justice and Human Rights*. New Delhi, 2004.

Kaur, Ravinder. *Brand New Nation: Capitalist Dreams and Nationalist Designs in Twenty-First-Century India*. Stanford, 2020.

Khosla, Madhav. *India's Founding Moment: The Constitution of a Most Surprising Democracy*. Cambridge, 2020.

Komirredi, S. *Malevolent Republic: A Short History of the New India*. London, 2019.

Kothari, Rajni. *Memoirs: Uneasy is the Life of the Mind*. New Delhi, 2002.

Mander, Harsh. *Locking Down the Poor: The Pandemic and India's Moral Centre*. New Delhi, 2020.

Michelutti, Lucia. *The Vernacularisation of Democracy: Politics, Caste and Religion in India*. New Delhi, 2008.

Miller, Joshua. *Democratic Temperament: The Legacy of William James*. Kansas, 1997.

Nag, Kingshuk. *The Saffron Tide*. New Delhi, 2014.

Nandy, Ashis, *Bonfire of Creeds: The Essential Ashis Nandy*. New Delhi, 2004.

Nayar, Kuldip. *The Judgement: Inside Story of the Emergency of India*. New Delhi, 1977.

Nilsen, Alf Gunvald, Nielsen, Kenneth Bo, and Vaidya, Anand. *Indian Democracy: Origins, Trajectories, Contestations*. London, 2019.

Nussbaum, Martha C. *The Clash Within: Democracy, Religious Violence, and India's Future*. Cambridge, Massachusetts, 2007.

Patel, Aakar. *Our Hindu Rashtra: What It Is. How We Got Here*. Bangalore, 2020.

Quraishi, S.Y. *The Great March of Democracy: Seven Decades of India's Elections*. New Delhi, 2019.

Rajshekhar, M. *Despite the State: Why India Lets Its People Down and How They Cope*. Chennai, 2021.

Roy, Arundhati. *Listening to Grasshoppers. Field Notes on Democracy*. London, 2009.

Roy, Prannoy and Sopariwala, Dorab. *The Verdict: Decoding India's Elections*. New Delhi, 2019.

Sanyal, Paromita and Rao, Vijayendra. *Oral Democracy: Deliberation in Indian Village Assemblies*. Cambridge and New York, 2018.

Sen, Amartya. *Identity and Violence*. New York and London, 2006.

Shani, Ornit. *How India Became Democratic: Citizenship and the Making of the Universal Franchise*. Cambridge, 2018.

Sharma, Ruchir. *Democracy on the Road: A 25-Year Journey Through India*. New Delhi, 2019.

Shastri, Sandeep, Suri, K.C., and Yadav, Yogendra. *Electoral Politics in India: Lok Sabha Elections in 2004 and Beyond*. New Delhi, 2009.

Shekhar, Hansda Sowvendra. *The Adivasi Will Not Dance: Stories*. New Delhi, 2015.

Thapar, Romila, Ram N, Bhatia, Gautam and Patel Gautam. *On Citizenship*. New Delhi, 2021.

Thorat, Sukhadeo and Newman Katherine (eds.). *Blocked by Caste: Economic Discrimination in Modern India*. New Delhi, 2009.

Vaishnav, Milan, and Hintson, Jamie. *India's Fourth Party System*. Washington, DC, 2019.

Vanaik, Achin. *The Rise of Hindu Authoritarianism: Secular Claims, Communal Realities*. New York, 2017.

Varshney, Ashutosh. *Battles Half Won: India's Improbable Democracy*. Gurgaon, 2013.

Yengde, Suraj. *Caste Matters*. Gurgaon, 2019.

Zelliott, Eleanor. *Ambedkar's World: The Making of Babasaheb and the Dalit Movement*. New Delhi, 2013.

Photo and Illustration Credits

1. Ministry of Information & Broadcasting, Government of India, via Wikimedia Commons
2. Wikimedia Commons
3. The White House
4. Unidentified photographer
5. The World Happiness Report 2020
6. Courtesy of Anindya Chattopadhyay
7. Courtesy of Abhinav Chaturvedi
8. Our World in Data
9. Courtesy of Anindito Mukherjee
10. Photo by Sandeep Yadav © Karwan e Mohabbat
11. Photo by Debasish Roy Chowdhury
12. Courtesy of Shiv Shankar Chatterjee
13. Courtesy of Anindya Chattopadhyay
14. Courtesy of Anindya Chattopadhyay
15. Courtesy of Dadarao Bilhore
16. Photo by Debasish Roy Chowdhury
17. Courtesy of World Development Report 2018
18. Courtesy of Sanjay Borade
19. Courtesy of Ishan Tankha
20. © ILO/J. Urmila 2018
21. Courtesy of Abhinav Chaturvedi
22. Courtesy of Anindya Chattopadhyay

23. Photo by Debasish Roy Chowdhury

24. Photo by Debasish Roy Chowdhury

25. Photo by Debasish Roy Chowdhury

26. Courtesy of Anindya Chattopadhyay

27. Courtesy of Kashif Masood

28. PRS Legislative Research data/IndiaSpend

29. Photo by Debasish Roy Chowdhury

30. © Smita Chakraburtty/Paar

31. Courtesy of Amnesty International India

32. Courtesy of Mitali Gupta

33. Courtesy of Indranil Bhoumik

34. Courtesy of Anushka Shah, MIT Media Lab

35. Courtesy of Press Information Bureau

36. Courtesy of Amnesty International India

37. Courtesy of Furquan Ameen

The publisher and the authors apologize for any errors or omissions in the above list. If contacted they will be pleased to rectify these at the earliest opportunity.

Index